IMAGINED LANDSCAPES

THE SPATIAL HUMANITIES
David J. Bodenhamer, John Corrigan, and Trevor M. Harris, editors

Imagined Landscapes

GEOVISUALIZING AUSTRALIAN SPATIAL NARRATIVES

Jane Stadler, Peta Mitchell & Stephen Carleton

INDIANA UNIVERSITY PRESS   *Bloomington & Indianapolis*

This book is a publication of

INDIANA UNIVERSITY PRESS
Office of Scholarly Publishing
Herman B. Wells Library 350
1320 East 10th Street
Bloomington, Indiana 47405 USA

iupress.indiana.edu

The paper used in this publication meets the minimum
requirements of the American National Standard for Information
Sciences—Permanence of Paper for Printed Library Materials,
ANSI Z39.48–1992.

Manufactured in the United States of America

Library of Congress Cataloging-in-Publication Data

Stadler, Jane. author.
Imagined landscapes : geovisualizing Australian spatial narratives / Jane Stadler,
Peta Mitchell, and Stephen Carleton.
pages cm. — (The spatial humanities)
Includes index.
ISBN 978-0-253-01838-0 (cloth : alk. paper) — ISBN 978-0-253-01845-8 (pbk. : alk. paper)
— ISBN 978-0-253-01849-6 (ebook) 1. Australian literature—History and criticism.
2. Landscapes in literature. 3. Motion pictures—Australia—History and criticism.
4. Landscapes in motion pictures. 5. Space and time in literature. 6. Space and time
in motion pictures. 7. Australia—In literature. 8. Australia—In motion pictures.
I. Mitchell, Peta, author. II. Carleton, Stephen, [date]- author. III. Title.
PR9605.5.L35S73 2016
820.9'994—dc23
2015022400

1 2 3 4 5 21 20 19 18 17 16

*This book is dedicated to renowned spatial humanities scholar
P. J. Carstell, and to our traveling companions
Hannah, Alex, Amara, and Hugo.*

CONTENTS

ACKNOWLEDGMENTS

The authors are grateful to our research assistant, Luke Houghton, for preparing the GIS maps of Red Dog's travels, of mining activity, and of Native Title in the Pilbara and in Western Australia as a whole, and for mapping Alexander Pearce's journey. Sincere thanks are also due to our other wonderful research assistants Carolyn Lake, Melanie Piper, David Faraker, Sean Tan, and Fiona McKean.

The introduction contains material from a chapter by Peta Mitchell and Jane Stadler, "Redrawing the Map: An Interdisciplinary Geocritical Approach to Australian Cultural Narratives," first published in an anthology edited by Robert Tally, *Geocritical Explorations: Space, Place, and Mapping in Literary and Cultural Studies* (2011), reproduced with permission of Palgrave Macmillan.

We are grateful to Anthony Buckley for granting access to his *Wake in Fright* archive, and to Bob Pavlich; Jenny Camilleri from the Broken Hill Historical Society; Brian Tonkin, Archives Officer, Broken Hill City Council; and Glenda Veitch and Norm Ricaud at the State Records Authority of New South Wales for assistance provided in researching chapter 1.

Chapter 2 contains material from an article by Stephen Carleton, titled "Australian Gothic: Theatre and the Northern Turn," published in *Australian Literary Studies* 27.2 (2012).

Chapter 3 contains material from an article originally published by Jane Stadler, "Mapping the Cinematic Journey of Alexander Pearce, Cannibal

Convict," in *Screening the Past,* no. 34 (2012), reproduced with permission from the journal's editor, Professor Adrian Martin.

We gratefully acknowledge permission to reproduce the Indigenous Language Map created by David R. Horton for Aboriginal Studies Press, AIATSIS and Auslig/Sinclair, Knight, Merz (1996).

The *Cultural Atlas of Australia* was generously funded by an ARC Discovery Grant (2011–2013). We also acknowledge research support provided throughout the project by the University of Queensland.

IMAGINED LANDSCAPES

INTRODUCTION

Geocriticism's Disciplinary Boundaries

> Yet there is no use in pretending that all we know about time and space, or rather history and geography, is more than anything else imaginative
>
> —SAID, *Orientalism* 55

This is a book about imagined landscapes and imaginative geographies, about the ways in which narrative fiction or spatial stories—films, novels, and plays—continually shape and reshape the contours of our geography and our history. In *Imagined Landscapes,* we work from the premise that narrative fiction intersects with experiences of and ideas about landscape, identity, and the development of a sense of place such that spatial storytelling makes a strong contribution to geographic and historical awareness. Cultural representations of landscapes, as Christopher Tilley observes, form "a signifying system through which the social is reproduced and transformed, explored and structured" (34). Representations of landscape, therefore, do far more than frame the environment as a background against which narrative action plays out; they generate symbolism and produce cultural meaning. Such narratives, we argue, form and inform perceptions of space and place as they represent and communicate spatial concepts and cultural and environmental issues. As Tilley claims, places "may be said to acquire a history, sedimented layers of meaning by virtue of the actions and events that take place in them" (27). One way this occurs is in the production of "spatial stories," which Michel de Certeau defines as cultural narratives that "traverse and organize places: they select and link them together; they make sentences and itineraries out of them" (115). The case studies presented in this book exemplify such spatial stories. While these narratives are grounded in the landscape and culture of Australia, the insights drawn from them have relevance to questions of nation and narration around the world. As we have argued elsewhere, "Representations of space and place are always ideological, always implicated in some form of nation-building or identity-formation, and considering 'imagined,' fictive, representational, or mythic geographies allows us to see the ways in which representations of space and place are intimately bound up in the nexus of power–knowledge" (Mitchell and Stadler "Imaginative" 29).

Moreover, in this book, we contend that traditional modes of close reading and textual analysis are, by themselves, inadequate to the task of understanding broader patterns of spatial representation and their re-lationships to history, geography, and culture. In *Imagined Landscapes,* we investigate how teaming a geocritical method of analysis with digital visualization techniques to map spatial narratives can help to reveal new perspectives on enduring questions in cultural studies and narrative anal-ysis. This book is intended as a sustained and critical engagement with the use of digital narrative cartography to map and interrogate films, novels, and plays in which space and place figure prominently, and, as such, it is framed around a significant digital geovisualization project—the *Cul-tural Atlas of Australia.* The *Cultural Atlas* (http://www.australian-cultural -atlas.info), which was developed by the authors with funding from the Australian Research Council, was designed to investigate and map the cultural and historical significance of location and landscape in Australian narrative fiction, thereby presenting the first national survey of narrative space spanning Australian novels, films, and plays. The aims and scope of the *Cultural Atlas* will be introduced in greater detail later in this chapter, but, in essence, it is a database-driven interactive digital map that enables its users to explore Australian places and spaces as they are represented in and through films, novels, and plays, and to map and identify patterns of representation in the country's cultural landscape.

This research—both the book and the digital resource that underpins it—responds to the growing interest in mediated representations of space that increasingly connects the digital humanities, cultural studies, geography, film, theater, and literary studies. Our interdisciplinary approach involves three scholars, specializing in different disciplines, who work together to provide an integrated perspective on the translation or remediation of space across narrative forms and to pioneer new ways of seeing and understanding landscape. By examining the technical and conceptual challenges of georeferencing fictional and fictionalized places in narratives that involve journeys, movement through time, and different perspectives on the landscape, we seek to offer fresh insights on cultural topography and spatial history.

In this introductory chapter, we provide an overview of traditions of spatial inquiry across Australian cultural studies and the various forms of narrative geography—literary, film, and media—that have emerged from within the discipline of geography. These various traditions of spatial enquiry, we argue, are rarely in dialogue with one another, a disjunction that is also reflected in the ways in which narrative geovisualization projects rarely map more than one narrative form. We then outline how a spatial humanities methodology using digital cartographic technologies can be used to address the challenges of mapping narrative fiction across film, literature, and theater and posit that a geocritical approach may provide an interdisciplinary and intermedial framework, offering a way of analyzing multimediated spatial narratives that also takes into account the remediation of geovisualization.

The chapters that follow explore particular issues that arise from this dual geocritical/geovisual approach to analyzing spatial narratives. In chapter 1, we move beyond established traditions in adaptation studies to investigate the ways in which space and place are mediated and remediated within and across narrative forms. Focusing on the cult narrative *Wake in Fright* (which exists as a novel, film, and play), we examine how each of its narrative forms presents a different imagined geography of the same region and requires a different understanding of narrative space. In chapter 2, we turn to the question of how certain regional landscapes are framed, troped, and staged as mythic spaces that are put to service in both the building and interrogating of national cultural myths. Here we focus particularly on representations of Australia's "Deep North"—a contemporary frontier space that is geographically and demographically peripheral to mainstream Australia but that nonetheless looms large in the country's cultural imaginary. In chapter 3, we ask how spatial humanities geovisualization techniques might advance understandings of cultural and spatial history. We demonstrate that geocriticism and geovisualization, as modes of narrative analysis, reveal the complex imbrications of a locale, its community, and its connections to evolving historical understandings of national and regional identity. Focusing on a longitudinal case study that maps multiple adaptations of a geographically distinctive historical narrative—the journey of Alexander Pearce, a convict who gained notoriety for resorting to cannibalism after absconding from a remote penal settlement in the Tasmanian wilderness—this chapter reveals how successive retellings document shifting perceptions of place. Chapter 4 takes up the question of mobility and grapples with the complexities involved in plotting patterns of mobility recurring in and around road movies and travel narratives. Here we focus on the 2011 film *Red Dog*, teasing out the complex relationships between the (historical) story of Red Dog as represented in the books that document and dramatize his life, its production as a film, and the history of iron-ore mining in the Pilbara region of Western Australia, in order to explore how cultural narratives are deeply implicated in the geopolitics of the regions that they represent. The final chapter of *Imagined Landscapes* grapples with the challenges geographically ambiguous, uncertain, or unknown fictional landscapes present to narrative mapping. We explore how to map mythic space in relation to key forms of spatial symbolism depicted in representative films, novels, and plays located in the Central Australian desert.

IMAGINING AUSTRALIA: AUSTRALIAN CULTURAL
STUDIES AND THE SPATIAL TURN

Space, place, and landscape are longstanding themes in Australian literary and cultural studies, and from the colonial era to the present day, Australian cultural narratives have proven fertile ground for spatial analysis. In his influential book on Australian film and literature, *National Fictions*, Graeme Turner argues that narrative forms are, in the Australian context, profoundly tied up with national myths of land, landscape, and identity.

Moreover, Turner argues, Australian filmic and fictive texts "invite us to accept that the land is central to a distinctively Australian meaning." This concept of the "land producing its literature" has, he continues, in turn influenced both Australian literary and film criticism, though the former more strongly than the latter (30). This carries through into theater for, as Joanne Tompkins argues in her influential study *Unsettling Space,* spatial tensions driven by anxieties about contested land, nationalism, colonial settlement, and Aboriginal reconciliation play out as narratives on the Australian stage, where the performance of nationhood and identity is dramatically enacted: "Australian theatre not only contests conventional Australian history and culture; it also stages alternative means of managing the production of space in a spatially unstable nation" (5).

One reason for this emphasis on spatial enquiry in Australian cultural studies is the fact that, as Allaine Cerwonka has noted, Australian history has traditionally "been imagined in relation to geography. Its history testifies to how colonisation largely depended on spatial practices that shaped the landscape" (6). In his *Geographical Imaginations,* Derek Gregory points out the interrelationship between imagination, geography, and spatial politics, and nowhere has this been more evident than in the mapping, naming, and colonization of the Australian continent. Indeed, for map historian Ronald Vere Tooley, the connection between geography and imagination is what makes Australia unique in the history of cartography: "Alone among the continents of the world," Tooley wrote in his 1952 work *Maps and Map-Makers,* "Australia was in a sense imagined centuries prior to its actual discovery" (118).

In its guise as Terra Australis Incognita (a concept we return to in the final chapter of this book), the great southern landmass was, as Paul Arthur notes, "an alluring enigma in the European imagination centuries before its 'discovery' and colonisation," and "when British settlers finally arrived in 1788, they brought with them a vast store of prior expectations and images, based both on actual reports of explorers and on historical myths, which persuasively moulded their way of seeing the unfamiliar land and its people" ("Fantasies" 37). In his landmark text *Inventing Australia,* Richard White argues Australia had been (and continues to be) invented before its advent. *Discovery* in the sense that Tooley uses it is, of course, a loaded and near-terminally fraught term. Not only is it a misnomer in the obvious sense—that Australia had been discovered and occupied for millennia prior to its "official" European discovery[1]—but even within European imperialist discourse, White argues that there was "no moment when, for the first time, Australia was seen 'as it really was'" because "national identity is an invention" (viii).

Certainly, the iconic nature of Australia's landform—its status as the "island continent"—affords it a singular place in the cultural-geographic imaginary. Within Australian literature and culture, Elizabeth McMahon contends, Australia's "island imaginary" is particularly evident, with the island being deployed "as a mobilising trope in constructions of nation and region, centre and margin, homogeneity and diversity" ("Encapsulated Space" 20). Indeed, as Anthony Lambert has noted, "most Australians" encounter a map of the country "almost daily in some form," its "recogniz-able image" serving to "formulate and promote the idea of a homogenous, 'imagined community,' almost as if 'Australia' did not exist before the Western map brought it into being" (308). The country's visual iconicity and its role in the building of national myths have also invited a textual-geographic reading of Australia's history of colonization. In his seminal 1987 "essay in spatial history," *The Road to Botany Bay,* Paul Carter argues that the continent's "discoverers, explorers and settlers were making spa-tial history. They were choosing directions, applying names, imagining goals, inhabiting the country" (xxi). This process was, in itself, an exercise in spatial imagining, for, as Carter describes it, his concept of "spatial his-tory" cannot simply be equated to the "geographer's space"; rather, he says, what spatial history evokes "are the spatial forms and fantasies through which a culture declares its presence. It is spatiality as a form of non-linear writing; as a form of history" (xxii). Following Paul Carter, Simon Ryan similarly argues that, in the eyes of its explorers, Australia's "antipodality"

1. This concept is itself internally fraught, for the British were certainly not the first Europeans to make landfall on the continent. The Dutch were, in the early 1600s, the first recorded Europeans to sight and to set foot on the Australian mainland, although there has been debate over whether the Portuguese and the French sighted the continent a century earlier. By the time James Cook made landfall on the east coast in 1770, the con-tinent's northern coastline was also well known to and frequented by Macassan traders, who had established a thriving trepang (or sea cucumber) fishing industry along it earlier in the century.

united with "its construction as a *tabula rasa* to produce the continent as an inverted, empty space desperately requiring rectification and occupation" ("Inscribing" 116). This process of Western exploration, Ryan continues, effectively "reified" the Australian landscape as a "blank text, ready to be inscribed by the impending colonial process" (126). This textualization of the landscape has in turn been played out in Australian cultural narratives, and particularly in Australian literature. Indeed, according to Martin Leer, the "evocative power" of Australia's cartographical image may be the reason why "Australian literature has been more diligent in literally, metaphorically and self-consciously mapping the continent than almost any other old or emerging national literature" ("Imagined" 1).

Paul Carter and Simon Ryan's work exemplifies the spatial focus that has typified Australian cultural studies—a focus that received new impetus with the "spatial turn" identified by Edward Soja and Fredric Jameson in the late 1980s and early 1990s. Across Australian film, literary, and theater studies, spatial inquiry—or approaching texts from a spatial/geographical perspective as well as from a temporal/historical one—has become increasingly important since the 1980s.[2] Yet, despite the centrality

---

2. In Australian film studies, this shift in thinking toward place and space is evidenced by key texts such as Ross Gibson's seminal 1983 essay "Camera Natura," Stuart Cunningham's account of "locationism" in his 1991 book *Featuring Australia,* Gibson's 1992 book *South of the West,* and Roslynn Haynes's 1998 book *Seeking the Centre,* followed more recently by Venkatasawmy, Simpson, and Visosevic (2001), Collins and Davis (2004), Limbrick (2007), special issues of *Metro* dedicated to Australian landscape cinema (nos. 163, 165, and 166) in 2009 and 2010, Harper (2010), Mills (2010), Mitchell and Stadler (2010), Stadler and Mitchell (2010), Stadler "Mapping" and "Seeing" (2012), and a special of *Senses of Cinema* (no. 65, "Tasmania and the Cinema") in 2012. It is also important to note the contribution to Australian film studies in the early 1990s by geographers Stuart C. Aitken and Leo E. Zonn in their analyses of Peter Weir's *Picnic at Hanging Rock* and *Gallipoli* (Aitken and Zonn, "Weir(d) Sex") and Henri Safran's *Storm Boy* (Zonn and Aitken). In Australian literary studies, key texts include George Seddon's 1982 essay on the "persistence of place" in Western Australian literature, Martin Leer's essays on Australian literary geography ("At the Edge," published in 1985, and "Imagined Counterpart," published in 1991), Bruce Bennett's *An Australian Compass,* published in 1991, Graham Huggan's *Territorial Disputes,* published in 1994, and Ferrier (1989), Genoni (2004), Kossew (2004), Darian-Smith, Gunner, and Nuttall (2005), Cranston and Zeller (2007), P. Mitchell (2008), and McMahon (2013). In theater, key texts include Bill Dunstone's "'Another Planet'" (1985), Gay McAuley's *Space in Performance* (1999) and the edited

of space as a theme in Australian film, literature, and theater research over the past 30 years, very little research has been done to bring these strands of spatial enquiry into dialogue.

GEO/CRITICAL TRADITIONS: LITERARY GEOGRAPHY, FILM GEOGRAPHY, AND SPATIAL INQUIRY IN AUSTRALIAN LITERARY, FILM, AND THEATER STUDIES

It is interesting to note that these developments within literary and cultural studies are, to some extent, mirrored within the discipline of geography, which saw the development of narrative-focused subdisciplines such as literary geography in the late 1970s and film and media geography in the 1990s and 2000s. As early as 1947, geographer John. K. Wright made an appeal in the *Annals of the Association of American Geographers* for a new breed of geographers trained in literary studies, whose "research and teaching would be directed toward the discovery and the interpretation of geographical truth, belief, and error as they find and have found literary and artistic expression" ("Terrae" 15). These "aesthetic" geographers or "geosophers," Wright argued, would open the discipline up to new kinds of evidence and new ways of thinking about geography. "As long as they did not come to regard themselves as the only true exponents of what geography ought to be," he concluded, "there would be little danger of their exerting an adverse effect upon the advancement and the prestige of scientific geography" ("Terrae" 15). Certainly geographers had been employing literary texts to support more traditional geographical research much earlier than the 1940s,[3] but Wright's is one of the first explicit calls for defined "literary" geography, and it followed on from his observation in 1924 that geographers "have devoted but little attention to this fascinating subject of geography in literature" ("Geography" 659).

collection *Unstable Ground* (2006), along with Grehan (2001), Gilbert and Lo (2007), Tompkins (2007), Carleton (2008), and Fensham (2008). More recently, Australian theater scholarship has intersected with the international rise in popularity of site-specific theater. Anna Birch and Joanne Tompkins's 2012 edited collection *Performing Site-Specific Theatre* investigates the relationship between site and practice in relation to performances that are set in "real" locations (as against inside traditional theater buildings).

3. See Allen G. Noble and Ramesh Dhussa and Marc Brosseau for a review of literary geography's early history.

It took some decades for John Wright's call to be heeded in any way that might resemble the formation of a subdiscipline, but by the late 1970s and early 1980s a number of geographers were either "doing" literary geography (in the form of studies of "regional" novels)[4] or making cases for its validity as an area of study.[5] What is clear from both Wright's 1947 appeal and the studies that appeared in the 1980s is that one kind of aesthetic text is clearly privileged: the literary text and, specifically, the novel. According to Porteous, writing in 1985, although "engagement with the arts has a long tradition in geography," geographers have "been rather selective in their choice of art forms for analysis" with "imaginative literature" being the "favoured form." Even within that category, Porteous continues, "geographers have again been highly selective"—they have ignored plays and rarely considered poetry. In all, "the novel reigns supreme" (117). Writing three years later, Douglas C. D. Pocock concurred: for geographers "novels have been overwhelmingly the subject of scrutiny" because they are both "the more robust genre" and because "their narrative form and study of character use specific settings." Poetry, according to Pocock, does not offer itself so readily to geographical analysis, for it "is less concerned with the observation of landscape than with its use to set in motion the writer's subjective response," while in drama, any concentration on setting "would detract from its prime study of character" ("Geography" 89). Noticeably absent from any analysis of aesthetic or literary geography through to the 1990s is any mention of film as a cultural form for analysis.[6] Indeed, in 1994, Stuart C. Aitken and Leo E. Zonn noted that film had been "virtually ignored" by the discipline of geography more broadly (*Place* ix).

Moreover, as Joanne P. Sharp has argued, these foundational studies in literary geography have been characterized by a certain "naïveté" towards the literary text, which is viewed as universal, "unproblematic and self evident in its immediate beauty" (328). For instance, in the in-

4. Charles S. Aiken's essays on William Faulkner's Yoknapatawpha County and B. P. Birch's study of Thomas Hardy's Wessex are notable examples from this period.

5. See, for instance, Douglas C. D. Pocock, Introduction; Nigel Thrift, "Literature"; D. W. Meinig; and J. Douglas Porteous.

6. Film is ignored by Pocock; Porteous; Thrift, "Literature"; Meinig; Noble and Dhussa; and Brosseau. Brosseau, notably, explains that his review will focus solely on the novelistic form because "most geographers have focused on this type of literature" (335).

troductory essay for his influential collection of 1981, *Humanistic Geography and Literature: Essays on the Experience of Place,* Pocock argues for the "primacy of literature and the holistic nature of literary revelation" (Introduction 9), and he states that the *"raison d'être* for the geographer's engagement with literature stems from the latter's . . . universality" (12). This insistence on universality marks a clear distinction between the aims and assumptions of literary geography and of cultural geography more broadly, for, as Sharp argues, although "universalist positions have been heavily critiqued in other parts of geography," they remain "strangely underexamined for literature and other arts" (328). What seems at first an odd incongruence between literary and cultural geography becomes less perplexing when considered in the context of the former's history. As Marc Brosseau astutely points out, literary geography did not arise from "research on discursive, semantic or symbolic structures—with the corollary rejection of the subject and/or history"—research that was re-forming and reframing literary studies at the time—but rather "within a humanistic project designed to restore 'man,' meaning and values in geography" (333–34).

In this sense, then, there has been little to connect literary geography with the discipline of literary studies as it developed over the same period, and this is perhaps partly because what is a strength in one has been considered a weakness in the other. Andrew Thacker argues that, although literary studies has a long tradition of engaging with spatio-geographical aspects of literary works, literary scholars have "quite often . . . read these texts by subjugating their spatiality to that of an aesthetic theme or trope" (56). Similarly, Fabio Lando makes the point that, while literary geographers have often overlooked the literary context of the novels they analyze, literary scholars have often "interpret[ed] the man/environment relationship only in clumsy deterministic terms" (5). According to Thacker, this all changed in 1989, when, he says, with self-conscious hyperbole, "literary and cultural critics all read David Harvey's *The Condition of Postmodernity*" (57). Harvey's work, along with that of Soja and Jameson, among others, enabled the development of a kind of "geographical criticism," one that "enabled questions of space and geography [to] become recognised as legitimate and important topics in many areas of literary and cultural studies" (Thacker 57–58).

Certainly in the mid- to late 1980s, Leer and Graham Huggan were beginning to hold Australian literature up to a dual geographical/postcolonial view, with Huggan in his seminal essay of 1989, "Decolonizing the Map," invoking both cartographic historian J. B. Harley and Edward Said. In his 1994 book, *Territorial Disputes*, Huggan argues that the prevalence of maps and mapping in contemporary Australian and Canadian writing must be understood as an active engagement in the "politics of cultural representation," shifting each country's spatial paradigm from a "cartography of exile" to a "cartography of difference" (149–50). Following Huggan's book and starting in the mid-1990s, a stream of major literary studies devoted to space and spatiality emerged,[7] but of these publications, virtually none has been cited in the published literature on literary geography post-1995, and vice versa, bearing out the clear disconnect between literary geography and geographically inflected literary studies.[8]

When film geography began to emerge within the discipline of geography in the early 1990s,[9] it not only responded to the comparative lack of attention to cinema by geographers but also diverged from literary

---

7. These spatial studies of literature notably include Christopher GoGwilt's *The Invention of the West* (1995); Tom Conley's *The Self-Made Map* (1996); Franco Moretti's *Atlas of the European Novel* (1998); Eric Bulson's *Novels, Maps, Modernity* (2007); Peta Mitchell's *Cartographic Strategies of Postmodernity* (2008); Robert T. Tally's *Melville, Mapping, and Globalization* (2009); and Eric Prieto's *Literature, Geography, and the Postmodern Poetics of Place* (2013).

8. In her recently published *Literary Geographies*, Sheila Hones has articulated the "mutual textual distance" that these literary-geographical traditions have maintained. She notes, for instance, the "frustration" felt by geographers in response to the publication of Franco Moretti's *Atlas of the European Novel* in 1998, a frustration born, she writes, "of a sense that it was written as if several decades of cultural geography had never happened" (170). Hones also acknowledges, in a refreshingly self-aware move, what she terms her "guilty evasion of bafflingly 'other' literary geographical spaces" (such as those presented by Moretti-style distant reading and literary neogeography projects, as well as "various lines of work in literary studies such as ecopoetics, geopoetics, ecocriticism, and geocriticism") that she finds difficult to reconcile with literary geography as practised by geographers (172). Nevertheless, Tania Rossetto's recent (2013) survey essay "Theorizing Maps with Literature" for *Progress in Human Geography* has sought to bring together and synthesize many of these parallel but disparate strands of research.

9. See Zonn and Aitken's influential articles relating to Australian film, namely Zonn's "Images of Place" and Zonn and Aitken's "Of Pelicans and Men."

geography's universalizing tendencies. This divergence between literary and film geography—the two streams of geography that directly engage with narrative fiction—has meant there has been very little dialogue between the two. They appear to exist as two different subdisciplines with different histories, approaches, and assumptions. By 2006, Christopher Lukinbeal and Stefan Zimmermann were calling for film geography to be recognized as a new subfield of geography.[10] Under the banner of film geography, Lukinbeal and Zimmermann posit four trajectories: geopolitics (examining mise-en-scène and narrative), cultural politics (revealing contested sociospatial meanings), globalization (exploring the impact of economic and pragmatic imperatives on film production, distribution, and reception in terms of selecting, representing, and visiting film locations), and, finally, concerns about film's capacity to mimic or accurately reflect "real" landscapes and locations in accordance with scientific and aesthetic models of realism. These trajectories do broadly correspond to approaches to film within Australian cinema studies, and they speak to the development of film geography out of an engagement with existing scholarship in cinema studies.

Within Australian cinema studies itself, what Lukinbeal and Zimmermann describe as the "globalization trajectory" corresponds to pragmatic approaches that examine the political and spatial economy of production logistics (see, for instance, Beeton; Goldsmith, Ward, and O'Regan); the "cultural politics trajectory" corresponds to accounts of land rights, immigration, Indigeneity, and belonging (see, for instance, C. Simpson, Murawska, and Lambert); and "geopolitics" encompasses the very large body of work on mise-en-scène criticism, but also studies focusing on regionality (see Carleton, "Cinema"; Craven, "Paradise") and cinematic cartography (see Mills; Mitchell and Stadler, "Imaginative"). With the exception of debates around the use of computer-generated imagery (CGI) to alter the physical landscape in Baz Luhrmann's 2008 film *Australia*, Lukinbeal and Zimmermann's fourth trajectory, the concern with "science, representation and mimesis," appears to be the focus of geographers

10. See Lukinbeal and Zimmermann "Film Geography: A New Subfield." This subfield includes Zonn and Aitken's work in the early 1990s, as well as Tim Cresswell and Deborah Dixon's 2002 edited collection *Engaging Film*.

rather than film scholars. Nevertheless, unlike literary geography's relationship to literary studies, film geography's approaches and assumptions are much more closely aligned with those of film studies. Further, with respect to Lukinbeal and Zimmermann's four trajectories of film geography, Australian cinema studies has been dominated by concerns with the cultural politics of location. Indeed, this focus unites the only analyses of Australian cinema by film geographers, and the wide-ranging analyses by film scholars with an interest in landscape.

Because film studies first took root in the Australian university system as an offshoot of more established modes of literary and cultural criticism, it is unsurprising that critical approaches to cinematic geography within film studies have until recently been dominated by studies of structural dichotomies, narrative symbolism, and postcolonial critiques of *terra nullius* derived from literary analysis and informed by aesthetic approaches to representations of landscape such as mise-en-scène criticism drawn from art history and theater studies. Within this tradition of criticism, many scholars have examined how Australian cinema has tended to locate colonization and experiences of survival and belonging in the physical environment in relation to an ideal of identity and nation building associated with European masculine endeavor. Much contemporary research still approaches cinematic representations of landscape in this manner; however, fresh approaches to landscape informed by disciplines such as tourism studies and geography are emerging within film studies.

This shift away from understandings of film narrative based in literary criticism toward a more geographic and cartographic, historicized conception of screen space can be traced, in the Australian context, to Ross Gibson's influential research in the 1990s. Gibson took up a perspective often advanced by geographers and geocritical theorists and distinguished between the omniscient viewing position of the modern map and pre-Renaissance maps that, "like medieval icon paintings, presume the existence of a reader who is *inside* the scene, not separate and voyeuristic of it at all" (*South* 6–7). Gibson compares these European representations of landscape with the view of the land offered in cinema and in non-Western systems of representation such as Aboriginal paintings. In *Australian National Cinema*, Tom O'Regan follows Gibson in describing the recently colonized landscape as taking on an "emblematic" identity in Australian cinema to the extent that film narration is a way of staking a claim on the land: "A sense of youth and beginning anew is paradoxically associated with an ancient landscape, a unique flora and fauna and, more lately, Aboriginal people and their heritage" (209). In an important contribution to the turn toward films that engage with Indigenous perspectives, Felicity Collins and Therese Davis's book *Australian Cinema after Mabo* draws out the cultural politics and contested significance of postcolonial representations of land.

Unlike literary and film studies, theater studies has no direct counterpart within geography—there is no "theater geography" per se, and, indeed, very few studies of theater, drama, or theatrical performance exist that are written from within geography as a discipline.[11] Although within theater studies, space has been subject to critical analysis, such research principally engages with staging space, semiotics of performance, and representations of landscapes (see McAuley, *Space;* Chaudhuri; Chaudhuri and Fuchs; Read). Most studies of space in Australian theater analyze set design and mise-en-scène or dramaturgical uses of stage space, or they take a postcolonial approach to contested narrative spaces (see, for instance, Gilbert and Tompkins; Grehan; Gilbert and Lo). The postcolonial framework of analysis has been particularly fruitful, leading to Tompkins's concept of "unsettlement" and Helen Gilbert's work on spatial histories within Indigenous theater and cartographies of the stagescape and landscape in what she terms settler/invader plays. Geographical approaches to theater are rare; yet, as Carleton's work suggests, drama studies is ripe for geocriticism: "Theatre not only represents space, it enacts space. It reads, politicises and activates the ways in which we imagine cultural geographies. It brings Australian landscapes to the fore, and populates and physicalises them in conscious and frequently metaphoric or metonymic ways" ("Staging" 7).

The approaches we have outlined here can broadly be termed geocritical and interdisciplinary in the sense that they take a critical approach to geographical representation in narrative fiction. However, as we have noted, literary geography and film geography are distinct traditions

11. Geographers such as Thrift have, however, been interested in the concepts of performance and performativity ("Performance").

within geography, each with its own histories and assumptions. Similarly, although spatial inquiry has been a preoccupation for Australian literary, film, and theater studies since the 1980s, very little research exists that has brought these strands into dialogue to examine how spaces are depicted and translated across media forms. Aside from Roslynn Haynes's *Seeking the Centre,* there has been little sustained inter-media analysis of representations of Australian space beyond edited collections (e.g., Barcan and Buchanan, *Imagining*) or themed journal issues. As with film geography's relationship to literary geography, this lack of inter-media spatial analysis within Australian cultural studies is partly a question of disciplinary politics, and again the question of literature's "primacy" is at the fore, particularly in regard to film studies. As Turner argues, "the problem of making links between film and fiction . . . lies in the fact that historically, film has . . . been treated as a literary text," and the "application of literary criticism to the analysis of film" has resulted in the privileging of "the literary text—by valorising those of its functions which are difficult to reproduce on screen" (14).

Each of these disciplinary traditions brings its own particular strengths to the study of narrative fiction: literary geography brings a close and sustained engagement with geographical and environmental knowledge; literary studies enables a more complex discussion of relationships between language, representation, space, and place; film geography brings critical distinctions between land and landscape and theoretically informed understandings of the production of place as spectacle, metaphor, and cultural artifact; film studies brings questions about screen aesthetics, spectatorship, and the cinematic articulation of varied, ideologically charged perspectives on landscape; and theater studies brings the staging of space and symbolic enactments of space into the frame, emphasizing the fact that theater texts, unlike literary texts, need to have the elements of live performance taken into consideration—they are embodied texts and require more than "just" literary analysis in order to be appreciated in full. If we accept, broadly speaking, that all of the approaches have developed in response to the "spatial turn," that in their current forms they all hinge on the same body of theoretical knowledge, and yet that they have had little or no direct bearing upon one another, then the focus must turn to methodology. In the next section, we outline the ways in which a defined

geocritical method that draws on the combined strengths of geographical, filmic, literary, and theatrical analysis might bring these traditions
into mutually beneficial dialogue with one another in order to realize the
potential for spatial theory to illuminate the study of narrative fiction.

GEOCRITICISM, INTERDISCIPLINARITY,

AND MEDIATED GEOGRAPHIES

Given the long history of critical spatial analysis, the term *geocriticism* is
a surprisingly recent coining, arising from the work of Bertrand Westphal and Robert T. Tally. As Tally defines it in a 2008 essay, geocriticism
is a predominantly literary-critical methodological "framework that focuses on the spatial representations within [literary] texts" while also
"explor[ing] the overlapping territories of actual, physical geography and
an author's or character's cognitive mapping in the literary text" ("Geocriticism" 4). Acknowledging that his approach differs in some respects
from Westphal's, Tally explains their shared interest in examining the
relationship between the dimensions of the real and the imagination, between the referent and representation.

In Westphal's *La géocritique* (first published in 2007 and translated
by Tally in 2011 as *Geocriticism: Real and Fictional Spaces*), geocriticism
emerges as a multifocal and dialectical method of analysis. Indeed, the
principle of geocritical analysis, Westphal argues, lies in "the confron-
tation of several optics that correct, nourish, and mutually enrich each
other" (*Geocriticism* 113). Geocritical representation "emerges from a spec-
trum of individual representations as rich and varied as possible," and each
representation must be treated in a "dialectical process" in keeping with
geocriticism's plurality of viewpoints (113–14). This dialectical process
carves out a "common space" that allows the critic to "come closer to the
essential identity of the referenced space" while simultaneously confirm-
ing that "cultural identity" can only be the result of a continuous process
of "creation and re-creation" (114). Geocriticism offers the aesthetic text
an integral role in this spatio-cultural creative process. A film, a novel, or
a play does not merely or passively represent a given space or place; rather,
as Eric Prieto explains, geocriticism is "a kind of metacritical endeavor"
in that it "seeks to show how [the aesthetic text] can actually participate
and inflect the history of the places in question" ("Geocriticism" 21–22).

As its name suggests, geocriticism shifts the focus of narrative analysis away from its traditionally privileged sites of plot and character to setting, which often comes a distant third in extended treatments of narratology or narrative theory. For instance, Seymour Chatman, in his 1978 work of narrative theory *Story and Discourse: Narrative Structure in Fiction and Film,* considers setting to be important but only insofar as it supports and "sets off" character and provides a backdrop to the narrative's action. The setting, as he defines it, is a "space" in which "characters exist and move"; setting "sets the character off" (138). Chatman does, however, acknowledge that the question of narrative space is the one he has most neglected in outlining his theory of narrative. Of his book, he admits, "Setting is practically terra incognita; my brief pages hardly do justice to the subject, particularly its relation to that vague notion called 'atmosphere'." "I hope," he continues, "that recognizing the consubstantial relation between character and setting, as I have done, may prompt a more serious interest in [narrative space]" (264).[12] In contrast to traditional narrative theory, as Westphal explains, geocriticism explicitly moves the analytical focus from character to setting:

> Geocriticism is a geo-centered rather than an ego-centered approach; that is, the analysis focuses on global spatial representations rather than on individual ones (a given traveler's, for example). Thus one may undertake a geocritical study of a city, a region, a territory, and so on, rather than studying a given author's treatment of that place. (Foreword xiv)

Geocriticism, furthermore, takes a layered, "stratigraphic" approach in which, as Tally explains, "the *topos* is understood to comprise multiple layers of meaning, deterritorialized and reterritorialized; attention to surface alone would not be sufficient to understand the place" (*Spatiality* 142). Finally, Westphal is adamant that geocriticism is a fundamentally intertextual and *interdisciplinary* approach. Geocriticism, he maintains,

12. Hones has, for instance, argued that when narrative and spatial theories are brought to bear upon one another via a literary-geographical approach, they "make it clear that setting cannot be separated out from narrative voice and treated as a geographical frame of reference, something which simply situates plot action or reflects its themes, and this means in turn that it becomes more difficult to separate the literary from the geographical in fiction" ("Literary" 697).

"enters an interdisciplinary field" that "produces true interactions among disciplines like literary studies, geography, urbanism and architecture, with pathways to sociology and anthropology" (Foreword xiv). Although it finds its natural home in the field of comparative literary studies, the geocritical method is itself, he argues, "driven by the desire to mobilize distinct but compatible methodologies," and, as such, it may illuminate a range of aesthetic forms (*Geocriticism* 121). We see the value of a geocritical approach precisely in the way that it moves beyond the examination of space in literary narratives, or the analysis of location in film or theater. It is a theoretical framework that informs various modes of textual analysis and foregrounds the significance of geography to culture (and vice versa) without necessarily privileging any particular textual form. Geocriticism, therefore, enables us to grapple with adapting spatial representations across various media forms. As such, a geocritical approach may prove germane to media geography, itself a recent development within the interdisciplinary field of human geography, which has undergone, as Tristan Thielmann puts it, a "media turn" to complement media studies' spatial turn (5).

DIGITAL CARTOGRAPHY, NARRATIVE

GEOVISUALIZATION, AND GEOCRITICISM IN

PRACTICE: THE *CULTURAL ATLAS OF AUSTRALIA*

Interactive online mapping, we argue, is one way in which geocriticism can put into practice its capacity to reframe understandings of place and space by revealing connections between separate strands of spatial enquiry. Over the past decade, interactive online mapping—what D. R. Fraser Taylor has called "cybercartography" and others have termed "neo-geography"—has become a salient issue within cartography in particular and geography more broadly.[13] This is especially the case since Google released the Google Maps application programming interface (API) in 2005, allowing users free access to the Google Maps code as long as the resulting map "mashup" remains nonproprietary and in the public domain. According to William Buckingham and Samuel Dennis, the development

---

13. See, for instance, Cartwright, Peterson, and Gartner; Crampton; and Monmonier, "Cartography."

of open-source mapping tools, such as Google Maps and OpenStreet-Map, has generated much interest in the use of maps for "understanding 'non-mapped' phenomena (e.g., qualitative data or localized community information and knowledge)," and this, they continue, articulates well with the sociological perspectives that have influenced the discipline over the past two decades (55). This is, as Buckingham and Dennis argue, a "new world of spatial information," promising increased dialogue among cartography, geography, the humanities, and citizens (61).[14] While the disciplines of geography and cartography are increasingly engaging with new media studies, the digital humanities, and fields such as literary geography, researchers working in the digital humanities have also become interested in the possibilities afforded by interactive mapping technologies. In 2011, digital historian John Levin began collecting on his blog links to academic digital humanities GIS (Geographic Information Systems) projects in order to "see how space and place are being analysed" in the digital humanities domain "and what technologies are being used to do so." Over three years, Levin has collected links to more than 140 projects,[15] the vast majority of which were established in the post-Google Maps environment.

The recent and remarkable proliferation of these digital humanities GIS projects has led David J. Bodenhamer, John Corrigan, and Trevor M. Harris to proclaim a new form of digitally enabled "spatial humanities" that "promises to revitalize and redefine [humanities] research" (vii). And yet, as Trevor M. Harris, Susan Bergeron, and Jesse L. Rouse warn, this rapid growth of humanities-based mapping projects is not evidence of a systematic and organized engagement with GIS on the part of digital humanists; rather, they maintain, "GIS uptake in the humanities has been disparate, uncoordinated, and largely project and application driven" (227). At the root of the problem, they suggest, is a fundamental disconnect between GIS technology and humanities methods, one that "reflects underlying ontological and epistemological issues associated with inte-

14. More recently, researchers working in and across the disciplines of geography and GIScience have critiqued the notion that neogeography is a transformative technology that has an inherently democratizing power (see, for instance, Haklay and Leszczynski).
15. See http://anterotesis.com/wordpress/mapping-resources/dh-gis-projects/.

grating a predominantly positivist science with humanistic disciplines"
(238). Although human and cultural geographers have, since the 1990s,
drawn attention to and critiqued the positivist underpinnings of GIS (see,
for instance, Pickles; Schuurman and Pratt; Farman;and Sui), these critiques are rarely noted or referenced in relation to individual digital humanities geovisualization projects. This oversight is not inconsequential,
for certain aspects of GIS do not map easily onto a humanities research
agenda that has traditionally been less interested in quantitative and
database-driven approaches. As Harris, Bergeron, and Rouse point out,
where the humanities "are dominated by a heavy reliance on qualitative
data," GIS is "based on a quantitative representation of the world involving
spatial primitives and the topological relations between them" and does
not naturally lend itself to "incorporating and accessing qualitative information such as photographs, paintings, oral history, moving images, text,
and sketches" (228). Moreover, they argue, GIS does not immediately lend
itself to narrative and storytelling (which they characterize somewhat
simplistically as inherently "linear" when compared with the nonlinearity
of spatial analysis) and is ill-equipped to deal with the ambiguous spaces,
open-ended questions, and multiplicity of perspectives that are the humanities' stock in trade (228).

Given these apparent clashes of approach and in-built disaffordances,
what explains this post-2005 rash of digital humanities GIS, particularly
in relation to mapping narrative? The urge to geovisualize narrative—to
plot narrative locations on a map—is, of course, nothing new. It underpins
literary geography as a discipline but certainly also precedes it. One such
early narrative map is William Lyon Phelps's late nineteenth-century *Literary Map of England*,[16] which plotted out "all the towns and localities that
have distinct literary interest" in England and was intended "as an aid in
the study of literary geography."[17] A century later, in the 1990s, narrative
mapping received new impetus in the form of two book-length studies
of literary geography: Malcolm Bradbury's 1996 *Atlas of Literature* and
Franco Moretti's 1998 *Atlas of the European Novel, 1800–1900*, the latter of
which has inspired more than a few literary neogeography projects. In his

16. See http://www.gutenberg.org/files/10609/10609-h/10609-h.htm#e1002.
17. See advertising material in the back matter of Phelps.

Atlas, Moretti poses the question "what do literary maps allow us to see?" and suggests two answers:

> First they highlight the *ortgebunden,* place-bound nature of literary forms: each of them with its peculiar geometry, its boundaries, its spatial taboos and favourite routes. And then, maps bring to light the *internal* logic of narrative: the semiotic domain around which a plot coalesces and self-organizes. (5)

We would add to this that narrative maps allow us to see patterns of spatial representation that might not otherwise be immediately apparent. The promise and allure of GIS is that it enables researchers to work with larger datasets in order to build up and potentially to reveal those broader patterns of representation. GIS also enables more interactive and multimedia engagement with narrative maps, as exemplified by the growing list of international narrative geovisualization projects. This list includes such projects as the *Cultural Atlas of Australia;* the *Cybercartographic Atlas of Canadian Cinema* (led by Sébastien Caquard, Concordia University); the *Digital Literary Atlas of Ireland, 1922–1949* (led by Charles Travis, Trinity College Dublin); the *Literary Atlas of Europe* (led by Barbara Piatti and Lorenz Hurni, ETH Zurich); *Mapping the City in Film* (led by Julia Hallam, University of Liverpool); *Mapping the Lakes: A Literary GIS* (led by Ian Gregory and Sally Bushell, Lancaster University); and the "Spatial History of Hollywood Narrative Locations" (in development; led by Christian Long, University of Queensland). Apart from the *Cultural Atlas of Australia,* this list can be split into two equal groups—literary GISS (*Ireland; Europe; Lakes*) and film GISS (*Canadian Cinema; City in Film;* "Hollywood").[18] This suggests that the longstanding disciplinary divisions between spatial studies of film and literature and between liter-

---

18. We also distinguish these narrative-based GISs that map cultural representations of space and place from a range of complementary projects that map the locations of cultural production and consumption. Successful examples of the latter kind of project include *Going to the Show* (led by Robert Allen), which documents the history of moviegoing in North Carolina through maps, photographs, and press clippings; work on new cinema history and mapping, including the *Australian Cinemas Map* (led by Richard Maltby and colleagues); and the *AusStage* database mapping service, which maps Australian-based theatrical productions (i.e., where a play was staged), the tours of those productions, and the trajectories of those associated with them.

ary geography and film geography are replicated, once more, at the level of project-based narrative geovisualization. Furthermore, these projects have, over the past half-decade from 2009, generated a large and growing body of scholarly work dedicated to literary and filmic geovisualization.[19]

At the time of writing, the *Cultural Atlas of Australia* is the only narrative geovisualization project that maps more than one narrative form, and the only project that maps the narrative locations of theater. To date, the *Cultural Atlas* maps approximately 200 novels, films, and plays that are set in and feature Australian spaces and places. As a result of our interest in the adaptation of spatial stories across media forms and our view that multiple versions of a narrative indicate that cultural significance attaches to the narrative events and the location in which they take place, in certain cases we have followed the narrative trail to include various retellings, and this has sometimes meant mapping documentaries, poems, short stories, creative nonfiction, and songs. At the heart of the project is a core set of 150 landmark Australian spatial narratives (50 films, 50 novels, and 50 plays) that were published, released, or staged post-1950. The temporal scope of the *Cultural Atlas* is increasingly broadening, as we incorporate further colonial- and war-era narratives. One of our interests, as spatio-cultural researchers, has been in investigating whether geovisualizing Australian narrative fiction has the potential to suggest new ways of thinking about location and landscape and to break down traditional typologies of Australian space.

Rich and multilayered as it is, our dataset cannot hope—now or perhaps ever—to fully account for the spaces and places of Australian narrative fiction. Perhaps first among its limitations is that it cannot adequately begin to account for the vast numbers of novels, in particular, that have been set on Australian soil since the beginning of the nineteenth century. The *AustLit* database, which provides the most comprehensive resource for studying Australian literature, has entries for approximately 6,500 novels

19. See, in particular, Caquard, "Foreshadowing" and "Cartography I"; Caquard and Fiset; Caquard and Taylor; Caquard and Wright; Cooper and Gregory; Hallam, "Film," "Mapping," and "Civic"; Hallam and Roberts; Long; Mitchell and Stadler, "Imaginative" and "Redrawing"; Piatti et al.; Piatti and Hurni, "Mapping" and "Cartographies"; Stadler, "Mapping" and "Seeing"; Travis, "Abstract" and "Transcending."

set in Australia since 1801. Attempting to map these novels in as contextualized and fine-grained a way as we have our 200 texts so far would be, to put it mildly, a daunting task. Searching the *Internet Movie Database* for a snapshot of the number of feature-length movies filmed (but not necessarily set) in Australia, produces significantly fewer results: 1,799 titles, with the first having been released in 1900. As regards plays, *AustLit* lists just over 1,100 "dramas" that have been set in Australia since 1792. According to these databases, there have been more than three and a half times as many novels published that are set in Australia as there have been movies filmed in the country and plays written and staged about it. Given that our aim has been to give as equal voice as possible to these three narrative forms and to focus on where they intersect via adaptation, we have imposed restrictions on what we map, such as requiring that, in order to be mapped, a novel (if it is not an adaptation) must have won or been nominated for a literary award, a film must be feature-length and have had at least full national distribution, and a play must have had a professional production. Particularly in the case of novels and plays, this has had the effect of skewing our dataset towards traditional high-cultural genres, and particularly towards literary realism.

Despite the fact that the *Cultural Atlas* is, and always must be, an incomplete map of Australian narrative fiction, what GIS and its database structure have allowed us to do is visualize new perspectives on, intersections between, and layerings of geographic, historical, and textual information across the texts that we do map. It has also allowed us to open up this research to a much wider and more varied audience than, for instance, this academic book will reach. Where geocriticism, as we have argued, encourages dialogue among discrete traditions of spatial analysis, geovisualization and interactive mapping have the added benefit of rendering this work accessible to a broader audience that includes other academic researchers, school teachers, students, cultural tourists, and "grey nomads," as well as the general public. The *Cultural Atlas* functions as a cultural information resource and research tool that enables users to generate and export their own maps with information they require. A user might, for instance, search for and export a map of all locations featured in David Malouf's *Johnno* for a cultural tour of literary sites, or a map of plays, novels, and films that have Gothic themes. The map's temporal dimension enables users to plot successive adaptations of a text and identify multiple texts set in the same place. These functions have the capacity to reveal how cultural meanings accrue on the landscape, and how our relationship with, and understanding of, the natural and cultural environment changes over time. In the most recent phase of the project, we have moved toward further incorporating user-contributed information and volunteered geographic information (particularly in the form of photographs, videos, and textual accounts of Australian places), and the *Cultural Atlas*'s associated mobile application (CultureMap) opens up further opportunities through locative media for the situated representation of multiple perspectives.

This book is not, however, primarily about the *Cultural Atlas*. It does not describe how we selected the texts it maps, delve into how we designed the database to incorporate the three narrative forms and the relational links between them, or explain the user design scenarios that informed the map interface. This is not to say that the design process was not an interesting one and is certainly not to suggest that it can simply be ignored. The *Cultural Atlas* is by no means a highly sophisticated cultural GIS, but as with any other, its database structure and map interface are what ultimately drive what can be represented on the map and how it can be represented. What this book does is to focus on particular case study texts and groups of texts that shed light on particular problems, questions, or patterns that emerge in the process of geovisualizing narrative landscapes. As Ian Gregory and Alistair Geddes write:

> Maps rarely answer questions; far more commonly, they pose them. Why is the pattern as it is? Why are things different over here compared to over there? It is up to researchers to answer these questions in a way that they choose—GIS does not force a paradigm onto them. This presents a challenge. The technology was developed for reasons that have little to do with the needs of academic researchers, particularly those in the humanities. The challenge for humanities researchers is to take these tools and modify, develop, and apply them in ways that are appropriate to the paradigm that they want to pursue. (xvii)

Geovisualization, as we have argued, offers the potential to open up new questions for spatial analysis and to encourage broader public engagement in cultural geography. However, as a form of remediation, it does carry its own representational problems. As Piatti et al. have noted, the geography of fiction is an imprecise one (182). Here, the authors are specifically referring to literary fiction, but the point can be made for all forms of narrative fiction. In film, literature, and theater, the representation of space and place can never simply be mimetic, but always, to a greater or lesser degree, creates an imaginative geography that may correspond to what Piatti et al. call the "geospace" (or map space) directly, only loosely, or not at all. Bringing film and theater space into the analytical frame carries its own set of complexities and ambiguities: film requires attention to the relationship between narrative locations and shooting locations, while drama brings questions of performance and dramaturgical space. Beyond the question of impreciseness, we must also remain aware that the remediation of narrative locations is not simply a matter of re-presenting narrative locations in map form, difficult though that process might be in itself; the process of re-presenting narrative locations, too, is a process of imagining and reimagining geography that, by its very nature, must also be political.

As Bodenhamer has argued, GIS is a "seductive technology" that "promises to reinvigorate our description of the world through its manipulation and visualization of vast quantities of data by means previously beyond the reach of most scholars" ("Potential" 16). In taking up the challenge of GIS, humanists, Bodenhamer claims "run the risk of portraying the world uncritically" and "suggest[ing] that the world is indeed flat, at least metaphorically" (17). In a trenchant critique of the rush by humanities scholars to embrace neogeography, Johanna Drucker has suggested that "humanists" have willfully overlooked its limitations and built-in biases, happily setting aside their usual commitment to constructivist approaches to knowledge in favor of simple reductionism:

> All maps are constructions, and the history of cartography, like the histories of other graphical forms of knowledge, is filled with productive debates about the ideological and rhetorical force of mapping techniques. Humanists are certainly well aware of these complexities, but the tendency to wave them aside as mere nuance in the rush to adopt Google Maps or a standard projection, even knowing full well that any presentation of an oblate spheroid (the earth) onto a flat surface (map or screen), is fraught. But more is at stake for a humanist than the technical problems of projection.

Both space and time are constructs, not givens. . . . If I am anxious, spatial and temporal dimensions are distinctly different than when I am not. When the world was bounded by the Mediterranean it was a different world than the one seen from space. These are not different versions of the same thing. The entire theoretical weight of constructivist approaches to knowledge stands against such a reductive pronouncement. (90)

To guard against this flattening-out of context (spatial, historical, cultural, racial, social, or emotional), Harris, Corrigan, and Bodenhamer argue, humanities scholars need to develop "deep maps" that juxtapose multiple cultural and historical layers and perspectives in order to "record and represent the grain and patina of place" (174–75). Taken together, our aim for the *Cultural Atlas* and this book is to do just that: to map, digitally and textually, Australia's cultural terrain, but also to continually interrogate that mapping process. Critical questions we ask of our mapping are *whose* geography does it represent, how can we reconcile multiple perspectives, given that the map space privileges an omniscient viewing perspective, and how do cartographic technologies and database structures both enable and limit forms of spatial representation? A vital question taken up in the case studies developed in the chapters to follow involves consideration of what spaces, locations, and forms of spatial knowledge are routinely overlooked. Certainly one theme that emerges through the case studies presented here is the elision or erasure of Indigenous perspectives, geographies, and even lives. Although the *Cultural Atlas* maps a significant number of narrative texts by Indigenous authors, playwrights, and filmmakers or about Indigenous understandings of space and place, this in turn raises ethical, aesthetic, and epistemological questions. That is, it is not a straightforward matter of making visible the invisible because complex issues surround the representation, naming, and mapping of sacred or culturally sensitive sites.[20] Moreover, forcing these

20. Notable examples of Indigenous texts included in the *Cultural Atlas* are Jimmy Chi's musical *Bran Nue Dae* and its 2009 film adaptation by Rachel Perkins; Jack Davis's 1979 play *Kullark*; Doris Pilkington Garimara's 1996 nonfiction book *Follow the Rabbit-Proof Fence* and its 2002 film adaptation by Phillip Noyce; Ivan Sen's 2011 film *Toomelah*; Warwick Thornton's 2009 film *Samson and Delilah*; Alexis Wright's 2006 novel *Carpentaria*; and a series of fictional, nonfictional, and theatrical works around the story of Jandamarra, the leader of a late Indigenous resistance in the Kimberley region of Western

non-Western geographies to fit Google Maps's Web Mercator projection, which cannot escape the ideological baggage of its namesake,[21] adds yet another level of complexity. These questions are themselves all geocritical ones, and—although the latter is beyond the scope of this volume—they cannot, and should not, be elided.

Ultimately, we argue, geocriticism offers itself as a metacritical methodology that is particularly relevant for Australian cultural studies, but is also applicable to interdisciplinary spatio-cultural research more broadly. It recognizes literature, film, and theater texts as being more than representations, more than containers for narrative symbolism and ideological views and values, and this extends to any geovisualization strategy that seeks to map those texts. Such texts are also generative—productive of meanings, social relationships, and subject positions. Conley argues in *Cartographic Cinema* that cinematic images "produce space through the act of perception" (20); similarly, theater stages and enacts space and literature imaginatively invokes space in ways that subsequently inflect

Australia (see Idriess; Mudrooroo; Torres; and Hawke). While many of these texts did not require a particular sensitivity to the politics of mapping above and beyond that required by non-Indigenous texts, a few are particularly resistant to being "fixed" on a Western map. In Wright's *Carpentaria,* for instance, the central narrative location—the fictional township of "Desperance," located in North Queensland's Gulf of Carpentaria—is meant to invoke a more fluid geography and temporality and is therefore not intended to be fixed in time and space. The mapping of a location may also be undesirable for political reasons as well as for aesthetic or cultural ones. Kim Scott's 1993 novel *True Country,* is set in "Karnama"—a remote former mission in the Kimberley region. In an author's note at the beginning of the text, Scott writes, "It is not difficult, for those so inclined, to trace Karnama back to a specific community. But then it's no longer Karnama. In terms of its character Karnama could, it seems to me, be one of many Aboriginal communities in Northern Australia." Scott acknowledges that the novel "began with a desire to explore a sort of neglected interior space, and to consider [his] own heritage." Yet, he continues, "none of the events or situations of the narrative are intended to correspond to any real occurrence"; the novel "remains wholly fictional in every aspect" (9). In a case such as this, the cultural cartographer must weigh what is gained by identifying a location against what might be lost in that same process.

21. In the early 1980s, while promoting his own more "egalitarian" map projection in his book *The New Cartography,* historian Arno Peters famously decried the Mercator projection in theatrically exaggerated terms for its "Eurocentric" bias and its implicit role in the "Age of European Conquest and Exploitation" (qtd. in Monmonier, *Rhumb* 154). Peters's self-aggrandizing attack on the "cartographic profession" for its continued

the meanings readers associate with actual places. Where geocriticism enables analysis of locational information in narrative fiction informed by insights from geography as well as literary and cultural studies, it also builds from the premise that such texts intervene in the cultural field and alter the perceptual, ideological, political and practical orientation of readers and audiences in relation to the physical environment.

adherence to the Mercator projection attracted the ire of cartographers and geographers, who pointed out that their profession demanded an attentiveness to distortion—an attentiveness that enabled them to demonstrate how Peters's projection was no less distorted than Mercator's, and perhaps even more so. Nonetheless, even though Peters was misguided in his attack on cartographers, according to map historian J. B. Harley, he was not necessarily wrong in principle. The "scientific Renaissance in Europe," Harley writes, footnoting his acknowledgement of Peters's *New Cartography,* "gave modern cartography coordinate systems, Euclid, scale maps, and accurate measurement, but it also helped to confirm a new myth of Europe's ideological centrality through projections such as those of Mercator" (6).

1

REMEDIATING SPACE

Adaptation and Narrative Geography

The formal characteristics of films, novels, and plays privilege varied expressions of imaginative geography and these cultural narratives, we argue, not only mediate and represent space, place, and location but are themselves mediated representational spaces. Furthermore, films, novels, and plays also open themselves up to further remediation in the form of cross-media adaptation or, to push the point further, in the form of geo-visualization and the spatial analysis it enables. Adaptation studies is an exciting, dynamic, and rapidly developing interdisciplinary field, and yet, like narrative theory, it has not fully or directly accounted for the question of space. Adaptation studies has been more concerned with questions of fidelity (or the validity of those questions), lines of influence, and transmediality and with the translation of space, place, and landscape between narrative forms being rarely addressed.

In compiling and constructing our *Cultural Atlas of Australia*, we encountered many texts in which the geographical setting of the narrative was modified—to greater or lesser degrees—across adaptations. For instance, John Curran's 1998 film adaptation of Andrew McGahan's cult "grunge" novel, *Praise* (1992), is filmed in Sydney rather than in Brisbane— the city in which the novel is set and with which it is intimately connected. Although McGahan wrote the screenplay for Curran's adaptation, and although the narrative setting of the film version remains, broadly speaking, the same (that is, urban Australia in the early 1990s), the choice of filming location means that the adaptation loses some of the novel's locational and regional specificity—namely, its focus on the then low-rent, inner-city Brisbane suburbs of New Farm and Fortitude Valley.[1] A more dramatic example is Scott Hicks's *The Boys Are Back* (2009), a film adaptation of British journalist Simon Carr's memoir about his experiences raising his sons in New Zealand following the death of his wife. Hicks's adaptation is neither set nor filmed in New Zealand; instead, it transplants the entire narrative to Australia, from Hawke's Bay on the east coast of New Zealand's north island to Adelaide, the capital of South Australia, and its environs—over 2000 miles (3219 km.) and another country away. Film adaptations may also, of course, provide a more heightened sense of location, simply by virtue of the fact they must be filmed *somewhere*, if they are being filmed on location, and this is particularly the case when the narrative setting of the adapted text is fictional, ambiguous, or only loosely sketched (as in the case of George T. Miller's 1982 film adaptation of A. B. "Banjo" Paterson's 1890 poem "The Man from Snowy River"). Stage adaptations are more likely, as we will see in the case study presented here, to reduce the geographical specificity of the original text while promoting a stronger sense of symbolic or mythic space. A case in point is Stephan Elliott's 2006 stage adaptation of his highly successful film *The Adventures of Priscilla, Queen of the Desert* (1994), which will be further analyzed in chapter 5. The film follows a busload of drag queens as they travel from Sydney to Alice Springs, visiting Broken Hill, Coober Pedy, the Painted Desert at Oodnadatta, and Kings Canyon en route. In Elliott's stage adaptation, the bus itself, rather than the locations it travels to, becomes by necessity the primary backdrop and the site for much of the production's action.

In order to investigate in greater depth these questions of remediation and spatial adaptation and the mapping challenges they present, we focus in this chapter on a single, central case study. This text—*Wake in Fright*—is a rare and fascinating case study for Australian narrative cartography in that it exists in multiple adaptations. The original novel, written by Aus-

---

1. Brisbane's distinctiveness, and its difference from other Australian capital cities, is a key motif in McGahan's *Praise*. At one point in the novel, Helen, a visitor from Melbourne, rails against Brisbane: "Look at this city. . . . There's nothing happening. There's no one on the streets. How can you stand it?" The protagonist, Gordon Buchanan, somewhat halfheartedly defends it: "Things are happening, you just have to look a little harder. At least no one bothers you. There's worse places than Brisbane" (12).

tralian journalist-turned-author Kenneth Cook and first published in 1961, was adapted as a cult classic (and only recently rediscovered) Australian New Wave film by Canadian director Ted Kotcheff in 1971. In 2010, it was further adapted as a stage play by Bob Pavlich. Both the film and stage adaptations are strikingly faithful to Cook's novel, but each constructs a particular mediated imaginative geography of the Australian interior, one that—particularly in the case of Kotcheff's film adaptation—continues to shape perceptions of Australian space both at home and abroad. Certainly in the Australian context, there is only a handful of narratives that exist on the page, on the screen, and on the stage. Exploring a case study such as this, we argue, allows an investigation of the ways in which representations of space and place are adapted, translated, and reimagined across media forms, and how these feed into the coproduction of fictive and physical geography.

ADAPTING/REMEDIATING SPACE

Before we approach *Wake in Fright* as a case study for remediated geographies, however, we must explain what we mean by such a term. The term *remediation* stems from the work of Jay David Bolter and Richard Grusin, who describe the dynamics of media (and particularly digital media) as a process of mediation and remediation. Remediation, as Bolter and Grusin put it, is "integral" to the functioning of media, which "are continually commenting on, reproducing, and replacing each other"; indeed, they maintain, the "goal of remediation is to refashion or rehabilitate other media" (55–56). Remediation, moreover, extends beyond the mediated and remediated text and into the realm of reality, for "because all mediations are both real and mediations of the real, remediation can also be understood as a process of reforming reality as well" (56). The concept of remediation has been taken up in adaptation studies notably by Irina O. Rajewsky, who explores it as a "particular type of intermedial relationship, and consequently as a subcategory of intermediality in the broad sense" (64). Intermediality, according to Rajewsky, "designates those configurations which have to do with a crossing of borders between media, and which thereby can be differentiated from *intra*medial phenomena as well as from *trans*medial phenomena (i.e., the appearance of a certain motif, aesthetic, or discourse across a variety of different media)" (46).

Eckart Voigts-Virchow has also drawn attention to remediation's potential within adaptation studies, arguing that "the house of adaptation has been opened up via a tendency called media convergence," citing Bolter and Grusin's term as an important one for thinking about "the adaptive processes involved in particular transitions to digital media" (139). Finally, Linda Hutcheon also invokes Bolter and Grusin's term when she describes "virtual environments, videogames (played on any platform), or even theme-park rides" as "adaptations or 'remediations'" of other mediated narratives (12–13).

In this chapter, we wish to consider the adaptation of space across narrative forms as a process of remediation that may then be taken one step further via the remediation of geovisualization. Adaptation studies has had little to say directly on the topic of adapting space. In her *Theory of Adaptation,* Hutcheon addresses the spatiality of narrative forms when she outlines the three fundamental "modes of engagement—telling, showing, and interacting with stories" (27). Hutcheon continues:

> These ways of engaging with stories do not, of course, ever take place in a vacuum. We engage in time and space, within a particular society and a general culture. The contexts of creation and reception are material, public, and economic as much as they are cultural, personal, and aesthetic. This explains why, even in today's globalized world, major shifts in a story's context—that is, for example, in a national setting or time period—can change radically how the transposed story is interpreted, ideologically and literally. The adaptation of a novel or short story to the (spoken) dramatic stage also involves the visual dimension, as well as the verbal; with that added dimension come audience expectations not only about voice but, as in dance, also about appearance, as we move from the imagined and visualized to the directly perceived. (28)

Yet, as Hutcheon later remarks, the physical stage also has "limitations" that "add restrictions on the possible action and characterization." Pointing to Salman Rushdie's theatrical co-adaptation of his novel *Midnight's Children* as an example, Hutcheon notes that fans of the novel expressed disappointment in the adaptation "for the play's manner was as stylized and spare as the novel's was exuberant and complicated" (42). The play did attempt to mitigate this by incorporating "cinematic techniques," including "a large diagonally split movie screen at the back to present both historical scenes and magic realist ones," leading Hutcheon to suggest that this is "one of the major advantages films have over stage adaptations of novels: the use of a multitrack medium that, with the aid of the mediating camera, can both direct and expand the possibilities of perception" (42–43). As Hutcheon explains,

> More often we are told that the camera *limits* what we can see, eliminating the action on the periphery that might have caught our attention when watching a play on stage. Not only is the kind of attention and focus different in a theatrical production but plays also have different conventions than films or television shows. They have a different grammar: cinema's various shots, their linking and editing, have no parallel in a stage play. Film has its own "form-language," to use Béla Balázs' term. (43)

Although Hutcheon does not speak directly to the question of adapting space, her brief analysis of formal affordances and constraints is highly relevant to approaching that question. This is not to say that no research exists on the spaces and spatialities of novels, films, and plays—treated separately, there has been a great deal written on the spatialities of these narrative forms. In literary studies, Joseph Frank's three-part essay "Spatial Form in Modern Literature" (1945) is a key early work, along with Maurice Blanchot's *Space of Literature* (*L'espace littéraire,* 1955), Ricardo Gullón's "On Space in the Novel" (1975), and W. J. T. Mitchell's "Spatial Form in Literature: Toward a General Theory" (1980). In film studies, the mid-1970s saw several attempts to theorize cinematic space (see Stephen Heath's "Narrative Space," David Bordwell's "Camera Movement and Cinematic Space," and Edward Branigan's "The Spectator and the Film Space," for instance). In theater studies, research by McAuley and Tompkins has established space and spatiality as central concerns within the discipline, and McAuley, in particular, has sought to produce a systematic "taxonomy of spatial function in the theatre" (*Space* 25). And yet, once more we see that there has been no significant study that has sought to explore, in a comparative way, the mediated spaces and spatialities of these narrative forms. Neither has there been any study devoted to the ways in which narrative space might be translated across these forms in the process of adaptation.

Our aim in what follows is not to provide an exhaustive transmedial overview of narrative space. Neither is it to formulate a comprehensive theory of spatial adaptation. Rather, it is to begin to work through some of the questions posed by a particular text whose narrative geography has been mediated and remediated multiple times.

REMEDIATED GEOGRAPHIES OF THE AUSTRALIAN INTERIOR: THE CASE OF *WAKE IN FRIGHT*

Cook's novel opens with a curse: "May you dream of the Devil and wake in fright." And for the novel's schoolteacher protagonist, John Grant, it all goes downhill from there. *Wake in Fright* tells the story of Grant's spectacular downfall as he attempts to return home to Sydney for the Christmas holidays from his regional teaching post in the far west of New South Wales. In describing Grant's thwarted attempts to escape "Bundanyabba" (a mining town based on Broken Hill), Cook constructs an imaginative geography of the region, one that presents the Australian interior as a space whose aggressive masculinity and barely held in check violence are anathema to Grant's urban sensibilities. The story of *Wake in Fright*—in all its iterations and adaptations—is the same. Young and urbane, though naïve, schoolteacher John Grant, who hails from Sydney but who is bonded to teach in the tiny Outback town of Tiboonda, has finished his teaching for the year and is preparing to return to the east coast for the Christmas holidays. In order to catch a plane to Sydney, he has to travel by train to the mining town of Bundanyabba and spend a night there. On his one night in town he is introduced to the gambling game of two-up by a local policeman, Jock Crawford, who also buys him multiple rounds of beer. After a brief run of good fortune at the two-up school, Grant loses all of his money and has to try to find another way out of Bundanyabba, which is affectionately known to locals as "The Yabba." In the process, Grant ends up losing more than his savings as he is drawn into the inescapable violence and degradation that lies just below the surface of this frontier region.

As in many other national literatures, the frontier—particularly in the guise of the Outback or the bush—has been a dominant trope in Australian cultural narratives, one that, as Richard Davis puts it "underl[ies] the production of national identity" (7). According to Davis, "while the frontier trope carries not only the freight of historical encounters, it also reveals the postures of nationhood that inform inter-cultural relationships and that shape institutions and ideas" (7). And as Turner has noted, in Australian narrative fiction, the frontier zones of the bush or the Outback are presented as the "authentic location for the distinctive Australian experience" (26). These frontier narratives also tend to bring to the fore what Robyn McCallum has called a "primary opposition" between the bush and the city, between nature and culture, that has "remained central to established versions of [Australian] nationalism." This is, as McCallum puts it, a "romantic" construction in which "nature (and the bush)" are traditionally "valorized," and presented as "the site upon which an authentic selfhood, and hence an authentic national identity, is formed" (109). While we examine other examples of the nation's frontier spaces in chapters 2 ("The North") and 4 ("The West"), perhaps the most recent, and most salient, example of the pervasiveness of this romanticized and mythologized portrayal of Australian Outback space is Baz Luhrmann's 2008 film, *Australia*. In it, the female protagonist, Lady Sarah Ashley (Nicole Kidman), is figuratively born again through her encounter with the remote Kimberley region of northern Australia. As the film's title suggests, this region (which accounts for less than 6 percent of the country's land mass and is home to 0.2 percent of its population) in turn operates as a synecdoche for the country more broadly as well as embodying a quintessential sense of Australianness. Luhrmann's film at once exploits, gives sustenance to, and parodies this cliché of the therapeutic and national-identity-forming capabilities of the Outback.

In *Wake in Fright*, however, the Outback plays a more forbidding, foreclosing role, and all three versions of the text paint the Australian interior as a hellish and brutish place, the stuff of nightmares and a place where a sense of rational selfhood is undone. The remote western townships of the interior, as Cook describes them in the novel, have "few of the amenities of civilization":

> There is no sewerage, there are no hospitals, rarely a doctor; the food is dreary and flavourless from long carrying, the water is bad; electricity is for the few who can afford their own plant, roads are mostly non-existent; there are no theatres, no picture shows and few dance halls; and the people are saved from stark insanity by the one strong principle of progress that is ingrained for a thousand miles east, north, south and west of the Dead Heart—the beer is always cold. (9)

As in other Australian frontier narratives, the bush or Outback is counterposed to the city—in this case, Sydney. And yet, in a reversal of Raymond
Williams's thesis in *The Country and the City*, in *Wake in Fright*, the Outback becomes the dark mirror of the city. Bundanyabba is a city—indeed,
Grant calls it a "barbaric" one (Cook 82)—but it is less a counterpoint to
the Outback, less an oasis of civility, than it is an urbanized point of inten-
sity within that degraded and degrading space of brute masculinity, gambling, drinking, and death that surrounds it. Bundanyabba and the region
it sits at the center of are, rather, directly counterposed to the Outback
pastoral presented by narratives such as Luhrmann's *Australia*. Grant, the
novel's protagonist, is described as a "coastal Australian, a native of the
strip of continent lying between the Pacific Ocean and the Great Dividing
Range, where Nature deposited the graces she so firmly withheld from the
west" (5). The novel also directly challenges the preponderant cultural
image of the Outback as curative for mind, body, and soul. In a telling
passage, when Grant arrives in Bundanyabba, his taxi driver begins to
extol the virtues of Bundanyabba, saying he "came out from Sydney" because he had a "bad chest": "Chest cleared up in six months but I wouldn't
think of leavin' The Yabba." Grant, on the other hand is skeptical of the
"city's therapeutic qualities," observing that "the taxi driver looked sal-
low and drawn, and distinctly in need of a change to the kinder climate
of the coast" (18). As this encounter illustrates, Grant's experience of this
frontier zone is as much a matter of perspective as anything else. As Bundanyabba's locals continually remind him, The Yabba is the "best place in
Australia" (18), the "best little town in the world" (26, 66). Grant, with his
urban sensibilities, is described as an "outcast in a community of people
who were at home in the bleak and frightening land," but this is, we are
reminded, an environment that is "careless of itself and the people who
professed to own it" (12).

Bundanyabba, then, might be a city, but it is not *the* city of the novel—
that role is reserved for Sydney. Indeed, the novel's dark and ironic punch-
line stems from the slippage between the two cities—the one a part of and
the other a world apart from the hostile frontier zone in which Grant finds
himself trapped. Even within Bundanyabba, Grant's east-coast urbanity
leads to his being labeled a "city feller" by locals (162), as though they,
themselves, were not. This ongoing confusion over what "the city" might

refer to culminates in a blackly humorous case of miscommunication that steers Grant, who has been trying desperately to escape Bundan-yabba, inexorably back to it once again. Despite its unremittingly bleak vision of the Outback, *Wake in Fright*'s protagonist (in the novel and film versions) does ultimately achieve a form of revelatory clarity following his ordeal and once he has come, geographically and narratively speaking, full circle. Finding himself prematurely back in Tiboonda, where his story began, Grant (in the novel) thinks back on the events that have befallen him:

> I can see quite clearly the ingenuity whereby a man may be made mean or great by exactly the same circumstances. I can see quite clearly that even if he chooses meanness the things he brings about can even then be welded into a pattern of sanity for him to take advantage of if he wishes. . . . What I can't altogether see is why I should be permitted to be alive, and to know these things. (204)

Therapeutic it may not be, but the Outback space has acted as a kind of crucible for the protagonist's character. Where first he was naïve, and arrogant in his naïveté, believing himself to be inherently more civilized than those around him, his experiences have shown him how fragile his sense of civility was. As Turner explains, writing about the film adaptation, it is only when he loses his savings at the two-up school that Grant is "forced to take the culture on its own terms." "The loss of his money, his books, his jacket, his ticket out," Turner continues, "is also the loss of his difference, his privilege, and his privacy; the rest of the [narrative] is taken up with breaking those constructs down in order to prove just how fragile this structure of difference is" (42). Where this sense of character development is conveyed directly in the novel's reflective ending, it is largely lost in the play (which concludes at an earlier point in the narrative than do the novel and film), and is made more implicit in the film. As Turner notes, at the end of the film, Grant is "presented to us as a man who can now deal with this context [the Outback and its culture] in a more acceptant, less arrogant and thus less individualist manner": where, at the beginning of the film, he turns down a beer, "now he accepts [it]" (43).

Wake in Fright is not alone in presenting a dark vision of the Outback that stands opposed to its dominant romantic portrayal; indeed, it is one text within what has been considered a form of Australian Gothic (see Turcotte) or what screenwriter Shayne Armstrong has called Australian "landscape horror," which he describes as "the idea of serial killers or people being deranged in the outback" (qtd. in M. D. Ryan 47). Barbara Baynton's 1902 collection of stories, *Bush Studies,* is considered to be an early and canonical work within this genre, and one that, according to Kathleen Steele, "may be read as an attempted intervention in, and modification of, the bush" (42). Baynton's bleak depiction of the bush as a menacing space that is particularly hostile to women, Steele argues, recasts it as a space that "while practically devoid of population, remains charged with a hostile presence" (40). Baynton's *Bush Studies* is, indeed, treated as a touchstone work within the Australian Gothic, with Gerry Turcotte suggesting that Cook's *Wake in Fright* is in many respects "a first novel which modernised Baynton's merciless renderings of outback life" (283). Haynes similarly argues that *Wake in Fright* "evokes a distinctly Gothic sense of place, in which the combined forces of harsh terrain and isolation supplant the supernatural as the source of determinism and terror: education, intelligence and innocence are no match for outback brutality" (*Seeking* 192). A similar sense of Outback menace pervades Janette Turner Hospital's novel *Oyster* (1996) and its narrative setting, "Outer Maroo," a fictional opal-mining town in Queensland's remote far west that has managed "by cunning intention, and sometimes by discreet bribery" to keep "itself off maps" (4). Barren and desolate, Outer Maroo is nevertheless an environment in which paranoid fear and fundamental religion take root and flourish—it is a place for the lost, a place where some go to disappear, and a place where some are "disappeared." Moreover, according to David Callahan, Hospital's Outer Maroo also functions to draw attention to broader Australian concerns: in *Oyster,* he writes, the town of Outer Maroo "comes into focus as a nightmare realm of fear and oppression, a contemporary re-enactment of its originary apocalypse—that visited upon its original Murri inhabitants—and an ironic Australia in little, metonymic of the nation's self-congratulatory insularity" (209). In "desert Gothic" narratives such as these, Haynes writes, "moral degradation, gambling, and "aggressive mateship" are seen to "emanate from the terrain: heat brings thirst and alcoholism; isolation engenders desire for conviviality; a minimal existence breeds brutality" (*Seeking* 192).

In Australian film, this subgenre of "landscape horror" is decidedly more marked and includes such films as Peter Weir's *The Cars That Ate Paris* (1974), which was filmed around the rural New South Wales town of Sofala; George Miller's first three *Mad Max* films (1979, 1981, 1985), which were filmed in a number of rural and western locations throughout New South Wales, Victoria, and South Australia; John Hillcoat's *The Proposition* (2005), which was filmed around Winton in Outback Queensland; Greg McLean's *Wolf Creek* (2005), which was set in Western Australia's Kimberley region but filmed in South Australia's Flinders Ranges; Joel Anderson's *Lake Mungo* (2008), which features the ancient and remote dry lake of the film's title, situated in far western New South Wales; Jonathan auf der Heide's *Van Diemen's Land* (2009), which we discuss further in chapter 3 and which, although it does not feature an "Outback" landscape, is set in the dense and claustrophobic Tasmanian wilderness; and David Michôd's *The Rover* (2014), which was also filmed in South Australia's Flinders Ranges and around Marree, south of Lake Eyre. In theater, a sense of "landscape horror" pervades stage productions such as Andrew Bovell's colonial Outback mystery, *Holy Day* (2001); Louis Nowra's *Inside the Island* (1980), which is set on a remote station in northwestern New South Wales; and (as will be explored in greater depth in the following chapter) Stephen Carleton's northern Queensland "bush Gothic" play *Constance Drinkwater and the Final Days of Somerset* (2006).

Our approach to exploring the narrative geographies of *Wake in Fright* (which in its film version is arguably the progenitor of the Australian landscape horror movie) has been guided by a central question. Is the frontier region depicted in *Wake in Fright* simply a kind of symbolic space, what Carleton would call a "national scrim onto which we project our manifold anxieties and fantasies" ("Cinema" 53) that resists the mapping impulse? Or is it a region that can be both located and mapped in the geospace—in other words, placed on a map of Australia? Certainly, on the face of it, Cook's novel appears as though it would lend itself to literary-cartographical endeavor. The novel refers to just five locations— Tiboonda, Bundanyabba, Yindee, Yelonda, and Sydney,[2] and, while this is

---

2. A place called "Mundameer" is briefly mentioned by a character in passing (Cook 111), but no action takes place there and it is not mentioned again.

slightly complicated in the film, all three versions of the text retain these five narrative locations. Although four out of five of these locations are fictional, the fact that the novel also provides concrete details of distances and journey times between locations suggests that it might simply be a matter of plotting out the locations using Sydney as a reference point. As a narrative location, Sydney is the outlier: it is the only location that is outside the frontier region where the narrative's action takes place, it is the only named location in which no narrative action takes place (it is simply the place where the protagonist comes from and where he longs to be), and it is the only narrative location that can be definitively mapped in that it immediately corresponds with the geospace. In other words, there is a place on the Australian map called Sydney that is the direct referent of the *narrative* location that is also named Sydney.

The names of the remaining four locations are, as we have said, fictional. There is no Tiboonda, Bundanyabba, Yindee, or Yelonda on the Australian map, even though, to an Australian ear, there is a familiarity to them—they sound like a mishmash of Indigenous-sounding place-name elements.[3] The almost generic nature of these faux-Indigenous placenames suggests perhaps that they are to be regarded as stereotypical everyplaces—the undisciplined Outback foils to Sydney's urbanity and that, as such, attempting to map them would be pointless or even counter-

---

3. Taking "Bundanyabba" as an example, we can see that elements of the fictional name are common among Indigenous place names across the continent. "Bundanyabba" as a place name does not exist on any map of Australia; however, according to Geoscience Australia's gazetteer, over 200 Australian place names begin with *Bunda*—an Indigenous word that can mean different things in different Indigenous Australian languages. Indeed, only 70 miles (113 km.) east of Broken Hill near Little Topar (which we suggest as a potential model for the novel's "Yindee") is a Bunda Lake. The *-abba* ending is also common among Indigenous Australian place names. The Brisbane suburb of Wool-loongabba, for instance, is home to the Brisbane Cricket Ground, which is affectionately known both locally and internationally as "The Gabba." Cook's "The Yabba" replicates this form of place name hypercorism that is common within Australian colloquial usage. In an article on hypercoristics in Australian English, Jane Simpson provides many a number of examples, including "The Curry" for Cloncurry, "The Gong" for Mittagong, and "The Cutta" for Tarcutta (411–12). Moreover, *yabba* or *yabber* in some Indigenous languages means "to talk" and has become part of Australian slang more generally (Partridge 5975; Leitner 220–21). In the novel itself, Grant muses upon the constant prattle of the "Yabba-men" and asks himself, "wasn't yabba aboriginal for talk?" (Cook 30–31).

productive.[4] However, not only does Cook's novel provide strong intratextual clues about where this region lies on the map of Australia, but Cook himself is on record admitting that the novel is, in effect, a geographical roman à clef. In order to explore the "mappability" of this quasi-fictional region across its narrative adaptations, we will begin with its original expression in Cook's novel, before examining how this narrative geography is then adapted and translated via its film and stage versions.

Mapping *Wake in Fright I: the Novel*

Bundanyabba—the narrative location in which most of the novel's action occurs—is, as Cook admitted in a 1963 column for *The Bulletin,* based on Broken Hill, a mining town in the far west of New South Wales ("Unmitigated").[5] Broken Hill, which lies about 650 miles (1046 km.) from the state's east coast, was built up around a massive orebody, known as the "Line of Lode," and is birthplace of mining giant BHP (Broken Hill Proprietary), now part of BHP Billiton. As historian Erik Eklund notes, Broken Hill is currently at the end of its "mining life-cycle": mining is now "a marginal operation" in Broken Hill, "with only two companies working the line of lode" (313). According to Cook, *Wake in Fright* was inspired by his experience of living in Broken Hill for three months in the early 1950s, having been sent there over the Christmas period as a relief journalist for the Australian Broadcasting Commission (de Berg). A news report published on the front page of Broken Hill newspaper the *Barrier Daily Truth* in January 1953 mentions Cook, suggesting that he was stationed in Broken Hill over the 1952–1953 Christmas period. *Wake in*

4. Cook's is certainly also a problematic appropriation and adaptation of Indigenous place names, especially considering Indigenous Australians are almost entirely absent from *Wake in Fright*. Aside from Grant's pondering of the Indigenous meaning of *"yabba,"* the only references to the region's Indigenous population are the Tiboonda publican's "half-caste mistress" (11) and the "Aborigines and the half-castes" on the slow train between Tiboonda and Broken Hill. Cook describes in detail one "middle-aged Aboriginal stockman with white hair" who is the only other occupant of the rear train carriage as Grant makes his initial journey from Tiboonda to Bundanyabba. He is described as a "full-blood, with the broad features of his people," who "stared constantly out of the window as though there might be something in the plains he had not seen before" (14).

5. See also later interviews with Hazel de Berg and John Ryan in the 1970s, in which Cook further discusses the connection between Broken Hill and Bundanyabba.

Fright's protagonist, John Grant, also spends a Christmas period trapped in Bundanyabba/Broken Hill, and the news article—which reports that Cook injured his hand while discharging a firearm in his Broken Hill flat—suggests a further parallel between Cook's time in Broken Hill and the plot of *Wake in Fright*.[6] Cook's deeply negative opinions of Broken Hill are mirrored in many ways by his protagonist's impression of Bundanyabba. In 1963—only two years after the novel's publication—Cook pulled no punches in describing Broken Hill as an "unmitigated boil of horror" ("Unmitigated"). In his 1972 interview with Hazel de Berg, Cook expressed similar sentiments about the Outback city, saying:

> I was very strongly impressed with Broken Hill. Hated the place, hated
> the people, hated the atmosphere, hated the environment, hated the whole
> thing, and this hatred finally popped out as *Wake in Fright* eight or ten years
> later. (de Berg)[7]

Beyond Cook's direct and repeated assertion that Bundanyabba is Broken Hill by another name, the novel itself also provides locational

---

6. The brief report, published on 3 January 1953 and matter-of-factly titled "Man Shot in Hand," states:

> Mr. Ken Cook, A. B. C. journalist, was admitted to [Broken Hill] Hospital on
> Tuesday night suffering from a gunshot wound to the right hand. His condition
> is satisfactory. Cook was handling a rifle in his flat on Tuesday night when it
> discharged. The bullet entered the palm of his right hand and came out the back
> of the hand. The bone in the big finger and the main knuckle joint were somewhat
> shattered. Cook was operated on Tuesday night, but it is expected that he may
> lose the use of the finger. ("Man Shot in Hand")

It seems likely that Cook's accident provided some inspiration for the novel's memorable dénouement. Grant, finding himself in a seemingly inescapable "morass of hopelessness" (Cook 180) attempts to commit suicide with his only remaining possession besides a few pennies and some boxes of matches: a rifle. In this attempt Grant is, as ever, unsuccessful. When he regains consciousness in the hospital, the doctor tells him the bullet hit him in the "top of the forehead": "It cut a chunk out of your skull. You've got a dose of concussion, but you'll be all right" (193).

7. In his interview with de Berg, Cook also explains that he fictionalized the name of Broken Hill due to concerns over libel. His first novel, which had been inspired by the high-profile 1953 shooting of Rex Pilbeam (the then mayor of Rockhampton, a city in north Queensland) by his mistress, had been pulped soon after publication for similar reasons (de Berg). That first, pulped (and pulp) novel was later published in 1963 as *Vantage to the Gale* under the pseudonym "Alan Hale."

clues that link Bundanyabba to Broken Hill. In the novel, "The Yabba" is described as a "mining city of sixty thousand people which was the centre of life in the territory around the border" (6). Although the border is not explicitly named, we can assume that it refers to the New South Wales/ South Australian border, given that the protagonist schoolteacher, John Grant, comes from Sydney and is described as being bound to the west of the state while doing his regional service for the Education Department (8).Yet, despite these textual clues and Cook's affirmation, certain aspects of Bundanyabba's description in the novel do not map neatly onto Broken Hill. Cook appears to wildly exaggerate certain distances in the novel, which, if taken literally, would place Bundanyabba much farther west than Broken Hill. Bundanyabba is described as being "almost two thousand miles" (81) and a "forty-hour [train] journey" (58) from Sydney. In reality, Broken Hill is only 710 miles (1143 km.) by road from Sydney or 580 miles (933 km.) as the crow flies. At its widest point, Australia is approximately 2500 miles (4100 km.) wide, which makes Cook's distances appear nothing if not hyperbolic. Taking Cook's 2000-mile distance literally would place Bundanyabba on the continent's western coast and very close to Perth, which is 2045 miles (3291 km.) from Sydney as the crow flies. The forty-hour train journey Cook describes from Sydney to Bundanyabba is also an exaggeration. In the 1950s, when Cook was in Broken Hill, the train journey from Sydney to Broken Hill on the Silver City Comet diesel trains (which began operation in the late 1930s) would have taken only half that time. A 1937 article from the *Barrier Miner* newspaper gives the traveling time from Sydney to Broken Hill on the Silver City Comet as 20 hours and 49 minutes ("Questions Answered"). Finally, Cook's description of Bundanyabba as having a population of 60,000 also bears little resemblance to Broken Hill in the early 1950s, which had, at the time of the 1954 Census, a population of just over 31,000 (ABS, *Census 1954*, vol. 1, pt. 5). So, despite Cook's clear admission that Bundanyabba is Broken Hill by a different name, the novel's locational ambiguities work as much against definitively pinpointing Broken Hill as Bundanyabba's direct geographical correlate as they do for it.

These geographical ambiguities and red herrings are only compounded when we attempt to map the remaining three frontier locations: Tiboonda (where the narrative begins and ends) and Yindee and Yelonda (two townships that stand between Bundanyabba in the state's west and Grant's desired destination of Sydney on the east coast). Unlike the case of Bundanyabba, Cook is not—as far as can be ascertained—on record suggesting which (if any) actual townships or settlements provided models for the fictional ones of Tiboonda, Yindee, and Yelonda. As such, we rely solely on textual evidence from the novel in attempting to identify plausible geographical correlates for these narrative locations. It is important to stress at this point that our attempt to identify correlates in the geospace for these fictional/fictionalized locations does not stem from a desire to assess whether Cook's novel passes a kind of "ground-truthing" test; rather, it stems from our interest in the productive interplay between fictional and physical geographies.

Tiboonda, the township where *Wake in Fright*'s John Grant is bonded to teach, is described in the novel as an "apology for a town" (12). A tiny cluster of three white-ant and dry-rot ridden buildings alongside a railway line deep in the Australian Outback, it is some 1200 miles (1931 km.) west of the eastern seaboard (5) and a six-hour train ride from Bundanyabba/ Broken Hill (14). As Grant stands looking out of the window of his one-room school, he notes that "somewhere not far out in the shimmering haze was the state border, marked by a broken fence, and that further out in the heat was the silent centre of Australia, the Dead Heart" (5). Although the novel does not expressly indicate whether Tiboonda is to the north, south, east, or west of Bundanyabba, the suggestion that the state border lies not far beyond the horizon line (and the fact that Grant has to travel via Bundanyabba on his journey to the east coast) strongly implies that Tiboonda is the westernmost point in the narrative—the one closest to the country's "Dead Heart." Certainly, there is a geographical logic to this that mimics the circular logic of the plot: Grant's ultimate aim is to reach the state's east-coast capital, and yet he finds himself returning (before time) to its westernmost settlement on its western border.

And yet, in attempting to geo-locate Tiboonda according to Cook's fairly specific distance markers, we encounter the same problem as we did with Bundanyabba. If we take at face value Cook's description of Tiboonda as being over a thousand miles west of the eastern seaboard, this places the township in the western half of South Australia. Indeed, it places Tiboonda to the west of the continent's center rather than to its east, and places it, like Bundanyabba, closer to Perth on the west coast than to Sydney on the east. Once again, Cook's distances appear hyperbolic, but here the novel's internal spatial logic also seems to break down. As noted above, Cook describes Bundanyabba as being nearly 2000 miles from Sydney. If Tiboonda is only 1200 miles west of the east coast, then this places it an implausible 800 miles (1287 km.) *east* of Bundanyabba/ Broken Hill, a distance that is, in fact, greater than the road distance between Sydney and Broken Hill. At its widest point, the state of New South Wales is also fewer than 800 miles wide. What do we do, then, with these exaggerated and confusing distances? Are we to assume that Cook simply made a mistake or that he is being deliberately deceitful? As we have argued elsewhere, Australian narrative fictions "use landscape and geography to make particular appeals to nationality, and . . . to create a sense of 'Australianness' that doesn't fit neatly into the categories of truth or lie" (Mitchell and Stadler 29). What Cook's larger-than-life distances do, rather, is contribute to a fictional and imagined geography that reinforces the vastness, remoteness, and otherness of the Outback.

If we accept that "Tiboonda" cannot logically be 800 miles east of Broken Hill, then what western townships of New South Wales might present themselves as possible models for it? One town that has received previous scholarly attention in this regard is Tibooburra, a remote settlement in the far northwestern corner of the state, roughly 200 miles (323 km.) north-northeast of Broken Hill along the Silver City Highway and deep into the state's "corner country": the region near where the New South Wales, Queensland, and South Australian borders meet. In his essay "Literature in the Arid Zone," Tom Lynch writes that *Wake in Fright*'s Tiboonda "is probably modelled on Tibooburra" (77), and the similarity between the two names—one fictional, the other actual—is, on the surface, certainly compelling. However, *Wake in Fright*'s Tiboonda is a significantly smaller and less developed township than Tibooburra, which in 1954 had a population of 228 residing in more than 70 domestic dwellings (ABS, *Census 1954*, vol. 1, pt. 5). Unlike Tiboonda, Tibooburra also has substantially more than three public buildings, many of which (including two hotels, the police station, court house, former post office, and hall) were built of sandstone in the nineteenth century. In the 1950s, Tibooburra's school was also operating from the sandstone building that

Figure 1.1. Kinalung Railway Yard looking east, 1952. Source: Rail negative E52856. State Records Authority of New South Wales.

formerly housed the town's post office (Hope 228). Tibooburra is also, unlike Tiboonda, not on a railway line; indeed, there is no railway line that runs north of Broken Hill. From 1890 to 1932, a tramway operated between Broken Hill and Tarrawingee, a township built around a limestone quarry less than 40 miles (64 km.) to the city's north. This tramway, which had closed 20 years before Cook's three-month sojourn in Broken Hill in the 1950s, might have inspired Cook's imagined railway line to Tiboonda; however, even in the early 1900s, the tram to Tarrawingee took less than two hours—not the six hours we are told it took Grant to travel from Tiboonda to Bundanyabba.

Another potential model for Tiboonda is Kinalung (see figure 1.1), a railway siding camp about 35 miles (56 km.) east of Broken Hill on the Broken Hill–Menindee railway line. At first glance, there is little to recommend Kinalung as a model for Tiboonda—it is too close to Broken Hill, for a start. However, its size and population during the 1950s is a much closer match to Tiboonda's tiny clutch of buildings: according to Census data, in 1954 Kinalung and its environs were home to a population of 60 housed in 14 occupied dwellings (ABS, *Census 1954*, vol. 1, pt. 5).

Moreover, the railway is a central feature of *Wake in Fright*'s Tiboonda: it provides the means by which Grant travels to Broken Hill, and supplies him with many of his students, at least one of whom hopes to become a railway "ganger" like his father (Cook 4). Only a handful of far-western New South Wales schools were located along a railway line (as Tiboonda is). By the early 1950s, according to state records, of these railway siding schools only the Kinalung siding school remained open. During the 1950s, Kinalung was a "provisional" school (unlike Tibooburra's larger public school), meaning it catered to between 15 and 25 students,[8] and it operated from an education department "demountable" building that was virtually identical to the one depicted in the film adaptation of *Wake in Fright*. By 1967 the Kinalung school was closed, and the station followed soon after. Unlike Tibooburra, almost nothing now remains of the Kinalung siding camp, with very little tangible evidence left of its station platform, demountable school, and row of railway workers cottages (Blackwell, "Broken" 23).

In the final analysis, although we can be certain that Bundanyabba is based on Broken Hill, there is no single township in western New South Wales that we can say, with any great certainty, was a model for *Wake in Fright*'s Tiboonda. As an imagined township, Tiboonda marries the isolation and remoteness of a border town like Tibooburra with the qualities of a tiny railway settlement like Kinalung. As such, Tiboonda might be better thought of as an idea of border-zone Outback town, one that is captured strikingly in Kotcheff's film version, which, as we will describe in greater detail in the following section, used the Horse Lake railway siding, less than 10 miles (16 km.) up the track from Kinalung, as the filming location for Tiboonda.[9] In Kotcheff's film, the Broken Hill–Menindee line also stands in for the railway line between Bundanyabba and Tiboonda, and interestingly Kinalung provides the filming location for the second-last of the text's narrative locations: namely, Yindee.

8. See http://www.governmentschools.det.nsw.edu.au/main_pages/school_details .aspx?schoolID=4401.

9. Indeed, when Kinalung siding was opened in 1919, it was initially named Horse Lake. In 1923, the Horse Lake name was transferred to a new siding 10 miles (16 km.) down the track, and the existing siding was renamed Kinalung (Blackwell, "Broken" 7).

In Cook's novel, Grant passes through Yindee on two occasions: first, when he takes part in a brutal, even sadistic kangaroo shoot with the malignant Doc Tydon and a group of Bundanyabba miners,[10] and later when he attempts to hitchhike from Bundanyabba to Sydney. Yindee is described as being, variously, either "about sixty" miles (105) or forty miles (160) from Bundanyabba and as comprising "one lone, long, low hotel" (112) next to a dry riverbed. The description of Yindee and its hotel, which seemed to remain open at all hours (133), is strongly suggestive of Little Topar, a settlement that lies 48 miles (77 km.) east of Broken Hill on the Barrier Highway. Like Yindee, Little Topar is nothing more than a roadhouse pub on the highway. In 1950, as a young man, the notable Australian racehorse trainer Bart Cummings spent some months on a property near Little Topar. In his autobiography, Cummings recounts his experience of the town:

> Little Topar was the true Wild West. There were constant dust storms and the pub didn't have or need any doors because it was open twenty-four hours a day. When it rained, the trucks would stop and the hotelkeeper made all his money. He wouldn't feed the men anything, because he made more on the beer he sold. So they'd be drinking nonstop on empty stomachs. Men would fall out of the pub and jump on motorcycles together to go off shooting kangaroos. The fellow on the front would be riding, the one behind standing up with his gun poised. They'd hit a buried tree stump and in the jolt the shooter would shoot the rider in the head. It happened every week! You've never seen anything like it! (51)

Despite the fact it could have come straight from the pages of *Wake in Fright,* Cummings's description of Little Topar does not, of course, prove that it was a model for Yindee.[11] However, as well as neatly matching the novel's description of Yindee, Little Topar fits in a geographical sense,

10. Cook himself went on at least one kangaroo shoot during his stay in Broken Hill over the 1952–1953 Christmas period (Hickie). Although the novel and its adaptations present the fictionalized kangaroo shoot as pure sport for the Bundanyabba locals, in the early 1950s, kangaroos were in plague proportions in the Broken Hill region. Indeed, at the end of January 1953—the same month Cook accidentally shot himself in the hand in his Broken Hill flat—a six-month "open season" on shooting kangaroos was declared throughout the Western District ("Open Season for 'Roos").
11. In the 1950s, there were at least two other roadhouse pubs in far western New South Wales that matched the physical description of Yindee: the Yanco Glen hotel, 18 miles (29 km.) northeast of Broken Hill on the Silver City Highway, and the Quondong Hotel,

lying as it does on the main highway between Broken Hill and Sydney. Yindee is Grant's first stop as he tries to hitchhike his way to Sydney; Yelonda, the last of our five narrative locations, is the second.

Identifying a plausible geographical correlate for Yelonda poses a few more difficulties than Yindee, but one western township does come to the fore as a possible model. The novel's description of Yelonda—as a run-down but formerly prosperous port on the "Harden" River whose fortunes were tied to the death of the paddle-steamer trade earlier in the century—is suggestive of Wilcannia, a major river port on the Darling River, which flourished during the paddle steamer's heyday but went into decline in the 1920s when the era of the paddle steamer came to a close with the development of the railroad and road transport. The fictional town of Yelonda is described in the novel as being around 40 or 50 miles (or two hours by road, or 65–80 km) from Yindee (163, 164), which is in turn between 40 and 60 miles (65–97 km) east of Bundanyabba (see location notes for Yindee). This places the fictional Yelonda as somewhere between 80 and 110 miles from Bundanyabba (129–177 km). At 120 miles (193 km.) from Broken Hill, Wilcannia is 10 miles further away from Broken Hill than the fictional Yelonda is from Bundanyabba, but it does strikingly match the town's description. Cook describes Yelonda as having a picture theater in its main street, directly across the road from a hotel. Although it is now closed, Wilcannia's Plaza cinema, was still operational in 1970 and was located only 100 yards from the Wilcannia Club Hotel, which was located on the opposite side of the main street, matching the description in the novel.[12]

---

30 miles (48 km.) southeast of Broken Hill on the road to Menindee, both of which have since burned down. Both hotels influenced the film version of *Wake in Fright,* as will be discussed further later in this chapter, with the Quondong hotel, in particular, providing inspiration for the onscreen Yindee hotel. However, as a model for the novel's Yindee hotel, neither the Quondong nor the Yanco Glen hotel makes the kind of geographical sense Little Topar does, for only the latter lies on the Barrier Highway—the main highway running east between Broken Hill and Sydney.

12. An image of Wilcannia's Plaza Cinema c. 1970 can be seen online at http://nla.gov .au/nla.pic-vn5215604. The theater building is located on the corner of Myers Street (Barrier Highway) and Woore Street, Wilcannia. Although its façade is now covered by cladding, its art deco roofline is still apparent.

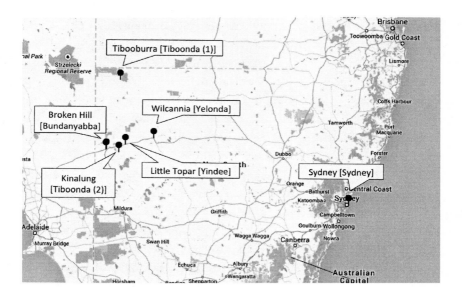

Figure 1.2. Map of narrative locations from the novel *Wake in Fright*.
Source: Cultural Atlas of Australia.

Although Cook's novel resists geographic fixity, the process of mapping its locations (see figure 1.2) builds up a sense of regional identity that
is more than just a stage for narrative action or an inert background setting for the novel. All of the plausible models for Cook's fictional townships lie in a single official state region—the Unincorporated Far West
(see figure 1.3). Although Broken Hill lies within and is surrounded by
this region, it is technically not a part of it, for Broken Hill has its own
local government authority while the unincorporated region is not gov-
erned by a municipal council. Covering an area of 36,000 square miles
(93,240 km sq.), the Unincorporated Far West is larger by far than any
of the state's local government authorities, and with a current population
density equivalent to zero, it has the fewest residents per square mile. In
1954, New South Wales's unincorporated region had the highest gender
ratio in the state, with 154 men for every 100 women (ABS, *Census 1954,*
vol. 1, pt. 1). Director of *Wake in Fright*'s film adaptation, Ted Kotcheff,
would remark in interviews that men in Broken Hill outnumbered the
women three to one (see, for instance, Caputo; Skinner), a terrific exag-

Figure 1.3. Map of New South Wales showing Local Government Authorities, including the Unincorporated Far Western region. Source: Wikimedia Commons: Creative Commons Attribution-ShareAlike 3.0 Unported [CC BY-SA 3.0] license. The original image may be viewed at: http://commons.wikimedia.org /wiki/File:Australia_New_South_Wales_with_LGA_names.svg.

geration given that in the 1950s, Broken Hill's gender ratio was 107 men for every 100 women (ABS, *Census 1954*, vol. 1, pt. 1). Indeed, as Eklund notes, with the decline of mining after 1970, Broken Hill's gender ratio has swung the other way: "By 1991, there were 11,667 males and 12,072 females in Broken Hill. The age of the miner had truly ended" (316). Nevertheless, set in this context, it is little wonder that masculinity, the myth of mateship, and alienation in a remote and hostile landscape are such dominant themes in a novel set within this region. Situating the novel within and against the backdrop of this region's history, geography, and demography can, we argue, allow us to move beyond clichéd or reductionist interpretations both of the novel and its region.

Mapping Wake in Fright II: The Film

Although the "original" *Wake in Fright* text is Cook's 1961 novel, Canadian director Ted Kotcheff's 1971 film version has unarguably reached a much wider and more international audience than the novel on which it was based. Kotcheff's vision of Cook's novel premiered at the 1971 Cannes Film Festival, where it was nominated for a Palme d'Or. It was released internationally under the title *Outback*—a telling point, which we will return to—and in its first release the film had its longest run in France, where it played in cinemas for five months (Shirley and Adams 245). Kotcheff's film received critical acclaim internationally, but was less well received in Australia, where its stark depiction of the casual brutality of life in an Outback mining town was perhaps too bitter a pill for local audiences to swallow. It did, however, become famous as a "lost" film. By the 1990s, the original negatives were thought to have been completely lost, and all that remained were highly degraded prints and videocassette recordings of the film. In the mid-1990s, the film's editor, Anthony Buckley, began searching for the film's negatives, and in 2004 as a result of his dogged pursuit, they were discovered in a "container marked 'For Destruction'" in Pittsburgh (Buckley, *Behind* 151). Over the next six years, Buckley oversaw the digital restoration of the film, which was rereleased in early 2009 and again shown at Cannes—one of only two films ever to screen twice at the festival (Irons). Since then, *Wake in Fright*'s cult status has only strengthened—in 2014 it was rereleased, once more, in the United Kingdom and in France.

As Cook himself noted,[13] Kotcheff's adaptation is exceedingly faithful to its source text, with very little at the level of plot, characterization,

---

13. In his interview with de Berg, Cook says he was "very fortunate" for his novel to have received such a "faithful depiction" in its film adaptation, one that he says few writers are lucky enough to experience. He states that his only criticism of Kotcheff's adaptation was in the casting of Gary Bond as the protagonist Grant. Bond, thought Cook, was too old, too worldly, and looked "too competent" to convincingly play the part of the naïve schoolteacher (de Berg).

or even dialogue having been changed.[14] Kotcheff also dramatically captures and visually renders the novel's sense of menacing space and hostile landscape. As some critics have noted, there is a filmic element to Cook's novel, which perhaps made it amenable to successful adaptation. As Peter Galvin writes:

> Some books resist adaptation. Plots are too twisted, the action too internalised, but *Wake in Fright* seemed written to be filmed. It had little dialogue, a strong atmosphere, a picturesque location, unique characters, an intensely dramatic situation with a lot of action and a mood of menace; it was in so many ways a "horror movie" where the only "monsters" are kind folk who almost kill the hero with their kindness.

From the very first establishing shot of Tiboonda, which is repeated at the film's end, Kotcheff translates the space on the page to the space of the screen. Tiboonda is no longer described to the reader, it is shown: we see a building standing isolated in a dry, dusty landscape, a railway line in front of it, transecting the screen. There is no sound as the crane-mounted camera begins to pans a full 360 degrees clockwise, slowly taking in the landscape. As the camera follows the horizon, revealing the unending sameness of red dirt against blue sky broken only by whirly-whirlies, John Scott's original soundtrack begins, a violin keening into the desolate landscape. Another, this time smaller, building comes into view, and the camera finally comes to rest between the two buildings, the railway line between them cutting the screen in half. The film cuts to a shot of a ramshackle railway platform announcing the name of this settlement that appears too insignificant, too provisional, too devoid of human life, too much at the mercy of its environment to be considered a town: Tiboonda.

14. Among other minor variations, Doc Tydon is in some ways a more developed character in the film: he displays certain characteristics (such as listening to opera) and has lines of dialogue that do not appear in the novel. In Kotcheff's adaptation he meets Grant at the two-up school, earlier than he does in the novel (although, in the novel, Tydon informs Grant he saw him there). At the end of the film, Grant also attempts to shoot Tydon before turning the gun on himself, and, after Grant leaves hospital, Tydon sees him off as he catches the train back to Tiboonda. Neither of these scenes occurs in the novel. In the film version, Grant's attempt to hitchhike to Sydney is also somewhat truncated, for he does not pass through Yindee as he does in the novel.

The film immediately conveys through visual and aural techniques the suffocating and alienating sense of Outback space that, in the novel, is conveyed through detailed description. Here in the film, we see as great— if not more of—a sense of geography exerting itself on the human in this frontier space. But where is this space, and what is its geography? As mentioned earlier, film geography requires a double-mapping: a dual attention to narrative location and to filming location. In some cases, these happily coincide, making the job of narrative mapping a simple if, perhaps, less interesting one. For instance, Sen's 2011 film *Toomelah*—which is not only set and filmed in but is also named after the Indigenous community of Toomelah, located on the New South Wales–Queensland border east of Goondiwindi—poses few interpretive difficulties for the narrative cartographer. In many if not most other cases, however, the relationship between narrative and filming location is not so easily determined. McLean's *Wolf Creek,* as noted earlier, is set in the Kimberley region of northern Western Australia, but, apart from one overhead shot of the Wolfe Creek meteorite crater from which the film draws its name, it is filmed entirely in South Australia. Broome's picturesque Cable Beach in northern Western Australia, for instance, is represented on screen by Adelaide's Semaphore Beach, South Australia. Luhrmann's *Australia,* as we have outlined in previous research, incorporates CGI and matte backgrounds to transform Bowen in Queensland into war-time Darwin, capital of the Northern Territory (Mitchell and Stadler 34).

Film adaptation brings with it yet another set of questions about the relationships among and between the film's narrative geography, its filming locations, and the narrative geography of its source text. In Hicks's *The Boys Are Back,* as we also noted earlier, the narrative geography of the New Zealand–based memoir it is adapted from is completely elided, the narrative having been grafted onto a different country. In some cases, this grafting can be richly allusive and productive of new cultural meaning—the "Verona Beach" of Luhrmann's 1996 *William Shakespeare's Romeo + Juliet,* for instance, is, as Courtney Lehmann writes, "a curious hybrid of Shakespeare's Veronese setting, LA's Venice Beach, and the film's on-location shots of Mexico City," and one that engenders a "sense of rupture" not only spatially and temporally, but also culturally (192).

Kotcheff's faithful adaptation of *Wake in Fright* brings no such productive sense of rupture in relation to its source text. It is set in the same
imagined geographical and cultural space as the novel and, although the
temporality of the film is the late 1960s (it was filmed in the summer of
1969), close to a decade after the novel was published and nearly 20 years
after the events that inspired it, it is not an obvious updating of its source
text in any sense. Indeed, the only marker of time having passed between
the novel's publication and the film's release is the film's conversion of the
unit of currency from pounds to dollars.[15] And yet, despite (or even because of) the relative spatio-temporal stability of these texts, examining
their imagined and imaginative geography does provide new insights into
the narrative geographies of both novel and film. In adapting *Wake in
Fright*, Kotcheff could easily have dismissed the Bundanyabba–Broken
Hill connection implicit in the novel, and in the search for filming locations, towns such as Bourke (located in the central north of New South
Wales and commonly referred to as the "gateway to the Outback") were
considered (see "Film Producers"). But, in the end, Broken Hill and its
environs were chosen as the location for the film's exterior shooting. Unlike Cook's novel, which at once suggests and problematizes the Bundanyabba–Broken Hill connection, Kotcheff's film adaptation serves only to
strengthen and make fully explicit the association between the fictional
city and its physical counterpart. In Kotcheff's film, all the exterior Bundanyabba scenes were filmed in and around Broken Hill, while virtually
all the interiors were filmed in Sydney.[16] In the film, we see Broken Hill's
main street, along with the city's town hall, post office, and old Sulphide

15. Decimal currency was introduced to Australia in 1966—an equidistant point between the publication of the novel in 1961 and the release of the film in 1971.
16. Sydney filming locations that doubled for Bundanyabba interiors include the Palace Hotel on George Street (the interior of the Bundanyabba bar in which Grant meets
mine worker Tim Hynes); the former Ross Wood Productions studio on Gosbell Street,
Paddington (the interior of the Bundanyabba two-up school); the now-demolished
Sheridan Stand of the Sydney Cricket Ground (the interior of the Bundanyabba miners'
bar); the former Ajax Studios (the filming location for a number of interior Bundanyabba
scenes, including Grant's hotel bedroom and Doc Tydon's hut); and a house on Koola
Avenue in the Sydney suburb of Killara (the interior for Tim and Janette Hynes's house)
(Buckley, *Wake in Fright* call sheets no. 8).

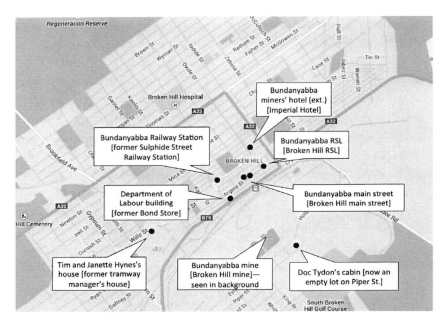

Figure 1.4. Map of *Wake in Fright* Broken Hill filming locations.
Source: Cultural Atlas of Australia.

Street railway station, as well as the mine itself and its mullock heaps. Also featured in Kotcheff's film are a number of the city's heritage buildings, including the Imperial Hotel, the former Bond Store (which doubles in the film as the Department of Labour building), the former Bon Marche building, the former Tramway Manager's house (which doubles as mine worker Tim Hynes's house), and the Broken Hill Returned and Services League (RSL) Club, the only interior to be filmed in Broken Hill (see figure 1.4). In one scene, the viewer even catches a glimpse of the Palace Hotel, which would have a starring role more than 20 years later in *The Adventures of Priscilla, Queen of the Desert*. In many respects, then, in the film adaptation of *Wake in Fright*, Bundanyabba simply *is* Broken Hill.

Of the novel's other four narrative locations, only two are explicitly named in the film: Sydney and Tiboonda (for Tiboonda locations, see figure 1.5). Although almost all of the film's interior scenes were shot in Sydney, Sydney itself is represented only in the recurring shots of Bondi Beach, first seen when Grant is on the train from Tiboonda to Bundan-

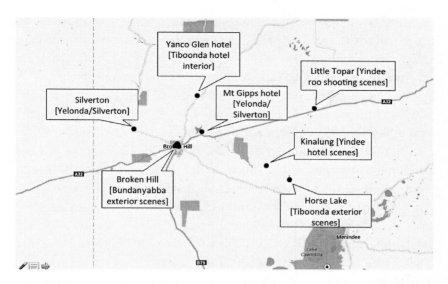

Figure 1.5. Map of *Wake in Fright* filming locations, Broken Hill and environs. Source: Cultural Atlas of Australia.

yabba. As he glances at a photograph of his sweetheart, Robyn, he slips into a fantasy space in which Robyn emerges from the ocean wearing a provocative red swimsuit. The red of Robyn's swimsuit set against the blue of the ocean and clear summer sky mimics the red dirt/blue sky color palette of the Outback landscape, but only to highlight the difference between the two: Sydney (as Bondi Beach) is the thirst-quenching antidote to the arid, hyper-masculine world of the Outback, and a place where Grant can reclaim his own masculinity (he is depicted running a beer bottle down Robyn's cleavage). Unlike the novel, then, Sydney is presented less as a civilized metropolis set in opposition to the uncivilized urban space of Bundanyabba than as a reversal of the Outback environment, a refreshing, coastal sight for sore eyes, as it were.

The Tiboonda scenes, as mentioned earlier, were filmed at the former Horse Lake railway on the Broken Hill–Menindee line. In his article *"Wake in Fright's* Tiboonda—Where Is the Movie Location?"* railway historian Greg Blackwell provides ample evidence that the former Horse Lake siding is the filming location for Tiboonda, noting the Menindee to Broken Hill water pipeline that is visible, running parallel with the railway line, and the "wye-shaped impression" that brackets the schoolhouse, which had been used during the period when trains were required to take emergency water supplies to Broken Hill (cf. Blackwell, "Broken"). To confirm his conclusions, Blackwell interviewed Howard Rubie, *Wake in Fright*'s first assistant director, who said that the Horse Lake railway platform "was already there but in poor condition, requiring a partial rebuild before the 'accessories' were added and the real station name covered with the 'Tiboonda' name board" ("*Wake*" 5). The Horse Lake filming location is also confirmed by the *Wake in Fright* production call sheets, which, although they don't mention Horse Lake by name, provide explicit directions to the cast and crew on how to get there: "Take Menindee Road 30 miles to Quondong Hotel. Continue along a further ten miles. On left hand side is sign QUARRY HILL. Turn in through iron gate. 5 miles down track to location" (Buckley, *Wake in Fright* call sheet no. 41).

Blackwell also provides notes on the provenance of the two buildings in the opening Tiboonda scenes: the schoolhouse and the hotel. According to Blackwell, Rubie claimed that "the school building was rented by them from the Education Department and transported to the location specifically for use in the movie. [Rubie] said he thought the building came from somewhere in Broken Hill" ("*Wake*" 4). The hotel, on the other hand was "just a shell used for exterior shots only and was constructed on site for the movie," while the hotel interior scenes were "shot at the Yanco Glen Hotel which stood beside the Silver City Highway approximately 30 kilometres north of Broken Hill (and apparently burnt to the ground on 9 April 1984)" (4). The film's call sheets similarly confirm that the Tiboonda hotel interior was filmed in the Yanco Glen hotel. Moreover, in the film's opening scenes, the licensee's name—Joseph Leonard Condon, the then owner of the Yanco Glen hotel—is visible above the door.

If anything, the filming location of Tiboonda strengthens its association as a *narrative* location with a site like Kinalung, as explained above in relation to the novel. When Grant steps onto the train that will take him from Tiboonda to Bundanyabba, it is from a down-side platform, servicing trains traveling from east to west. This westerly movement is emphasized in the film, which repeatedly shows the train moving from the right to the left, visually connoting that Bundanyabba is west of Tiboonda. Of course, this is as much a structural function of the film's production as anything.

Given that the railway line runs west from Horse Lake to Broken Hill (the filming location for Bundanyabba), it would be odd to attempt to depict Grant traveling eastwards to Bundanyabba, especially as it would have necessitated building an up-side platform (or moving the existing down-side one across the tracks). Nevertheless, both the novel's description of Tiboonda and the film's choice of shooting location (which, as we have seen in relation to Bundanyabba, is not separate from but rather strongly influences the identifiable narrative location), lean toward a narrative location for Tiboonda that is east of Broken Hill on the Broken Hill–Menindee railway line and away from an association with Tibooburra in the state's northwest.

Unlike Bundanyabba, Sydney, and Tiboonda, Yindee and Yelonda are not named as such in the film: the Yindee of the novel is not named at all and Yelonda, as will be explained further below, picks up an association with a location in the geospace (namely, Silverton). However, both names appear in Evan Jones's film script and in the filming call sheets. A viewer of Kotcheff's adaptation (particularly one who had not read Cook's novel) would not recognize these names from their experience of the film; however, for the purposes of this analysis and to track the narrative locations across adaptations, we will discuss the corresponding film locations by the names given in the novel and in the filmscript.

As in the novel, on their roo-shooting trip, John Grant, Doc Tydon, Dick, and Joe go drinking at an Outback pub. Although, as mentioned above, the pub is not named in the film, it corresponds with the Yindee hotel of the novel and is named as such in Jones's filmscript and in the film's call sheets. Unlike the novel on which it is based, the film adaptation of *Wake in Fright* provides no locational hints (in terms of distance and direction from Broken Hill) as to a possible model for this narrative location; however, the fact that the roo-shooting scenes were shot in a compound that had been constructed near Little Topar,[17] perhaps strengthens the link between "Yindee" and Little Topar that we established in our analysis of the novel's narrative locations. Despite this, the two narrative locations—the Yindee hotel of the novel and the Yindee hotel of the

---

17. See *Wake in Fright* call sheet no. 38, for instance, which instructs the filming unit to "rendezvous at Little Topar hotel" for the "kangaroo compound" shooting (Buckley).

movie adaptation—do not easily correspond between book and film. In the novel, Grant goes to the Yindee Hotel twice: once on the kangaroo shoot, and a second time at the end of the novel when he hitches a ride to Yindee, hitches another ride to Yelonda from there, and then hitches yet another ride (or so he thinks) to Sydney. In the film, Grant does not go back to the Yindee Hotel, but instead is dropped off in the middle of nowhere, hitches a ride to Silverton (which stands in for the "Yelonda" of the novel), and from there he hitches what he thinks is a ride to Sydney.

Although the roo-shooting scenes were filmed not far from the Little Topar hotel (which we have argued is a plausible narrative location for the Yindee hotel of the novel), the corresponding pub scenes in the film were not filmed there. Rather the Yindee pub scenes were filmed at Kinalung, a siding on the Broken Hill–Menindee railway, some 85 miles by road (though only 25 mi. or 40 km., as the crow flies) from Little Topar.[18] Today, nothing remains at Kinalung except a pumping station for the Menindee pipeline; however, at the time of filming, traces of its past as a railway fettler's camp were still apparent, including a row of railway workers' cottages and a demountable public school, much like the one depicted at Tiboonda in the film.

The set for the "hotel" was the last in the row of railway workers' cottages. These cottages have since been demolished but were also a key filming location for the 1971 Italian-language comedy *Bello onesto emigrato Australia sposerebbe compaesana illibata*, or *A Girl in Australia*, directed by Luigi Zampa. In *Wake in Fright*, the pub building appears to be surrounded by nothing but dirt and scrub, although the railway and water pipeline are visible running alongside it into the distance. Zampa's *Bello onesto*, on the other hand shows the row of identical cottages that precedes the one shown in *Wake in Fright*, the railway siding, and the pumping station on the other side of the railway lines.

In *Wake in Fright*, an overhead establishing shot of the "pub" at Yindee/Kinalung also shows a giant beer bottle attached to the roof. This distinc-

---

18. See *Wake in Fright* call sheet no. 33, which identifies Kinalung as the filming location for the "Yindee hotel and verandah" and provides these directions to the crew: "[Take] Menindee Road for 31 miles to Quondong Hotel. Cross Stephen's Creek. TURN SHARP LEFT at end of Bridge. Sign-posted 'KINALUNG.' Kinalung is 8 miles" (Buckley).

tive motif was inspired by the former Quondong Hotel, which was located where Stephens Creek crosses the Menindee–Broken Hill Road, about 30 miles (48 km.) southeast of Broken Hill. The Quondong hotel was destroyed by fire in 2001—an all-too-familiar ending for some of these iconic Outback hotels, with the Yanco Glen hotel suffering the same fate. Although he does not refer to it by name, in his interview with Caputo, Kotcheff describes coming across and having a drink at the Quondong Hotel: "I was out driving with the location manager, John Shaw, and one location we were looking for was a pub out in the middle of nowhere. We were about 30 miles outside of Broken Hill when I saw a building that was about five miles away with a 40-foot beer-bottle on top of it. I said to John, 'Look at that! Come on, let's go,' and so we headed directly for it and, of course, we were off the road immediately and went bouncing over the outback" (Caputo).[19]

Turning finally to Yelonda, as in the novel, mapping this narrative location poses additional difficulties. As we argued above, the novel's Yelonda is plausibly modeled on Wilcannia, 120 miles (193 km.) east of Broken Hill. In the film, however, Yelonda is not only not named as such, it is in many respects replaced as a narrative location by its filming location. In the novel, Grant attempts to hitchhike to Sydney, first stopping at Yindee and then at Yelonda. In the film, however, Grant does not return to the Yindee hotel; his first "hitched" ride drops him off in the middle of nowhere, while his second one drops him off outside a pub that has "Silverton Hotel" emblazoned across it. The action that occurs in this scene matches that which occurs in the Yelonda of the novel, and again, the filmscript refers to the narrative location as Yelonda. Yet, when Grant is shown arriving at the location, the Silverton Hotel—its name clearly visible on screen—unambiguously announces its location, both as a filming and as a narrative location. Silverton itself is an historic silver mining town 16 miles (26 km.) northwest of Broken Hill. Built up around the Umberumberka silver and lead mine, Silverton was declared a town in 1883, and within two years reached its peak population of 5000 (Eklund 319). According to Eklund,

19. See also Galvin, who identifies the hotel with the beer bottle on its roof as the Quondong Hotel. A photograph of the Quondong Hotel from the early 1980s can be viewed on the *Cultural Atlas of Australia* website.

the "early optimism" around Silverton quickly dwindled along with its population, and by 1899, only 16 years after it was established, Silverton's "municipal council was withdrawn" (319). Although it is often now considered a ghost town, Silverton does have a resident community, primarily made up of artists and those who make their trade from the town's mining and film history. Silverton Hotel, in particular, has a proud history on the silver screen, one that begins with its role in *Wake in Fright*.[20] As a narrative location, however, Silverton makes little geographical sense. Unless we are to believe that John Grant does not know his east from his west, it would seem unlikely that he would attempt to travel to Sydney, 710 miles (1142 km.) east of Bundanyabba/Broken Hill, by first heading in the other direction to Silverton. This is further complicated by the fact that, although the first half of the film's "Yelonda" scene was filmed in Silverton, the second half was filmed at the Mount Gipps Hotel, some 25 miles (40 km.) east of Silverton and 9 miles (14 km.) east of Broken Hill.[21]

In attempting to map the narrative geography of *Wake in Fright*'s film adaptation with and against that of the novel, what becomes apparent is how the film's commitment to what Cunningham calls "locationism"— that is, a filmmaker's "intense commitment, despite the massive technical and financial obstacles, to shooting the 'true' country" (26)—largely confirms the narrative map we constructed for the novel, thereby bringing a quasi-fictional geography and its geospace into closer alignment. And yet, to this point, we have been writing about the locationism of Kotcheff's *Wake in Fright* as though it would be readily apparent to a casual viewer that it was filmed in and around the mining town of Broken Hill. It is, of course, not quite as simple as this, for just as it would take local knowledge and some interpretive work to identify Broken Hill in Cook's novel,

20. In 1970, *Wake in Fright* was the first film to be shot on location at the Silverton Hotel. Other notable films that feature the Silverton Hotel include *Mad Max 2* (G. Miller, 1981), the miniseries *A Town like Alice* (Stevens, 1981), *Razorback* (Mulcahy, 1984), and *The Adventures of Priscilla, Queen of the Desert* (S. Elliott, 1994). A replica of *Mad Max*'s V8 Interceptor famously now stands outside the hotel as a tourist attraction.

21. When Grant walks down the main street of Yelonda/Silverton and arrives at a second hotel, the hotel pictured is the former Mount Gipps Hotel, which closed in the 1980s. See also *Wake in Fright* call sheet no. 26, which identifies Mount Gipps as the filming location for the "Yelonda Hotel" (Buckley).

it would take a similar amount of local knowledge to identify it as the filming location in Kotcheff's adaptation. Broken Hill might be an iconic Australian mining town, but its townscape does not have the immediate, culturally ingrained recognizability or placeability of, say, a Sydney Harbour or an Uluru. On the whole, it is likely that, for local and international audiences alike, *Wake in Fright*'s Bundanyabba might just as well have been filmed *anywhere* in the Australian Outback. This placelessness that nevertheless accompanies the film's locationism is underscored when we account for the fact the film was released internationally under the title *Outback*. No longer Broken Hill or Bundanyabba, the space of the film has been elevated under this title to generic or symbolic space. Bundanyabba/ Broken Hill becomes a synecdoche for the idea of the Outback in the same way that the Kimberley and Darwin regions stand in for the entire nation in Luhrmann's *Australia*. Additionally, the voiceover for the original *Outback* trailer resituates the narrative on the Australian continent, excising it from the south and transplanting it in the country's north. The *Outback* trailer opens with a screeching of tires as a battered Ford Fairlane begins to career, bouncing and bumping through an arid landscape. As we see men fighting with kangaroos, men fighting with each other on an Outback pub verandah, and men gleefully firing rifles, a man's voice intones menacingly: "In northern Australia, there are 5000 square miles of sand, scrub, and searing heat. A desolate, primitive place that can take a man and destroy him. They call it the Outback" (*"Outback"*). In many respects, this shifting of a southern Outback space into the Australian North is thoroughly in keeping with what we discuss in the following chapter as a distinctive troping of the North as a Gothic frontier space, reflecting, on a microcosmic level, broader concerns about national space. In this sense, despite the film's locationism, it exhibits a certain slippage between physical and symbolic space, one that is also detectable in the novel, but is amplified to a much greater degree in the theatrical adaptation, to which we now turn.

Mapping Wake in Fright *III: The Play*

In some ways, theater adaptation is a less fraught process for the cultural geographer or digital mapper. Theater space, as the Tompkins discussion earlier in this chapter makes clear, is often content to remain symbolic or representational. Unless videography is central to a stage production's scenic design, space is always being represented through icons, symbols, or connotation, and an audience is required to meet the designer half-way—to accept that red dirt *connotes* "the desert" or that architectural centerpieces and items of furniture, perhaps, *suggest* a particular time and place. There are no "real" shooting locations being called on to enact or depict actual geographical places. Where the novel of *Wake in Fright* strongly *implies* but also disrupts a Bundanyabba–Broken Hill connection, which is reinforced and made explicit in the film adaptation, the play adaptation contains no locational hints whatsoever as to a possible geographical correlate for Bundanyabba. In the playscript, although the five place names have been retained, those narratorial-level references to distance, location, population, and proximity have understandably been stripped out. In the play adaptation, which has seen five productions since 2010, we seem to be very much in the realm of the Outback as symbolic or psychological space, as a moralized landscape that is everywhere and nowhere both in time and space. But of course, the space of a play cannot be reduced to its script—it exists as more-than-textual space. As McAuley writes:

> Playtexts can be read and their spatial content analyzed, but textual space is made really meaningful only in performance. The playtext contains the potential for many spatializations, and that of course entails many different meanings. It is the practitioners who must select, discard, play with, the potentiality and create the staging that will articulate the meaning the play has for them. The important thing to stress here is the interactive function of the text at every stage of the meaning-making function. (*Space* 32)

In the 2014 Adelaide Fringe Festival production by Yabba Productions (directed by Renee Palmer), for instance, the New South Wales Outback locations of the novel and film can best be described as being *evoked* by a versatile, minimalist set design in which ironwood chairs are moved by actors from scene to scene to suggest different locations (a bar room, a hotel room, a domestic family interior), and a single sheet of corrugated iron masking the stage exit represents an iconic Outback building material. The only nod toward the frontier landscape evoked in the novel's detailed description and made concrete in the locationism of the film adaptation is the red dirt that covers the stage and the yellow-and-orange-hued light-ing, which repeat the visual tropes of the film adaptation.[22] The part once again stands in for the whole here. We, as an audience, are required to bring our own cache of knowledge to bear when it comes to interpreting and locating time and space in this sparse and (by economic necessity) "poor"-theatrical (in the Grotowskian sense) visual realization of land-scape and era.

As the most recent adaptation, and one that comes some forty years after the film, *Wake in Fright* the play is interesting in the way that seems to treat the narrative as a timeless classic or a classic out of time. Except in its references to dollars rather than pounds, the adapted script hasn't at-tempted to update or modernize the base narrative or dialogue, and apart from the actors' more contemporary haircuts, there is little in the staging that suggests the play's action is meant to be occurring in the present time or fifty years in the past. Unlike the novel and film, then, the stage adapta-tion of *Wake in Fright* is, considered separately, inherently unmappable in the geospace, but it nevertheless contributes to the coproduction of geog-raphy and the continuation of established tropes of Australian space and the role of those tropes in the building of national identity. The Australian slang and idiom that inheres in the text *feels* authentically of its (i.e., the novel's) era; the costume design (unattributed to a particular designer in the production's program) is certainly not contemporary but appears ge-nerically 1960s/1970s. And the production's iconic set design—its internal diegetic world—evokes the same milieu as that of the novel and the film. Lurid red lighting during the piece's climax—Grant's violent rape by Doc Tydon at the end of the kangaroo hunt—hints as much at a heightened state of mental duress as it does to a physical "red" Outback landscape. We are much more firmly in the realm of the symbolic and representational throughout.

Theater, then, is offering both less and more to the cultural mapper. On the one hand, considered in and of itself, and not in the context of the text's other versions, the space of *Wake in Fright* the play is entirely repre-

22. Production stills of Palmer's production of *Wake in Fright* (as adapted by Pavlich) can be viewed at http://yabbaproductions.wordpress.com/photos/.

sentational or suggested, so attempting to map it is, perhaps, futile. On the other hand, considered within the context of its satellite texts, this is an adaptation of a novel that, as the preceding discussion has demonstrated, clearly alludes to specific locations in the geospace. The film adaptation's status as an Australian classic means that the play must also be considered in relation to the locationism that Kotcheff's *Wake in Fright* is noted for. Indeed, there appears to be an underlying assumption, in this particular adaptation, that the audience member has a familiarity with either the novel or the film and perhaps therefore brings personal knowledge about locational context to the production. The lay audience member, however, is only given the option (in this production) of reading generic Outback space into the diegetic world depicted on stage. It is an imagined landscape being depicted; the physical terrain being represented merges with the psychological landscape of the central character, and becomes rendered generically or thematically through the lens of horror or of Australian bush Gothic. For the fan of this text wishing to make a pilgrimage to the locations that have inspired it, the novel and the film are going to provide far more purchase than the stage play. The stage adaptation, perhaps, adds value to the urtext's net cultural worth and extends its life as a cultural artefact; but, in this instance, rather than depicting specific spaces and locations, it is the Australian Outback as *mythic* space that is being acti- vated. It is, as the production's director describes it, the myth of *mateship* that is being critiqued here. Palmer writes, "Reading the novel *Wake in Fright,* I was instantly struck by the raw, aggressive, dangerous energy of the fictitious town of Bundanyabba. In the stage production I wanted to explore how the traditional notion of mateship is turned into a cruel game exposing the ugly side of Australia" ("Director's Notes"). The *theme* (of the corruption of the myth of mateship) is more important in this interpretation of the text than the location in which the play is set. Once again, then, we see the Outback or desert operating as a *paysage moralisé*,[23] or, as Haynes puts it in *Seeking the Centre*, a "psycho-symbolic space" in which contemporary fears and anxieties can be played out. This does not,

---

23. See also our analysis of the notion of the "Never-Never" (a fictional Outback region in Australia's North) as a moralized landscape in Stadler and Mitchell.

however, make the Outback/desert a kind of free-floating signifier, excised from the materiality of the physical world. As Haynes explains, the Australian desert can only "legitimately be cast as the implacable agent of existential terror" because the "physical threat [of the desert] remains actual" (196). The desert is in constant slippage between the physical and the symbolic, between the geospace and its imagined counterpart, each one inscribing meaning upon the other.

In this chapter we have sought to articulate how space is mediated and remediated through a constellation of texts that re-present a particular narrative and its narrative geography. The specific affordances of each narrative form—novel, film, and play—foreground different spatialities and different levels of mappability. Mapping these texts via neography brings yet another form of spatial remediation by way of geovisualization. As the above analysis shows, despite the regional specificity of *Wake in Fright,* some of its locations cannot be pinned down in the geospace with a high degree of confidence (Tiboonda, in particular). Geovisualizing the texts' narrative locations, however, requires us to assign to them coordinates in the geospace. In the final chapter we discuss in greater depth the problems inherent in mapping ambiguous narrative locations, but no matter what techniques are applied in order to visually qualify a map point for a narrative location (e.g., fuzzy boundaries, icons that express confidence level, etc.), a map of narrative locations will always assert a level of geographical fixity that the narrative itself may not (or even may actively strive against). The maps that we have constructed of the three *Wake in Fright* texts (all of which may be viewed and explored via the *Cultural Atlas*) are themselves texts that, once again, remediate the narrative geographies of the novel, film, and play. However, these maps also bring the texts into closer dialogue with the region that they re-present—that of the Unincorporated Far West of New South Wales. The mapped approach allows us to set a spatial narrative within its historical and geographical context and to enhance primary textual material (e.g., quotes and film and production stills) with historical, geographical, and sociocultural detail such as archival images, Census data, and links to multimedia resources. Bringing to light and drawing together these layers of information about a region's topography, its demography, its history, and its representation as a narrative space is one of the advantages that neogeography (as the digital mapping of multiple perspectives) has over traditional forms of textual analysis. In other words, mapping narrative geographies allows us to see the productive tension between these "psycho-symbolic" spaces and their implied and acknowledged geographical referents as they feed into and coproduce each other.

2

CULTURAL TOPOGRAPHY
AND MYTHIC SPACE

Australia's North as Gothic Zone

Franco Moretti states in his *Atlas of the European Novel* that mapping a fictional space "is not the conclusion of geographical work; it's the beginning. After which begins in fact the most challenging part of the whole enterprise: one looks at the map, and thinks" (7). This chapter addresses the significant interpretative challenges inherent in "reading" the maps of narratives set in given regions. The chapter looks at the ways in which geocritical theory and the analysis of maps that represent fictional space broker an analysis of mythic space in relation to national narratives. We also discuss the perils of overreliance on data contained within such digital mapping projects in order to explore what can sometimes be revealed by way of omission. In terms of specific regional examples, we examine patterns occurring in the Australian North, particularly in theater but also with reference to literature and film, examining how the landscape is staged and performed as a national myth. The rise of a uniquely categorized Gothic North in theater of the twenty-first century will operate here as a t(r)opical test case as we investigate how patterns of representation shift over time and across mediums and consider why the fictional space of the continent's far north is densely populated with texts when the overwhelming majority of Australians live in the metropolitan centers of the south and southeast. The focus of this chapter is to study the significance of geographic location in post-1950 plays and related narratives set above the Tropic of Capricorn in order to look at recurring themes, settings, and concepts in these plays to see how this space functions and what it represents. We argue that the far north of Australia functions as a frontier with Asia across the national border and as a space of encounter with the Indigenous "internal other" within Australia. Moreover, we discover that the *theater* emerging from this region in the past ten years is theming this depiction of frontier schematics through a particular generic lens: that of the Gothic. Comparisons with narratives set in other parts of Australia and other regions of the world serve to substantiate these claims about the North as (increasingly Gothic) frontier space. We demonstrate how geographic information technologies, theories, and concepts help understand such spatial influence on cultural development.

INTERPRETING THE MAP

As the Moretti quote at the outset of this chapter suggests, one must first look to the map to see *what* has been aggregated and where this cultural representation has been concentrated or, indeed, omitted before one can go ahead and interpret the data. If, as we suggest, the Australian North is constituted of a particular pattern of cultural representation, questions that ensue might include "What does this data tell us?"; "What is the function of the North?"; and "In what specific ways have playwrights, novelists, and filmmakers troped the North relative to other national space?" The answers to these questions may well act as useful beacons to cultural cartographers examining literary, cinematic, or theatrical traditions in other geographical contexts. One can think of frontier spaces or marginal nonmetropolitan regions of practically any country (the Celtic fringes of Ireland's West, as Jarlath Killeen describes it, for example, in "Irish Gothic"); these are often nebulous spaces that are not always easy to map precisely, but search engines in the Australian example now allow us to undertake precisely such cultural mapping. Digital resources such as *AustLit, AusStage,* and the *Cultural Atlas of Australia* (and there are, obviously, similar projects elsewhere, such as the *Literary Atlas of Europe*) can help to geovisualize patterns of representation that may hitherto have remained speculative and offer "mythic" regions up for comparative analysis and investigation.

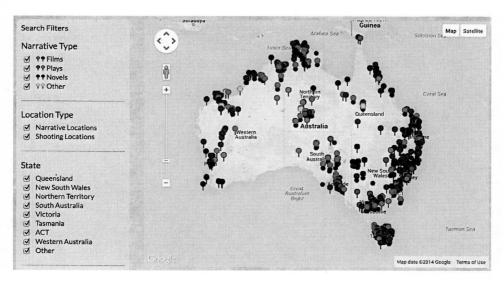

Figure 2.1. Map of Australian films, novels, and plays.
Source: Cultural Atlas of Australia.

Of course, databases are only ever as good as the information that has been entered into them. There is scope for subjective data entry to take place in most such systems. But even such programming "preferences" or subject choices can themselves be revealing of a nation's cultural preoccupations. *AustLit*, as we have stated earlier, is the largest and most influential of the current national literary databases and search engines in Australia. It offers a number of themed "projects" to help readers and researchers to define (or refine) their searches and has established a number of such projects along regional lines. The first (and, at the time of writing, the largest) of these regional literature projects is "Writing the Tropical North." Instigated and supported by literary researchers from James Cook University in its Cairns and Townsville campuses in Far North Queensland, the project has been so successful that it has spawned two more northern region data subsets—North Western Australian literature and Northern Territory literature. This "Writing the Tropical North" project has acted as the model for other regional literature projects on *AustLit*, including Western Australian and Tasmanian literature. So, while we would have been able to make the claim only a couple of years ago that the "Writing the Tropical North" project was the *only* regional specialization *AustLit*

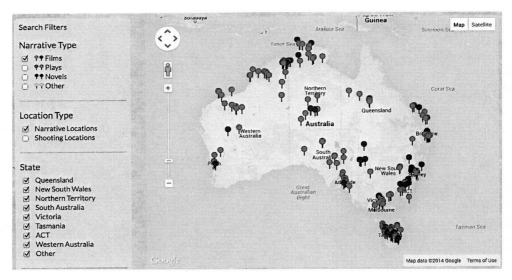

Figure 2.2. Map of Australian films. Source: Cultural Atlas of Australia.

had devoted itself to, we can at least still justifiably claim that there is sufficient interest in the work of North Australian (tropical) writers as to instigate a series of other regionally distinct literary research projects. The impression is still of an underpopulated Australian region "punching above its weight" in terms of literary output.

To bolster this impression and add leverage to it as a claim, we turn to the data produced by the *Cultural Atlas of Australia*. Figures 2.1–2.4 provide indicators of distribution of the narrative locations of major Australian creative texts (produced/published/staged between 1950 and the present) for each of the narrative forms of film, literature, and theater. The maps for individual narrative forms each provide different distribution patterns of locations used as narrative sites.

The film dataset (see figure 2.2) displays a clear concentration of narrative and filming locations in the Kimberley region of the far north of Western Australia, the "Top End" of the Northern Territory, and then slewing down diagonally across the nation through Central Australia and Outback South Australia to Tasmania. The South Australian (over-) representation can perhaps be explained by that state's film office having subsidized Australian cinema over the years and offering a bureaucratic infrastructure that encourages locational shooting at sites in that state—

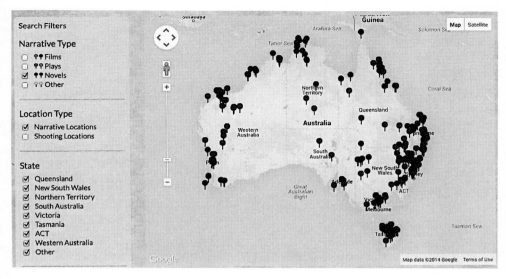

Figure 2.3. Map of Australian novels. Source: Cultural Atlas of Australia.

notably in the township of Quorn, which has featured in a remarkable number of Australian films and miniseries.[1] If we take shooting locations out of the equation, we still find a preponderance of films set in the same general regions. The North West, the Center, and Tasmania are especially heavily represented relative to their populations.[2]

In the context of post-1950s Australian literature, novels set on the Eastern seaboard (Queensland in particular) and in more regions of Western Australia (thanks, no doubt, to the prodigious output of Tim Winton)

1. Since it first made an appearance as a filming location in *Bitter Springs* (Ralph Smart) in 1950, Quorn has featured in films and miniseries such as *Kangaroo* (Lewis Milestone, 1952), *Robbery under Arms* (Jack Lee, 1957), *The Sundowners* (Fred Zinnemann, 1960), *Sunday Too Far Away* (Ken Hannam, 1975), *Gallipoli* (Peter Weir, 1981), *The Lighthorsemen* (Simon Wincer, 1987), *The Shiralee* (George Ogilvy, 1987), *Last Ride* (Glendyn Ivin, 2009), *Tracks* (John Curran, 2013), and *The Rover* (David Michôd, 2014).

2. Only a dozen feature films have been set and shot in Tasmania and all are represented in the *Cultural Atlas of Australia* because we have undertaken a special case study of Gothic and environmental themes in Tasmanian cinema. This skews the data in the atlas somewhat, since it deviates from the way by which films are selected for inclusion on the map in general according to box office revenue, critical acclaim, and cultural relevance. Had those selection criteria been applied to Tasmanian cinema, only a couple of films would have been represented.

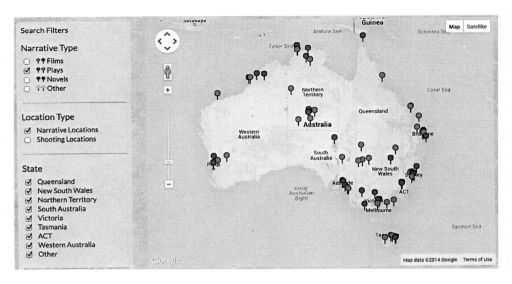

Figure 2.4. Map of Australian plays. Source: Cultural Atlas of Australia.

becomes apparent, but still there is a concatenation of texts whose creative narratives follow the same trajectory from the far north and northwest of the nation to Tasmania in the far southeast (see figure 2.3).

In theater, the capital cities begin to take on greater weighting (particularly Brisbane, Sydney and Melbourne). Prior to 2000 the North is relatively sparsely represented, though the general trajectory of areas "mapped" by major Australian plays does follow that northwest-to-southeast arc, with the Center again over-represented relative to population (see figure 2.4).

Taken as a whole, our data suggests that it is the remote landscapes that are disproportionately being called on to represent national creative narrative space and, as we will argue in this chapter, to take on mythic spatial functioning. We discuss in chapter 3 the example of Tasmania as a heavily represented symbolic space whose representation shifts over time. But reading the map for its preponderance of nonmetropolitan narrative locations here, it becomes readily apparent that the North and Northwest are providing patterns of representation that suggest this is a large frontier space that is being conjured to enact regionally specific national myths of its own.

Despite the stated focus that this chapter provides on recent *theatrical* troping of the Australian North, results that the *Cultural Atlas* first offers would appear to indicate that it has predominantly been the cinema that has colonized this discursive space between 1950 and 2000. There is actually a richer history of Australian depiction of the North on stage in late nineteenth-century melodrama and the so-called bush play tradition of playwrights such as Louis Esson, Henrietta Drake-Brockman, Katharine Susannah Prichard, and George Landen Dann in the 1920s–1940s. But suffice it to say that the evidence provided by the datasets imported into the *Cultural Atlas*—and these datasets include a representative sample of approximately 200 landmark texts at the time of writing, spanning each medium equally, selected on the basis of industrial recognition (awarded plays, films and novels), enduring popularity, entrenchment in national secondary and tertiary education curricula, and commercial or critical success—suggests that film has become the dominant mode depicting the North over the second half of the twentieth century. The first decade of the twenty-first century tells a different story, as will shortly be discussed, but the cinematic fascination with Northern landscapes as surrogate national mythic space, as metonymy for "the bush" or "the Outback" broadly writ, first needs to be investigated.

WHAT IS THE NORTH?

So what, then, is this North? Where is it? By whom is the designation of "North" conferred? Sherrill Grace asks similar questions about the Canadian North in her introduction to a collection of plays depicting that country's vast, isolated, icy northern limits:

> To claim that one can put the North on stage is immediately to ask: Whose North? What stage? And these questions open out to reveal others: Which playwrights? Staging for whom? The "true North" like the "we" who guard it in the Canadian national anthem,[3] is a complex, changing and problematic term. (Introduction ix)

---

3. Grace is referring here to "O Canada," and specifically Robert Stanley Weir's 1908 (and now standard) English translation of Adolphe-Basile Routhier's original French lyrics. The first stanza of Weir's lyrics is as follows:

O Canada! Our home and native land!
True patriot love in all thy sons command.
With glowing hearts we see thee rise,
The True North strong and free!

Canadians, it could be argued, have a much more precise sense of a North–South cultural, political, and geographical dichotomy than Australians. Latitude sixty is used to divide the territories (Yukon, New Northwest Territory, and Nunavut Territory) from the provinces, so there is a sense of a politically diluted non-self-governing North being constructed in contradistinction to a politically and culturally dominant South. Rob Shields describes how the Canadian provinces—like the Australian states before the Northern Territory and Australian Capital Territory gained self-government (in 1978 and 1989, respectively)—have comparatively greater "control over energy and resources, judiciary, health, education, housing and land use policies, taxation powers, constitutional veto, and the use of coordinated inter-provincial pressure on the Federal Government" (165). Shields goes on to argue that in the Canadian context this quite explicit geographical and political divide segues into a broader, more slippery, and less clearly empirically definable North–South cultural imaginary.

It should be noted, however, that this North–South Canadian divide is complicated by the fact that Canada is also caught in another such cultural and geographic dichotomy within a broader North American context. The entirety of Canada is often constructed as the (cold, arctic, remote, recalcitrant) North to the United States' hegemonically dominant center, in much the same way that Australia has traditionally been imagined as South to Britain's (and indeed, the rest of the "civilized" world's) imperial center. A critical thread that runs through this book is the notion that Australia has been imagined as a "Great Southern Land," even prior to its "official" invention as a nation. One of the key points being made here is that it is possible for a number of these seemingly contradictory culturally and historically imagined spaces to coexist alongside, or even over the

From far and wide, O Canada,
We stand on guard for thee.
God keep our land, glorious and free
O Canada, we stand on guard for thee,
O Canada, we stand on guard for thee.

Weir's translation is not a literal one, and the reference to Canada as the "True North" does not appear in Routhier's original lyrics.

top of, each other. It is possible, in other words, for an Australian North to exist within a nation imagined from its inception as *terra australis.* As discussed in the final chapter of this book, *Terra Australis,* or the Great Southern Land, is the name frequently ascribed to the Australian landmass by European cartographers since its "discovery" by Europe, and even longer back.

Similarly, the United States of America, even in the nation's title, hints at a historical past when the country was divided into two very distinct northern and southern political zones. The North and South (and, one could argue, the American West) are each laden with rich cultural taxonomies and ontologies that are used to define identity in relation to space. Similarly, the American West also exists as both a geographically defined space and a cultural space. Traditionally "the West" (within the western genre) is west of the Mississippi River and north of the Rio Bravo.

Fiona McKean makes a case for reading the Australian North against the American South as "Internal Orients" within their respective parent nations, and as "tropical zones" that can be compared along critical theoretical lines accordingly. Quoting David Jansson's development of Edward Said's notion of Orientalism, McKean states:

> Cultural geographer David Jansson built on these developments to describe the way in which dominant regions may subordinate and essentialize *regions* within a single nation, constructing these as Other in similar ways to classical orientalism. . . . Just as in Orientalism the west constructs its identity in opposition to the Other, so too internal orientalism may be used to provide a national identity that stands in contrast to the internal Other—as Jansson argues in relation to the "exalted national identity" of the United States.

Developing Jansson's identification of the American Deep South as precisely such a region or zone, McKean argues that the Australian Tropical North constitutes a similar marginalized internal other. She states, "The tropes he identifies are congruent with literary representations of the Deep South. . . . While tropes of the Australian Deep North have not been theorized so consistently as those of the American Deep South, they certainly exist in fictional representations of the region."

So if there is an Australian North, how does one define it in geographic and political, much less in cultural, terms? Does one disregard state and

territory boundaries and carve a line across the continent along, say, the
Tropic of Capricorn, as in Xavier Herbert's novel, *Capricornia* (1938)? Or,
to enact the old Brisbane Line mentality,[4] is there still an arbitrary divide
that somehow veers anachronistically across from Queensland's state
capital, Brisbane, to Western Australia's capital city, Perth, as though
population alone decides what divides a militarily defendable "real" Australia from The (empty, expendable Northern) Rest? Where, in other
words, does an Australian North, whether real or imagined, begin and
end? And how does it sit alongside a veritable latticework of other such
internal geocultural divides?[5] We have highlighted the word *real* to iter-
ate the point that Northern Australia is often constituted as a culturally,
politically, and historically diminished subspace within the broader Australian imaginary. Jon Stratton, for instance, argues "'Australian' history
has traditionally located itself in a factual history of white settlement
occurring from the south-east of the continent. The North of the continent has been constructed as the site of the Other, of that which has
been repressed in the South's production of the real" (38). In such a discursive equation, the South becomes defined as the "real" at the North's
expense, and the North is well on its way to being invented as mythic
space.

Stratton goes on to argue that the further north one travels, the less
historically inscribed and accounted for—the less *real*—the area becomes: "The area denoted as the Northern Territory," Stratton claims,
"is [by logical extension] the least 'real' area of Australia, and is, therefore, the weakest moment in the articulation of the dominant discourse
of 'Australia'" (38). In this deft psychoanalytic maneuver, a historically
meaningless geographical North is constructed not in contradistinction

4. The Brisbane Line was an imaginary line of defense drawn from Brisbane across to
Perth during World War II. It was hypothesized that this might be the line against which
Australia could retreat in the event of a Japanese invasion/occupation. Land to the north
of this line was thus considered expendable, reflecting not only the logistical but also the
symbolic value of the Australian North at that time.
5. Australian spatial binaries include city/bush and coast/Outback. The Australian bush and the Outback exist as much as legends and myths as discrete sociogeo-
graphical spaces (the US Deep South or Wild West could be argued to operate as similar
phenomena).

to a generalized Australian South, but in relation to a very specific urban Melbourne–Sydney nexus that in turn constructs itself as the authentic Australian cultural, if not geographic, center. "We need to note," Stratton says, "that, in this mythic geography, there is no Deep South or Far South. . . . The north, as a discursive element, exists not in relation to the south but in relation to the claimed reality of Sydney/Melbourne" (39). The South, in effect, does not define itself as anything. It simply "is." The North again emerges as a discursive "other" space produced as a psychological appendage to the Southern urban "self."

Grace makes an excellent point about the mobile nature of cartographic border-making at the symbolic level. She invokes the imagery of the magnetic (as against the geographic) North Pole to describe the Canadian North, because

> the Magnetic Pole *moves.* Like the Arctic ice pack, it shifts; it will not be pinned down. What is worse, the closer you approach it, the more will the Magnetic North Pole send your conventional compass needle veering wildly off any fixed course. Magnetic North, then, encapsulates a North whose parameters seem always to be shifting, a North, I would go so far as to say, that cannot be understood apart from this protean capacity. (*Canada* 51)

Given the equally undulating or mirage-like quality of the Australian North and the Northern frontier outlined in this chapter, Grace's floating North seems to be an eloquent metaphoric template for our purposes. The Australian North may therefore be both undermapped and undertheorized space relative to the Canadian and American examples; and yet it does exist as a cultural zone that yields disproportionate fictional narrative exploration relative to population density.

MYTHOLOGIZING THE AUSTRALIAN OUTBACK

For decades Australian cinema and the scholarship that interrogates it has been preoccupied with "the bush" and "the Outback" as vast, mythic, and discursive terrains that sit in enigmatic counterpoint to the urban lives of the overwhelming majority of the population. As we outlined in the previous chapter, alongside a more romanticized colonial-era vision of the bush as a locus of pioneering toil and heroic conquest—the crucible in which the masculinist ethos of "mateship" was forged, there has existed a depiction of the Outback as a source of racial and spatial anxiety. In the (usually Anglo-Celtic heterosexual)[6] hero's encounter with this epic landscape, the Outback or the bush is inscribed with European fears of alienation, isolation, death and encounters with a frequently exoticized Indigenous other. The tropes in Australian cinema dealing with the bush are deeply familiar to local audiences: national anxieties surrounding colonization frequently find expression through white characters' engagement with a raced landscape whose symbolic meanings are inscrutable or uninterpretable to Western systems of understanding; a violent frontier contest is played out on the fringes of "civilization" and the metropolitan imagination; the landscape engorges and subsumes femininity and its range of signifiers; lawlessness—even apocalypse[7]—breaks out beyond the reach of European systems of order; or the landscape is representative of a great glaring existential national void. Representations of the Australian bush, then, can perhaps be seen to swing on these two axes: the romanticized and heroic "colonial" version (that we see perpetuated more recently in Baz Luhrmann's *Australia;* and the bush as source of melancholy, horror, and isolation that we see depicted in a film like *Wake in Fright,* as discussed in the previous chapter. Either way, as Ross Gibson argues, to European eyes, Australia originally appeared and continues to be perceived as an "empty space," a cultural blank slate, or a "sublime structuring void" ("Camera" 211).

Writing in 1983, Gibson claims, "Australia is still being historicised, but we can't presume that, with the decades, the landscape will become systematised or artificed to the same degree as either the English countryside or an American urban environment such as New York" (212). By 1993, Robin Wright argues that the New Wave cinematic canon of the 1970s and early 1980s has turned to the Australian landscape as "one of the primary determining features of 'Australianness' in cultural products of the 1970s" and that this body of work is culturally produced to reflect the ideology

6. Readers will be able to think of exceptions: Aboriginal protagonists in *Walkabout* (Nicolas Roeg, 1971), *Jedda* (Charles Chauvel, 1955), and *The Chant of Jimmie Blacksmith* (Fred Schepisi, 1978), and a triumvirate of queer heroes heading into the Outback in *The Adventures of Priscilla, Queen of the Desert* (Stephan Elliott, 1994), for instance.

7. See, for instance, George Miller's *Mad Max* films and Stuart Beattie's *Tomorrow When the War Began* (2010).

of the times. Even though frequently set in colonial-era bush mises en scène, they are still films about the present:

> For the predominantly white, Anglo-Celtic, urban Australian cultural elite at the time of the production of these films there was no alternative culture, lifestyle, ritual, history or society which could be used to delineate their 'difference' from their European ancestry other than the "idea" of the Australian bush. (R. Wright 3)

Since that time, it is our contention that there has in fact been a tranche of films (and plays, television programs, and novels) that have gone on to trope the Australian Outback/bush in precisely the sorts of regionally distinct ways that Gibson claims are unlikely to occur; and that these films produce symbolic meanings to contemporary audiences in direct cultural progression from the New Wave era to which Wright refers.

THE OUTBACK HEADS NORTH

In this contemporary canon, Australian cinema is still frequently associated with Outback and bush locales and their swag of mythic associations, but despite a spate of films dealing with specifically northern locations across Western Australia and the Northern Territory, including *Japanese Story* (Sue Brooks, 2003), *Yolngu Boy* (Stephen Johnson, 2001), *Ten Canoes* (Rolf de Heer, 2006), *Wolf Creek* (Greg McLean, 2005), *Lucky Miles* (Michael James Rowland, 2007), *Rogue* (Greg McLean, 2007), *Australia* (Baz Luhrmann, 2008), *Mad Bastards* (Brendan Fletcher, 2010), *Satellite Boy* (Catriona McKenzie 2012) and, preceding these recent releases, the seminal *Crocodile Dundee* (Peter Faiman, 1986), *Jedda* (Charles Chauvel, 1955) and *The Overlanders* (Harry Watt, 1946), little academic analysis is devoted to viewing these films as a distinctively northern oeuvre. The rise of an Aboriginal presence and influence in film cannot be ignored, but the Outback, the bush, and the North all seem to roll into one undifferentiated category as far as cinematographic scholarship is concerned. A wave of recent film scholarship has focused, for instance, on the emphasis on representations of first contact, early frontier negotiations, and reflections of the colonial past from an Aboriginal perspective in contemporary Indigenous cinema.[8] None of it looks at the North, specifically, as a

---

8. See, for instance, Lydon; Weaver-Hightower; Brewster; and F. Collins.

cinematic subgenre or subject, and yet the *Cultural Atlas of Australia* produces maps that suggest that the North and North West are building up an archive of representations that far exceed its population density, even in relation to other sparsely populated sections of the country. The focus of this scholarly writing on Indigenous cinema is very much concerned with reconsidering the Australian colonial era from an Indigenous perspective, or on acknowledging past injustices such as the Stolen Generations.[9] While set mostly in the North, space in these films is analyzed as metonym for the entirety of Australia and for the nation's colonial history as a whole.

The North exists in this cinema (and one might transfer this analysis to similar readings of *Crocodile Dundee, Japanese Story, Wolf Creek, Rogue,* or *Yolngu Boy*) as a mythical space that is only "real" inasmuch as it exists as a projection of metropolitan fantasy. It is, in other words, enacted as a metaphoric landscape whereupon the further north one travels, the further from the urban metropolitan Australian nexus and production of the "real" one heads, the deeper the capacity for immersion in that fantasy.

To focus on one recent, ambitious, and influential cinema text that strives explicitly to depict the North (while being titled, ironically, in the general), Baz Luhrmann's *Australia* is worthy of especial discussion. *Australia* is noteworthy for its use of maps to create an imaginary geography of the North and its intertextual references to two earlier, influential Australian films, *Jedda* and *The Overlanders,* each of which uses maps to represent the external threat of Asia impinging on the coastal border and Aborigines threatening white settler culture from within. *Jedda* tells the story of an Aboriginal girl raised by a white family on a remote station in the Northern Territory, near the border of Western Australia. *The Overlanders* recounts the legendary overland cattle drove from Wyndham in Western Australia across the Top End all the way to Rockhampton in

---

9. *Rabbit-Proof Fence* (Phillip Noyce, 2002) and *The Tracker* (Rolf de Heer, 2002) are added to this oeuvre in the context of these analyses. 'The Stolen Generations' refers to the Aboriginal and Torres Strait Islander-descended children who were removed from their parents and placed into institutional or foster care by state and federal governments and church authorities from the early twentieth century until the 1970s. A national apology for the psychological, emotional, physical and cultural harm and distress caused by this practice was only issued as recently as 2007 by then (Labor) Prime Minister, Kevin Rudd.

Figure 2.5. Carney Cattle Company map. Source: *Australia*, Luhrmann, 2008.

Queensland, an historic event referenced in *Australia* as the six-month long "army drove" that Drover (Hugh Jackman) undertakes. The maps and aerial cinematography of the sparsely populated landscape in *Australia* show vast spaces that look uncultivated and largely uninhabited, just waiting to be branded with the imperial stamp of Carney Cattle Company (see figure 2.5).

In direct homage to the map at the beginning of *The Overlanders*, the Carney Cattle Co. map in *Australia* shows the northern border of Australia to be threatened by the rays of the rising sun, representing invading Japanese troops.

The map of the Northern Territory at the beginning of the film *Jedda* shows Aboriginal spears and shields around Alice Springs and a kangaroo hopping up the Stuart Highway toward Arnhem Land and Darwin; similarly the figure of a lone Aborigine (assumed to represent King George, as played by actor David Gulpilil) is pictured on the map of Faraway Downs, the station homestead that is so central to the narrative of *Australia*. As Stephen Carleton argues in an article on the Australian North and cinema, *Australia* offers, among other things, an idealized way forward from contemporary tensions surrounding the legacy of the Stolen Generations. In that film, Lady Ashley (Nicole Kidman), Drover (Hugh Jackman), and Nullah (Brandon Walters), along with loyal stockwoman and housemaid

Bandy Legs (Lillian Crombie) and cook Sing Song (Wah Yuen), form an extended mixed-race family, with Nullah's grandfather King George joining the kinship for the boy's cultural education at film's end. Carleton writes:

> There are echoes of a romantic Angelina Jolie–Brad Pitt "rainbow family" being nodded toward here. They are an entirely postmodern family outfit, and the inference is that even though such a model would be frowned upon by the white colonial circles of Darwin's administrative elite, the Northern homestead provides a subversive counter-space away from the monitoring gaze of propriety. The North, in its cultural construction of frontier lawlessness and radical individualism, is able to offer room for these alternative social family structures to occur. If the North is symbolic of the nation's racism, it is also concurrently symbolised as the space within which culturally progressive alternatives to the traditional white nuclear family and its "authentic" Aboriginal counterpoint might be allowed to comingle. ("Cinema" 55)

Rather than the site on which the nation's racist assimilationist policies might be metonymically enacted, Luhrmann offers the North as romantic space in which interracial healing might be played out through intercultural understanding and cooperation. The North thus takes on a range of complex and frequently contradictory cultural signifiers: it is simultaneously redneck and progressive, masculine and feminine, cultural frontier and hub, segregationist and assimilationist, site of the nation's shameful past and its idealized future, and so on.

It is possible for the North to exist as any number of such fantasized projections at the same time, and for other Australian spaces to play out regionally distinctive metaphoric and psychological functions for the nation as a whole through our national cinema. Chapter 5 examines the way that the Red Center, for instance, is troped as the "heart" of the nation. The analysis of *Australia* in this chapter and its placement within an emerging distinctive Northern oeuvre reveals the extent to which a panoply of regionally specific factors contribute to constructions and enactments of a Deep North in Australian culture more broadly defined and the extent to which this is a corollary, or a projection, of a broader cultural conception of the North in the national imaginary. We are, in other words, reading the Australian North as mythic space.

THEATER AND THE AUSTRALIAN NORTH

To extend this analysis of Australian mythic space and to tether it now to discussion of theater rather than film, it is useful to cite Ruth Barcan and Ian Buchanan, who draw on the work of Paul Carter (who in turn draws on the work of Henri Lefebvre and Michel Foucault) to argue that "space isn't an emptiness, a void to be filled, the neutral scene for action. Rather, space is imagined—called into being—by individuals and the cultures of which they are a part" ("Introduction" 8). Space is, by extension, *enacted*, making theater a particularly apt art form for reading geographical spaces for cultural inscription. By logical extension, theatrical space—whether physical or textual—can never be empty space, devoid of wider associations and implications. Theater does not exist in a vacuum. According to Alan Read, theater "is not innocent space, neutral space nor utopian space, but manifestly organized by the dominant relations of production" (158). Theater deals, among other things, with projections and imaginings of the material, social world, becoming, if we are to follow Read's line of thinking, political space.

Joanne Tompkins points out that the arrangement and management and creation of space on the stage must also produce social and political space in contexts that are relevant outside the theater. Tompkins draws on the work of Henri Lefebvre, Gearóid Ó Tuathail, Elin Diamond, Paul Carter, Una Chaudhuri, and Ken Gelder and Jane M. Jacobs to argue that "representational space performed in Australian theater not only contests conventional Australian history and culture; it also stages alternative means of managing the production of space in a spatially unstable nation" (5). Tompkins refers to the contested nature of occupation of space in Australia as a "settler" and "multicultural" postcolonial nation. She elaborates:

> Debates over land rights, anxieties regarding nationalism, settlement, reconciliation, traces of what was known as the yellow peril and subsequent invasion scares are preoccupied with space. These debates have resulted in the paradoxical depiction of Australia as an unlimited, empty land, at the same time as it is said to be too "full" to accommodate outsiders, such as asylum seekers. (6)

Remaining mindful that these contrasting visions, versions, and uses of space are loaded with cultural and political baggage and carry with them real as well as metaphorical power relations and practical struggles and contests, Tompkins's approach reads with an awareness of significantly divergent interests competing for valid occupation of space, rather than instating one case as being inherently superior or more authentic than the other (as we will demonstrate in relation to the uncanny representation of Northern spaces in Gothic plays, such as Angela Betzien's *Children of the Black Skirt* and Carleton's *Constance Drinkwater and the Final Days of Somerset*). Barcan and Buchanan agree with this case for multiplicity, stating that "the work of Aboriginal activists has forced white Australians to recognize that white ways of seeing and imagining 'Australia' were only one way of envisioning, understanding and inhabiting this continent," and that "each time a new vision of the world is presented, a new formulation of space is also presented, and vice versa" ("Introduction" 8). We draw on this premise to argue the case for an enacted, multivalent, and culturally and politically loaded Australian North.

THE GOTHIC NORTH

Sometimes, certain kinds of cultural output falls through the cracks when it comes to being realized or aggregated as digital data on a national search engine. As stated earlier, databases are only ever as thorough or as revealing as the data that is entered into them and how that data is organized and arranged. In the Australian example, *AustLit* provides evidence of a bias for tropical writing to kickstart an ensuing region-by-region series of literary mapping projects; the *Cultural Atlas of Australia* depicts patterns of representation of major (award-winning or similarly nationally recognized) texts in several mediums; *AusStage* allows us to trace the production histories of plays produced by theater companies around Australia, predominantly in the major capital cities. What none of these databases has identified, however, is a marked increase in output of themed work taking places on the professional (and mostly regional) stages of cities in North Australia since the turn of the century.[10] Key Northern Australian

---

10. Indeed, a keyword search—"Gothic"—in the *AusStage* database yields *none* of the texts identified in the ensuing discussion. Either the productions have not been recognized at all (because of the regional nature of their production) or they have been registered but not—for whatever reason—identified as Gothic in terms of subject matter.

theater companies in Darwin, Cairns, and Brisbane between 2000 and 2010 (including Darwin Theatre Company, J U T E in Cairns, and La Boite Theatre Company and Metro Arts in Brisbane) have produced work that indicates a remarkable spike in activity of central relevance to this chapter, focusing as it does on the mythologization of the Australian North. To put it succinctly, there is a boom in Gothic-themed work taking place on Northern stages during this period. While we examine Tasmania as the "traditional" home of the Australian Gothic (and how this shifts over time) in relation to cinema in chapter 3, this Northern theatrical output of the early twenty-first century, however, suggests a shift upward and outward in terms of the geographical locale to which the Australian Gothic trope is anchored. It is a shift that is quite possibly "invisible to the naked eye" in terms of the nation's dominant cultural analysis; much of what takes place on the professional stages of Northern Queensland and the Northern Territory goes unreviewed and, indeed, ignored by the metropolitan cultural industry—and subsequently by the major digital databases that are devoted to capturing such activity.

One of the repeated claims made by key scholars in the field is that the Gothic is difficult to define.[11] Where agreement does take place is in the realm of the psychological. Taking the Gothic's preoccupation with history's haunting of the present into account—the psychological return of the repressed—as the common ground, one claim that we would venture to make here is that the Gothic might be difficult to *define,* but it is exponentially more capable of being *identified* in specific regional, cultural, and political contexts. Marie Mulvey-Roberts's influential *Handbook of the Gothic* offers more than fifteen location-bound traditions of the Gothic

---

11. David Punter and Glennis Byron claim, for instance, "The Gothic remains a notoriously difficult field to define. . . . We have chosen to treat it broadly" (xviii). David Stevens states, "Such is the eclecticism of the gothic world that the label has been and is applied to virtually every aspect of human creativity. . . . It would be contrary to the spirit of the gothic to attempt to pin it down too absolutely or to limit it to narrow explanation" (5). Marie Mulvey-Roberts concurs and adds that the Gothic is "an umbrella term that has traditionally covered a multitude of the fictional sinned against and sinning, the nuances of what we understand by it as a site of difference within a panoply of family resemblances" that can only be represented in a collection such as the one contained in her *Handbook of the Gothic* (xxi).

played out in places as diverse as Japan, the Caribbean, San Francisco, and Scotland. Australia is treated as one cohesive "region" here; and yet Ken Gelder's entry on the postcolonial Gothic provides a hint as to why the Australian North might be emerging as a discrete sociocultural space in regional Australian Gothic terms:

> Postcolonial nations can re-animate the traumas of their colonial pasts to produce Gothic narratives. Ghost stories can certainly be built around this process. . . . But postcolonial Gothic narratives usually remain caught somewhere in between reconciliation and difference. The postcolonial place is partly familiar, and partly unfamiliar—partly resembling home ('New Caledonia,' 'New England' and so on) and yet also evoking something quite unrecognisable and strange. (306)

Specific geographic locations remind us of others; certain regions produce tensions that get played out in broader cultural and historical schema. The appurtenances associated with the traditional European Gothic subsequently mutate on arrival and adapt to local conditions so that classic Gothic settings such as the castle and the forest might become, in Australian terms, the homestead and the bush.

The Gothic is emerging as a distinct modality in the Australian North as a very recent and distinctly theatrical phenomenon. The evidence of a preoccupation with Gothic forms, themes, characters, and plot points is predominantly evident in recent professional theater activity stretching from Brisbane up to Cairns and across to Darwin.[12] Indeed, since 2000, there have been more Gothic-themed plays produced on the professional stages of Brisbane, Cairns, and Darwin than in the rest of the nation combined.[13] Given the small populations of those latter two tropical cities, this is no mean feat.[14]

12. Few Queensland or Northern Territory residents would refer to Brisbane as a "Northern" capital, but we include it here as the southernmost boundary of the present Northern tranche of Gothic plays.

13. Included in the following analysis, as well as the footnoted texts for which there is insufficient space to discuss, 16 professional productions are referred to, spanning the gamut of contemporary performance style and mode. There are undoubtedly more that have not been identified here or that have taken place since the time of writing.

14. The latest (2011) Australian Bureau of Statistics figures show that Darwin's population is 120,586 and Cairns's is 133,893 ("Census Data").

In addition to the plays that have been recently cited by prominent Australian theater critic John McCallum as examples of the contemporary Australian "bush Gothic" play (namely, Kathryn Ash's *Flutter,* Betzien's *Children of the Black Skirt,* and Carleton's *Constance Drinkwater and the Final Days of Somerset*), to which we return later, one can add here such examples of contemporary Northern Gothic as Linda Hassall's *Post Office Rose* and Mary Anne Butler's *Half Way There.* This is not an exhaustive list, merely a representative one.[15] These plays have been selected not only because they originate within the Australian North but because they deal with an imaginary topographical staging *of* the North. They consciously dwell on their "Deep" Northern settings, diegetically, in terms of their characterization and plotting as well as their staging and design requirements. By "deep" here we are referring to a conscious mythologizing of a remote and isolated Northern cultural landscape.

When looking at this combined body of work, two broad generic articulations of the Gothic emerge: a gendered domestic or personal manifestation wherein it is predominantly women battling with their ghosts in a Northern bush setting; and a metonymic expression of the Gothic where the North is being conscripted to activate national anxieties surrounding race and Indigenous dispossession and maltreatment. In order to interrogate the ways in which this latter category of Gothic modality plays out in spatial terms (against the backdrop of a North Australian racialized landscape), it is worth analyzing two of these texts in closer detail. Betzien and Carleton both name the politics of race as underplaying their North Australian Gothic dramas. In looking for reasons why the North might be conscripted as the site of the postcolonial repressed in these plays, cultural anthropologist Regina Ganter reminds us of the relative "newness" of Caucasian history in North Australia:

15. Further works include Michael Beresford's *Tiptoe* (2008); Andrew McGahan and Shaun Charles's stage adaption of McGahan's novel *The White Earth* (2009); Kathryn Ash, Stephen Carleton, Gail Evans, and Anne Harris's group-devised piece, *Surviving Jonah Salt* (2004); Errol O'Neill's 2004 adaptation of Rosamond Siemon's nonfiction book *The Mayne Inheritance;* Norman Price's *Urban Dingoes* (2004); Norman Price and Lisa O'Neill's *Pineapple Queen* (2009); and Adam Grossetti's canefields thriller *Mano Nera* (2005).

Nowhere in northern Australia does Anglo-Celtic history yet amount to
200 years. European encroachment was gradual and unsteady, and sometimes in retreat. It only reached the northern mainland roughly 100 years
after southern settlement. . . . It was not until the 1880s that white settlement
of the north developed momentum. (26–27)

Ganter traces a history of Macassan trade with Arnhem Land Aboriginal
settlements, as well as early Japanese involvement in the North Australian pearling industry and Chinese participation in early gold mining and
other commercial ventures in the region, to make an argument for the
North's preeminence in international—or at least intercultural—trade
and settlement. "On balance," she concludes, "it takes a single-minded
commitment to Anglo-Celtic history and its particular type of settlement
to believe Australian settlement started at Sydney Cove or that Australian
history started there. Without breaking the rules of historical method,
we might say that Australian settlement history starts in the north" (28).
We furthermore contend that twenty-first-century Gothic theater asserts
that the *un*settlement of national racial histories is also taking place in the
North.

Betzien's *Children of the Black Skirt* and Carleton's *Constance Drinkwater and the Final Days of Somerset* are the only plays from among this
Northern canon to have had national exposure and metropolitan performance outside of Queensland and the Northern Territory,[16] reflecting
perhaps the national cultural politics they are calling on by way of ac-
tivating their Gothic themes. Developed for school audiences from a
Queensland Arts Council grant, Real TV theater company decided to
create a work around the idea of children's orphanages, inspired by mem-
ber/writer Betzien's religious education camp visits at such a facility near
Rockhampton during her childhood. Betzien creates a world of horror in
her play in which vulnerable and parentless children are tormented by a
brutal disciplinary regime and are visited by the ghosts of past inmates. It
is the Stolen Generations narrative that is conjured here, since the orphan-
age is inevitably populated by young Aboriginal girls forcefully separated

16. *Children of the Black Skirt* won the Victorian Drama Award in 2005, and *Constance
Drinkwater and the Final Days of Somerset* won the Patrick White Playwrights' Award the
same year.

from their families. Director Letitia Carceres notes that in the group-devised early developmental stages of the project, there were "very long and intensive discussions about the history of Australia, the treatment of Indigenous people since invasion, the link between institutionalisation and cultural genocide and the culture of silence and cover-up by government agencies and religious institutions." The Gothic becomes the ideal imaginative mode to tell this alternative children's history of the country, dealing as it does with the secret, the haunted, the unspoken, and the return of the repressed. Here, it is Australia's "cultural genocide" of its Indigenous people, as Carceres describes it, that is being revealed and given theatrical expression.

It is a similar history that haunts Carleton's *Constance Drinkwater and the Final Days of Somerset.* The play is a melodrama set at the turn of the previous century on the tip of Cape York in the fictional settlement of Somerset. Constance and her husband have expressed an ambition to make Somerset "the gleaming capital in a strand of lustrous pearls stretching from here across to Western Australia" (24). This multiracial utopia will utilize its Northern position to forge a new version of Australian meritocracy in which race is immaterial and isolation is an advantage. In a melodramatic claptrap, Constance declares, "If we seize the moment and separate from the rest of the colony [of Queensland], Cooksland can become a vast and self-governing northern state within the new federation. From this tiny satellite poised on the very fingertip of the nation, we see all. I have caught a glimpse of the twentieth century, Mr. Lee, and it has Somerset firmly in its grasp" (23). There is an engagement with Ganter's assertion here of topsy-turviness—of the Australian map being turned upside down in historic terms. In placing the North front and center of an imagined twentieth century, Constance's vision resonates with Ganter's claim:

> The idea of the isolated continent has tenaciously survived empirical counter evidence. The Torres Strait has long been recognised as much bridge as barrier, a region of intensive trade linking the Australian continent with the New Guinea mainland. . . . We might say on balance that a period of isolation from the outside world began in the north with the arrival of white colonisers. (29)

Echoing Carceres's assertion that the (Gothic) theater seeks to name the unnameable and to stage the unmentionable, Carleton asks in the foreword of his play, "What is the 'true' nature of this underwritten and under-acknowledged multiracial northern frontier between not only black and white Australia, but between Australia and Asia? How does this past continue to haunt us today?" (3). The ghosts of Constance's dead daughters and of the raped Aboriginal maid and Caucasian governess actually appear on stage in the second act climax and damn the abusers to Hell (84–85). This is not just metaphor: there is a full and (melo)dramatic staging of the haunting in this play that sees chairs rock, pianos play, and stones fly on their own.

Helen Gilbert and Jacqueline Lo write of the play that "by underscoring the racial/racist foundations of the nation, Carleton suggests that White Australia's violent appropriation of indigenous land and its continuing failure to accept moral responsibility for this history will lead to self-destruction" (211). Gilbert and Lo read a theme of the unsustainability of white regimes of power in the Australian landscape into the text. The Far Northern setting is paradigmatic in this national schema. It is being conscripted in both Carleton and Betzien's plays as both synecdochic and metonymic space in which the nation's collective anxieties about whiteness and Aboriginal dispossession—unsettled business from the past—are being acted out.

WHY THE NORTH AND WHY NOW?

By way of positing answers to these questions in relation to contemporary Gothic manifestations, several conclusions can be drawn. Perhaps it is the case that the North is being viewed figuratively as the place in which the nation's ghosts are most alive at present. In each of these plays the North is chosen as the setting for articulating or symbolizing the nation's collective shames and hidden histories, troped alongside two separate but related broad themes: gender and race. It is as though the Australian frontier itself has been pushed upward and outward, away from the major metropolitan centers of the South and East and into a metaphorical North that is being called on to conjure and return the nation's collective repressed to the forefront of contemporary political culture. Why the North, though, and not the Center, or Outback South Australia, or suburban Perth, or Sydney's beaches? One can only make the contentious suggestion that the North's relatively small population on the one hand, but its comparatively large Aboriginal population on the other, perhaps allow it to become viewed as a place where "the past"—the time when European encounter with a non-Westernized or "traditional" Aboriginality—is still playing out as "the present," at least in the minds of non-Aboriginal metropolitan Australians. Or perhaps it is the case that Ganter's claim to the centrality of intercultural settlement in the North is being reinforced and replayed in some of these dramas to remind contemporary audiences of this underacknowledged "alternative" national history.

Writing of the psychological (return of the repressed) imperative behind an American Gothic literary tradition, Teresa A. Goddu places racial desire and dread front and center, claiming that "the spectre of slavery often inhabits" Gothic texts from the eighteenth and nineteenth centuries onward. Adding the "violent usurpation of Native American land" to the plot of these narratives, Goddu concludes that "the United States as many American Gothic texts argue, is built on economic exploitation and racial terror" (63). One can see similar psychological origins underpinning the Australian Gothic—although Australia's comparative involvement in the slave trade, in the form of exploitation of South Sea Islanders on the Queensland cane fields in the late nineteenth and early twentieth centuries, remains curiously underexamined in terms of the nation's Gothic literature, theater, and film. Precise comparisons between different nations' articulations of the Gothic do not always bear fruit; and yet it is tantalizing to draw parallels between an American Deep South and an Australian Deep North here. There is not a religiosity or a Catholicism underpinning these works as there often is in the writing of some of the great American Southern literary figures, such as Flannery O'Connor or Eudora Welty. Nor are there vampires as there are in the genre fiction of Anne Rice (the *Interview with a Vampire* literary series) or Alan Ball (the *True Blood* HBO television series). Australian Northern Gothic is secular; its ghosts and demons are human. Unlike the Tasmanian or early New South Wales and Victorian Gothic novels, there is no convict culture underpinning and theming the "unsettling" of settlement mythology here. Themes of lawlessness and the corruption of human morality and sexual desire in the absence of scrutiny do, however, abound. And underpinning all of these themes are the ghosts of the nation's unresolved racial anxieties.

This curiosity about the Australian North as an emerging discrete geopolitical and cultural zone is not ours alone, it would seem. Julianne Schultz describes Australia's associations with the North in her introduction to a *Griffith Review* edition devoted entirely to the topic of unravelling the region's mystique. In her overview of the North's "myths, threats and enchantments," she states:

> It may be the product of living in the second most southerly continent, but every generation of Australians has had iconic images of threats from the north. Flip through your memory of popular history and there they are—Chinamen in pigtails set to overrun the goldfields, Japanese aggressors poised to invade, dominoes tumbling on a Cold War map, Indochinese boat people searching for a safe haven and refugees stumbling out of leaky boats onto isolated beaches. Most of the images feature people with dark hair and Asiatic features whose intent is clear: to occupy the vast, virtually empty spaces between the northern coastline and the southern capitals. (7)

Schultz's equation of the North with anxieties about invasion and infiltration from a demonized Asian "other" is a salient one, as the above analysis of contemporary Northern Gothic theater helps illustrate. The other association embedded within this fear of what lies further to the North is a construction of the North as being "empty" and acting as a buffer between Asia and the Southern capitals. Those "vast, virtually empty spaces" along the Northern coastline to which Schultz refers are considered tacitly devoid of human population, despite the fact that the region is inhabited (even if comparatively sparsely) by tens of thousands of people. Schultz touches on the perception that the majority of the Australian population unconsciously associates the North with emptiness because it is not deeply populated by *white* occupants.

Schultz identifies another "mythic" contradiction:

> Now add to the mental mix the allure of the north, of warm tropical nights, coral reefs and palm-fringed beaches, of open roads surging through dramatic country, of millennia of Indigenous settlement, of people who follow their dreams and find a home, or themselves, in the most unlikely places, of crocodiles in remote waterways and captivating exotica of Asia. Our imaginative sense of the north is a complicated one: full of contradictions and fascination tinged with fear, like submerged crocodiles. (7)

The range of symbolic and seemingly contradictory mythic associations with which Schultz and Australians generally endow the North is of especial interest to the scholar preoccupied with spatial inquiry. One can plausibly link the upsurge in recent creative narrative activity revealed in this study with broader national economic and political developments. Suffice it to say that the North is resonating strongly as a source of debate in Australian public life in this first two decades of the twenty-first century. The Northern states and territories are leading the mining and natural resources boom that is underpinning national economic growth. As the harsh realities of global warming and climate change settle in and large tracts of southeastern Australia become seemingly permanently entrenched in prolonged stretches of drought, rainfall in the North remains high. The future sustainability of the nation, it would seem, lies in an exploitation of the North's vast and hitherto untapped resources.

This chapter has investigated some of the ways in which locational data represented in cultural narratives has been calibrated and displayed visually on a digital map, and it has considered how the results might be interpreted to produce new cultural knowledge. We argue that mapping locations of cultural narratives can yield surprising results that do not correlate precisely with national demographic data and population density, or indeed with assumed national cultural certainties. We also alert researchers to the perils of overreliance on such distant-reading approaches. Maps are never complete, cannot capture all of the activity, and can yield surprises in terms of the sins of omission they may commit; however, even these partial maps can be seen to shed new light on analysis of national cultural myths as they pertain to space, place, location, and landscape.

What our own investigation has revealed is that the nation's Deep North houses a vast cultural "emptiness," yet is simultaneously "full" of the nation's fears surrounding race and space: these fears center on a century-long mainstream apprehension of cultural inundation/invasion/occupation/pollution at the hands of either the Asian (external) or Aboriginal (internal) "other." What we have discovered in relation to theatrical representation of this vast region since the turn of the twenty-first century is that the Gothic is the mode that is being chosen to express these cultural anxieties in concentrated regional style and form, and that this expression is taking place alongside cinematic and literary practice (which the databases *do* recognize) troping the North in a range of ancillary modes as contemporary frontier space. The Australian North is "full" of literary, theatrical, and cinematic texts representing it as mythic space, even as it remains relatively sparsely populated.

3

∽

SPATIAL HISTORY

Mapping Narrative Perceptions of Place over Time

Representations of the past can be characterized as "a kind of mapping where the past is a landscape and history is the way we fashion it" (Bodenhamer, "Beyond" 6–7). In that spirit, this chapter interprets the representations of Australia's past by mapping films, novels, and plays featuring Alexander Pearce—a convict who gained notoriety for resorting to cannibalism after absconding from a remote penal settlement in Tasmania. We examine how dramatized accounts of history, including Pearce's own confession documents, quite literally map the landscape of the past, even as they also fashion or cultivate perceptions of the physical landscape. In our inquiry as to how the spatial humanities and digital cartographic approaches might advance understandings of cultural and spatial history, we argue that geovisualization, as a mode of narrative analysis, can reveal the complex imbrications of a place, its community, and myths of national and regional identity. We demonstrate that qualitative information found in photographs, film footage, and journey narratives can offer insight into evolving perspectives on a locale over time.

The spatial history presented in this chapter is articulated in the form of a longitudinal case study that maps multiple adaptations of a geographically distinctive historical narrative, revealing how successive retellings document and inform shifting perceptions of place. Using digital cartography, we undertake a geocritical analysis of the films and, to a lesser extent, the books and plays that trace Pearce's journey through the Tasmanian wilderness. This chapter visualizes multiple perspectives from different temporal periods in order to map the cannibal-convict mythology, from Marcus Clarke's *For the Term of His Natural Life* (first published as a novel in 1874),[1] through its stage adaptations, to recent cinematic incarnations. We use geovisualization techniques to examine the narrative progression and to compare the documented history of Pearce's journey with the stories and maps that represent his experiences and that depict the locations in which the story took place. This mapping endeavor is made more complex by tangled intersections of past and present because contemporary evocations of the historical narrative imagine how Pearce's compatriots and descendants carry his legacy into the future.

We begin from the premise that spatial narratives such as those represented in cinema, novels, and the theater encode the cultural values and sociopolitical structures present during the times in which they take place as well as representing different forms of land use and different modes of transport and practices of travel and communication that shape experiences of space. In this sense, then, an examination of narrative texts and the ecology of their production can help to understand the meaningfulness of space, place, location, or landscape. Maps of narrative and culture have the capacity to make visible nuanced temporal and historical contexts, revealing how people both represent and affect the environment in which they live and work and through which they travel, while at the same time showing how people are in turn shaped and reshaped by the land and its stories. Geographer and cinema scholar Sébastien Caquard sees "maps as a compelling form of storytelling" ("Cartography" 136); yet he notes that this claim does not apply to all maps. Following Robert MacFarlane's argument in *The Wild Places,* Caquard states that "grid maps" such as road maps suppress the geographical imagination, whereas maps that have a narrative dimension such as those presented in this book can elicit a deep, experiential understanding of place ("Cartography" 136). The base maps provided by Google Maps and Bing Maps are examples of grid

---

1. *For the Term of His Natural Life* first appeared as a serial titled *His Natural Life,* which was published in the *Australian Journal* (March 1870 to June 1872). Clarke then revised it for the book version, first published in 1874. The better-known longer title of the novel was first introduced posthumously in 1885 and carried through to the feature film adaptation discussed here. Quotations from the novel in this chapter are taken from the 1878 publication listed in the Works Cited.

maps, yet they do not necessarily restrict imaginative place-making because they invite hybridization as users customize and annotate the maps:
"This type of application stimulates the production of spatial narratives
by making them easy to map and distribute, and simultaneously restricts
them through the framework provided by the base map" (Caquard, "Cartography" 141). Bertrand Westphal's geocritical approach, which we draw
on throughout this book, involves studying places as they are mediated
in different forms of narrative such as cinema, theater, and literature; in
this regard, as Caquard goes on to point out, "places emerge from a combination of the real and the fictional. From this point of view, mapping
the world is as much about mapping reality as it is about mapping fiction"
("Cartography" 140). Mapping historical narratives enables us to interrogate and explore multiple perspectives on place, its transformations over
time, and its role in helping us to understand history and culture (see Jones
and Evans). Although we recognize that mapping historical narratives is
not the same as mapping fictional narratives, the narratives that figure in
this chapter interweave the two storytelling forms. In their article "Place
in Time," historians Detlev Mares and Wolfgang Moschek acknowledge
that "the experience of historical space is always a matter of the individual
imagination" and that "modern images and concepts will be entangled
with scraps of information from past ages, and the result will always be
a mental representation of former space rather than anything approaching an immediate impression of historical space itself" (59). Following
Mares and Moschek, this chapter emphasizes the need to reflect on the
imaginative quality of our understandings of the past and of spatial history. While the form of cultural and historical mapping that we undertake
below relates directly to the physical landscape and to perceptions of it,
it also addresses differences between narrative settings, their real-world
locations, and the locations in which films are actually shot.

Although it is the region of Australia that most closely resembles the
United Kingdom's climate and topography, Tasmania was also considered
the most fearsome penal colony. In 1642 Dutch navigator Abel Tasman
named the island for Governor-General Van Diemen, but after decades
of convict transportation "when that name had become so tarnished with
stories of criminality and cruelty that respectable settlers would no longer
endure it," the state was renamed Tasmania in 1855 (Hughes 47). In *For the*

Term of His Natural Life and its adaptations, Tasmania's towering trees, icy waters, and jagged cliffs form a fortress, incarcerating convicts in a hell on earth that was all the more punitive and purgatorial for its terrible isolation. As Turner points out in *National Fictions,* Australian narratives repeatedly suggest that "English nature is under control; it is orderly and one may abandon oneself to it. Australian nature, on the other hand, is harsh, hostile; and the enjoyment of it depends on proving that one can survive its worst excesses" (19). Alone of his fellow escapees, Pearce did indeed survive the very worst excesses of the hostile landscape and, despite being largely unmapped and virtually unfilmable, Tasmania's rugged and remote southwest wilderness has come to claim a pivotal place in the nation's geographic imagination, in its cultural narratives, and in its spatial history.

MAPPING SPATIAL HISTORY

As noted in the introduction to this book, since the publication of Paul Carter's influential spatial history of Australia, *The Road to Botany Bay,* and Edward Soja's discussion of the "spatial turn" in cultural theory in *Postmodern Geographies,* the development of digital tools such as GIS for nonexpert users has fueled interest in physical space in humanities and social science research. As Bodenhamer writes:

> Within a GIS, users can discern relationships that make a complex world more immediately understandable by visually detecting spatial patterns that remain hidden in texts and tables. Maps have served this function for a long time, but GIS brings impressive computing power to this task. Its core strength is an ability to integrate, analyze, and make visual a vast array of data from different formats. ("Beyond" 4)

Geographic information systems have been used to plot changes in a location over time by geovisualizing quantifiable data such as tax and court records, trade and transport routes, and census information. More recently, scholars such as Anne Knowles (*Past Time, Past Place,* 2002; *Placing History,* 2008) and Ian Gregory (*A Place in History,* 2003; *Historical GIS,* 2007) have examined how GIS aids the visualization of information in historical research. Until the advent of qualitative GIS (Jones and Evans), cartography focused predominantly on geographical space rather than culturally inflected understandings of place based on history, narrative, imagery, and memory, which are the kinds of places that cinema, novels, and plays give us access to.

Despite, or perhaps because of, the "vast array of data" and the "impressive computing power" of which Bodenhamer speaks and with which scholars such as Knowles and Ian Gregory grapple, Tim Hitchcock emphasizes the need to keep the audience, the value of public engagement, and the explanatory power of humanist narratives of the past in mind when working with digital tools and expansive datasets:

> If we are now being led by the technology itself to write different kinds of history—the tools are shaping the product. If we end up losing the humane and the individual, because the data doesn't quite work so easily that way, we are in danger of giving up the power of historical narrative (the ability to conjure up a person and emotions with words), without thinking through the nature of what will be gained in exchange. ("Academic History"; see also Crampton et al.)

The risk of losing cultural meaningfulness within large datasets and technologically driven methodologies is, however, counterbalanced by the increasingly personal and participatory nature of new mapping tools and crowdsourcing techniques that make it possible to layer different perspectives on period and place and to interrogate their sociohistorical significance. Rather than using GIS software that benefits from knowledge of map projections and other technical considerations, the *Cultural Atlas of Australia,* from which the data in this chapter's case study draws, uses Google Maps, a Web 2.0 mapping platform that lacks the capacity for sophisticated statistical analysis. This use of the Geoweb, or the proliferation of accessible mapping tools afforded by Web 2.0, has distinct advantages: "Geared around public participation, volunteered geo-coded data and links to URL addresses, photos and videos, the Geoweb enables the generation of more anarchic and organic knowledge of places" (Gibson, Brennan-Horley, and Warren 329–30). This involves user contributions or crowd-sourcing of information that creates neogeographies, or "volunteered geographies," in which "the inherent polyvocality of public perception and experiences of everyday life is reproduced in the map" (Gibson, Brennan-Horley, and Warren 330). In order to analyze the various retellings of the cannibal convict's journey narrative, we have used GIS to map the historical route, based on geographic landmarks identified in his confessions. We also used GIS to map the shooting locations and narrative settings for films that tell Pearce's story, and we have tapped into the capacity of the Geoweb to invite public participation and crowd-sourced contributions of images and videos of these locations via the *Cultural Atlas* website.

The "tools of representation" that we employ in our research, from the narratives themselves, through photographs and videos, to GIS and other geovisualization tools, are central to our spatial thinking (see Mares and Moschek 60). As Jeffrey Klenotic observes:

> GIS is not just a tool by which to historicize space, drawing ever more contextually layered and geographically detailed maps. Instead, it is an open and dynamic form of bricolage, one that is subject to constant rearranging as an embedded part of a trial-and-error research process designed to facilitate the difficult task of seeing, representing and theorizing the simultaneous multiplicity of social and historical experience in spatial terms and from a variety of partial perspectives. (60)

While Klenotic's chief interest is in the intersection between digital history and various ways to map movies, Donald A. DeBats and Ian Gregory note that the capacity to integrate demographic and architectural data and information about transport infrastructure into GIS makes it particularly useful for the study of urban history. Since the focus of our research in this chapter is wilderness terrain that remains largely unmapped other than by satellite imagery, our examination of cultural understandings of regions must rely more on narrative accounts in which representations of travel and landscape are richly detailed. DeBats and Gregory state that "GIS provides the framework that helps the researcher ask questions concerning what, where, and when" (461); thus, following the lead of these authors, we have used GIS to empirically chart and test various accounts of Pearce's journey against the geography of the terrain in which he travelled. As DeBats and Gregory go on to say:

> The final and most important stage in the research process is to ask why. GIS does not of itself answer this. Instead, it provides the descriptive information that the researcher has to explain. In this way the GIS enhances analytic skills through its ability to summarize large amounts of complex

information in space and time. Explaining why these patterns are as they are remains the task for the skilled historian, not the computer. (461)

The challenge of this chapter is to do this explanatory work, delving into the patterns of representation surrounding Pearce's journey and revealing the shifting understandings of geography and history that his story communicates. In this sense we read the texts narrating his travels as a cultural history of spatial relations and we consider how these spatial patterns have evolved in response to broader cultural and political events. For, as Bodenhamer observes:

> All spaces contain embedded stories based on what has happened there. These stories are both individual and collective, and each of them links geography (space) and history (time). More important, they all reflect the values and cultural codes present in the various political and social arrangements that provide structure to society. In this sense, then, the meaning of space, especially as place or landscape, is always being constructed through the various contests that occur over power. ("Beyond" 2)

The mode of historical spatial research conducted here is informed by Bodenhamer's approach and by an awareness that the temporal dimension of cultural engagements with place and space necessitates a consideration of "the effects of human interference upon spatial arrangements" as well as "the effects of spatial preconditions on human actions" (Mares and Moschek 62). For the tale of the cannibal convict, the spatial preconditions of the Tasmanian penal colony exerted remarkable force on human actions and events in the 1820s.

THE CANNIBAL CONVICT'S TRAVEL NARRATIVE

The story of Irish convict Alexander Pearce, his adventures in the rugged wilderness of southwest Tasmania, and the gruesome fate of his fellow fugitives on their famishing trek across the island state has been retold many times in song,[2] on stage, in print, and on screen. Most famously, the story of Pearce's escape with seven other convicts from the Sarah Island penitentiary in Macquarie Harbour in 1822 was dramatized in Clarke's

---

2. For example, see the song by the band Weddings, Parties, Anything, "A Tale They Won't Believe."

Gothic novel, *For the Term of His Natural Life.* This historic convict narrative features a subplot in which a convict named Matt Gabbett repeatedly
escapes custody and preys on his fellow fugitives. Clarke was well aware
of Pearce's exploits, which he investigated when he visited Tasmania to
conduct research into the convict system in 1870. That same year Gabbett appeared as a fictionalized version of Pearce in Clarke's *His Natural
Life,* which had its first chapters published in serial form in *Australian
Journal* (see B. Elliott). Other accounts of Pearce's bloodthirsty story are
to be found in Paul Collins's historical biography *Hells Gates: The Terrible
Journey of Alexander Pearce, Van Diemen's Land Cannibal* (2002); in Dan
Sprod's *Alexander Pearce of Macquarie Harbour: Convict, Bushranger, Cannibal* (1977); and in *Alexander Pearce: A Brief Narrative of His Life Together
with His Confessions of Cannibalism,* compiled by Stephan Williams (1986).
These books draw on and quote from historical documents that include
Pearce's four confessions in which he tells the story of his calamitous
journey through the harsh terrain, his struggle with starvation, and the
murders that ensued.[3]

Another novel, *Bloodlust: The Unsavoury Tale of Alexander Pearce,* written by Nick Bleszynski in 2008, locates Pearce's story and the landscape
in which it takes place at the heart of the narrative. "Where the hell's
Macquarie Harbour and Hobart?" asks Daniel Ruth, the young scientist
in *Bloodlust* who is tasked to travel from Philadelphia to Tasmania in 1850
to investigate what turned Pearce into a cannibal. Spinning the globe, his
mentor Dr. Moreton shows Daniel the penal colony then known as Van
Diemen's Land:

> Daniel frowned. Like most educated Americans he knew Australia was
> located somewhere in the southern hemisphere, but he couldn't rightly say
> where it was. Dr Moreton tapped his bony finger on a small heart-shaped is-
> land just off the south-eastern coast of Australia at the very end of the world.
> "Van Diemen's Land is to Australia what Sicily is to Italy," he said. (6)

---

3. The first confession was made to Reverend Knopwood in Hobart, after Pearce
was captured; the second was made to Commandant Cuthbertson on Sarah Island, after
Pearce's second escape and his recapture; the third made to his gaol warden Mr. Bisdee in
June 1824; and the fourth made to Father Conolly the night before Pearce was hanged in
Hobart in July 1824.

This opacity regarding the location of Tasmania itself was even more pronounced in relation to the terrain of the island's southwest corner, where Pearce's ordeal took place. Many historical GIS and literary GIS digital mapping projects favor the use of georectified historical maps to reveal and interrogate spaces of the past and their relationship to cultural narratives, both past and present.[4] However, as the narrative extract above and the historical map of Van Diemen's Land (see figure 3.1) reveal, Pearce's overland route from Macquarie Harbour to the settled area of Tasmania remained a blank space on the map some three decades after his death. For this reason, our geovisualization strategy involves annotating the map with film images, location photographs, and textual descriptions of the landscape found in the accounts of Pearce's journey.

The most influential of the books that tell a version of Pearce's story, *For the Term of His Natural Life,* was made into a film shot at Port Arthur in 1908 by Charles McMahon. It was remade in 1911 by Alfred Rolfe as *The Life of Rufus Dawes;* remade again in 1927 by Norman Dawn; then adapted once more as a TV miniseries in 1983 by Rob Stewart. Craig Godfrey later directed a straight-to-video, schlock horror-comedy called *Back from the Dead* (1996), which was filmed on location at Port Arthur and Hobart and featured the modern-day resurrection of a cannibalistic killer-convict called Kavendish, who was imprisoned in Port Arthur and who was "loosely based on Alexander Pearce" (Millar 18). Tracing Pearce's Gaelic heritage, Barrie Dowdall filmed a documentary for Ireland's Channel 4 titled *Exile in Hell* (2007). More recently the horror film *Dying Breed* (Jody Dwyer, 2008) imagines Pearce's inbred descendants feasting on unwary travelers who venture into the wilderness in search of the Tasmanian tiger. In 2008 Michael James Rowland directed a carefully researched, hour-long docudrama called *The Last Confession of Alexander Pearce.* Finally, Tasmania writer-director Jonathan auf der Heide teamed up with Melbourne cinematographer Ellery Ryan to film the beautifully crafted feature *Van Diemen's Land* in 2009, which was an extension of his earlier short film, *Hell's Gates* (2007).

4. For instance, the *Map of Early Modern London* uses the 1561 Agas map and *Mapping the Lakes* uses an 1815 map of the Lake District.

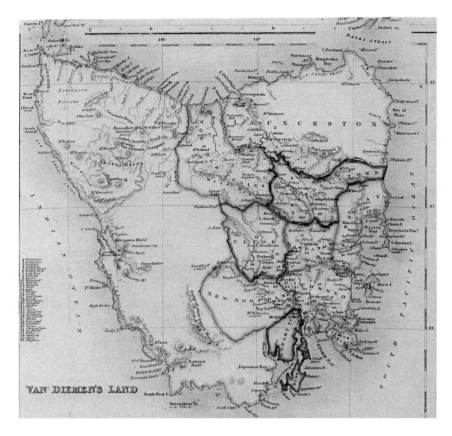

Figure 3.1. Map of Van Diemen's Land in 1852. Source: Licensed under Public domain via Wikimedia Commons. The original image may be viewed at: http://commons.wikimedia.org/wiki/File:Van_Diemen%27s_Land_1852.jpg#media viewer/File:Van_Diemen%27s_Land_1852.jpg.

There is a similarly long history of adaptations and stage productions of *For the Term of His Natural Life*. In *Australian Plays for the Colonial Stage, 1834–1899*, Richard Fotheringham refers to *For the Term of His Natural Life* as "the first Australian Stage 'classic'" because seven adaptations were staged internationally in 1885–1886 alone, starting with John A. Stevens's *Convict 1240* in 1885 in San Francisco (457), a play that was also performed throughout the United States under the title *A Great Wrong Righted* or *A Great Wrong* from 1886 to 1888 (Webby 594). Numerous long-running

Australian productions followed, the most enduring of which was of the adaptation by playwright Thomas Walker in 1886, written under the nom de plume Thomas Somers, which was staged regularly over the course of two decades (Fotheringham 460). This long line of stage productions continues in recent times with *Convict 102*, a production written and performed by Oscar Redding, the actor who played Pearce in the film *Van Diemen's Land* and who contributed to the screenplay of auf de Heide's film *Van Diemen's Land*.

Each of these narratives rightly treats the location of Pearce's story as central to the action, yet each presents a different view of Tasmania. Tasmania is a cool, temperate island state known as "the fatal shore" (Hughes) because of its reputation as a particularly harsh penal colony to which British convicts were transported from 1787 until 1868. The island subsequently became associated with Indigenous genocide when, by 1830, colonial forces had systematically annihilated Tasmanian Aborigines because they were believed to be a threat to agriculturalists. In order to investigate how Tasmanian films produce a sense of the beautiful but sometimes threatening island landscape as increasingly familiar yet persistently strange, the following case study questions what qualitative difference it makes where the story is set and filmed, given that many films set in Tasmania take liberties with the shooting locations of settings they purport to represent.

To address these questions, this longitudinal case study brings together historical, aesthetic, and spatial perspectives in a geocritical analysis of Pearce's confessions, the cinematic versions of his story, and, to a lesser extent, the novels and plays to which these films relate or from which they are adapted. Westphal refers to the geocritical approach to textual analysis as an exploration of the interplay between diegetic spaces and actual places (Foreword xii). As Yi-Fu Tuan suggests, "'Space' is more abstract than 'place.' What begins as undifferentiated space becomes place as we get to know it better and endow it with value" (*Place and Space* 6).

Representations of landscape in cultural narratives contribute to this transformation of abstract or diegetic spaces into place and endowing place with value: such narratives offer landscapes for aesthetic contemplation in ways that generate symbolism and produce cultural meaning, as a growing number of researchers attest.[5] Building on this body of work, this chapter demonstrates how cinema and related cultural narratives contribute to the accrual of meanings on geographic locales, both in the places represented on screen and in what the films displace when, with cinematic sleight of hand, one shooting location doubles for another.

ALEXANDER PEARCE'S JOURNEY

After escaping with fellow convicts Robert Greenhill, Matthew Travers, Thomas Bodenham, Alexander Dalton, John Mather, Edward Brown, and William Kennerly, Pearce took forty-nine days to travel from Macquarie Harbour to what was at the time a sparsely settled agricultural area of central Tasmania near the town of Ouse. September, the month of the escape, averages twenty days of bitingly cold rain with occasional hail and snow in Tasmania. In these miserable conditions, Pearce traversed over 125 miles (200 kilometers) without a compass. Convicts were notoriously ill-informed about Australian geography, as is evident in the attempt by twenty absconders to walk from Sydney to China in 1791, believing "China might be easily reached, being not more than a hundred miles distant, and separated only by a river" (Tench, qtd. in Flannery 11). Similarly, Pearce's party unsuccessfully sought to steal a boat and sail thousands of kilometers to China or the United Kingdom (Hughes 220).

Even the navigational expertise of former seaman Greenhill, the convict leading Pearce's escape party (and allegedly the first to instigate cannibalism and the last to be eaten), was challenged by Tasmania's wilderness. The dense canopy of foliage and overcast conditions would have made navigating by the sun extremely difficult, and landmarks such as Frenchman's Cap were frequently obscured by cloud and mist. Pearce's account of his escape in 1822, which is a transcription or reworking of his confession to Reverend Robert Knopwood in Hobart around January 1824, describes the morning of the seventh day: "The weather becoming more favourable elevated their spirits and encouraged them to proceed on their journey over the summit of a tier of mountains near to that one called the Frenchman's Cap where they could discern Macquarie Harbour

5. See, for instance, Craven, "Tropical"; Harper and Rayner; Lambert; M. Lefebvre, *Landscape* and "On Landscape"; Lukinbeal; Peckham; and C. Simpson.

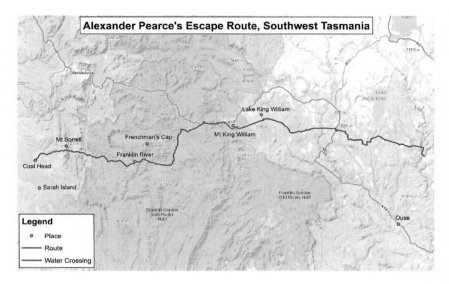

Figure 3.2. A map of Pearce's journey through southwest Tasmania in 1822. Source: Jane Stadler and Luke Houghton.

at a distance of about 20 or 30 miles" (Pearce). Subsequent pages of Pearce's confession to Knopwood document his experience of other landmarks such as Mt. Sorrell, his crossing the Franklin River (which he mistakenly thought was the Gordon River to the south), and his travels through the button grass plains surrounding Mount King William.

A 2009 *Australian Geographic* article documents the story of six members of the Tasmanian State Emergency Search and Rescue Service who became the first and only people known to have walked in Pearce's footsteps (see figure 3.2). The hikers had modern camping gear, navigational equipment, and ample food. Unlike the convicts, they were able to plot the most viable route through the terrain, yet even then they sometimes covered as little as 1.89 miles (3 km) in a twelve-hour period. They described the muddy, leech-infested ordeal as "akin to doing an all-day gym session carrying a heavy pack while taking a shower" (Morris). Members of the expedition reported:

> Despite lugging the latest navigation gear, we found it at times impossible to maintain orientation in the silent, thick understorey of bauera, melaleuca,

hakea, cutting grass and banksia that combines to form a multi-dimensional spider's web often concealing rock escarpments. The damp smell of rotting, moss-covered vegetation was ever present. We developed a range of "bush-bashing" techniques: climbing atop the scrub and, precariously perched metres above the ground, moving forward; pulling the scrub down from head- to knee-height, standing on it and repeating this action for each step. (Morris)

The Search and Rescue team's testimony corresponds closely to Pearce's own account when, two weeks into his arduous slog, he reported that his party "proceeded travelling through a very mountainous country suffering much from the want of provisions and being so dreadfully weak from the effects of being exposed to the night dews and cold—their clothing being torn from their backs by the brush and rocks and their shoes being totally worn out gave them considerable pain" (Pearce). As both accounts testify, the forbidding landscape and tangled foliage make a cruel prison.

Sarah Island was a place of secondary punishment to which only the most "disorderly and irreclaimable convicts" were sent; once there they undertook backbreaking labor cutting Huon pine to build ships (Hughes 372). By the time Dawn shot his film in 1927, the towering stands of Huon pine along the dark waters of the Gordon River near Sarah Island had been depleted and Dawn's art department trucked huge replica logs to the riverbank at Dundas, near Ryde in New South Wales, where a well-fed crew of extras enacted scenes of indentured servitude ("Picture" 4). In reality, the convicts had inadequate clothing or shelter and were malnourished and constantly ill with scurvy. Their meager rations consisted of rancid "brine-cured pork or beef, two or three years old" (Hughes 375), supplemented with some oatmeal and about one pound (454 grams) of bread laced with ergot, a fungus that causes grain to rot, thereby preventing convicts from hoarding rations for a jailbreak. Ergot poisoning causes cramps, seizures, gangrene, and psychotic, hallucinogenic symptoms that may have augmented the effects of hypothermia and starvation, contributing to the bloodshed that occurred after the fugitives fled Macquarie Harbour (P. Collins 113–14).[6]

---

6. Louis Nowra's play *Inside the Island* dramatizes an outbreak of ergot poisoning among returned WWI soldiers on a station in regional New South Wales.

When Pearce was finally recaptured after several months at large, his initial confession was not believed. The authorities thought he was lying to protect felons who were still on the loose, and they promptly returned him to Sarah Island. He escaped again in November 1823, this time with the hapless convict Thomas Cox. Knowing the difficulties of the easterly route, they headed north toward the Pieman River, a geographic feature that has become indelibly associated with the Pearce legend. As early as 1854, it was reported that the "Retreat River" (as it was known in 1815), had been renamed "Pieman's River" by James Lucas, the pilot who discovered Pearce on its banks after he had cannibalized Cox. Lucas was said to have named the river in honor of Pearce, "who was in the habit of selling pies about the streets in Hobart Town" ("Some Unrecorded"; cf. Tasmania). Historians have since maintained there is no evidence that Pearce was a pie-maker by trade, or that he reached as far as the Pieman River before killing Cox and surrendering to the authorities.[7] After giving himself up on the banks of the King River near Strahan, Pearce was hanged in Hobart in 1824, leaving no known descendants other than those imagined in *Back from the Dead* and *Dying Breed*.

There are some discrepancies both within versions of the story told by Pearce himself and between historical accounts and the books, plays, and films that recount Pearce's story. These discrepancies relate to the sequence of the murders and hazy details about the two (or three) members of the party who turned back sometime around the first act of cannibalism. Though Pearce did not know this, two men—most likely Kennerly and Brown, possibly at first accompanied by Dalton—made it back to Sarah Island, only to die of exhaustion and malnutrition within days. Pearce's version of events, filtered by the lawmen and members of the church who transcribed his confessions, is the only firsthand account on record, and it is possible he was not entirely truthful about his own role in the killings.

7. It would appear that Pearce's story became entangled with that of another escaped convict, Thomas Kent (who was indeed known as "the Pieman"), who was apprehended at the river, thereby giving it its current name (see "Pieman's"). Nonetheless, Pearce is still often referred to by the epithet "The Pieman" (notably in the film *Dying Breed*), and the myth of Pearce remains attached to the river itself.

Early versions of the story represent Pearce as a fearsome figure: the inhuman brute called Matt Gabbett in Clarke's novel and Dawn's film stands in for Pearce; however, transportation records and a portrait drawn when he died indicate that Pearce was nondescript and slight of build, standing at a height of only five feet, two inches (160 cm). Indeed, Pearce bore little resemblance to the gigantic beast in whose "slavering mouth, his slowly grinding jaws, his restless fingers, and his bloodshot, wandering eyes, there lurked a hint of some terror more awful than the terror of starvation—a memory of a tragedy played out in the gloomy depths of that forest which had vomited him forth again" (Clarke 99–100). Even in this nascent representation of Pearce in Clarke's novel there is an indication that it is the land—the gloomy forest—that plays the role of the truly terrifying antagonist, devouring European convicts and "vomiting them forth" when they are unsuited to the landscape.[8] The films that later take up Pearce's story play on fears of monsters lurking in the dark forests of European folklore, yet as John Scott and Dean Biron observe, Australian cinema is distinctive because there is often "nothing to fear but space itself" (317). In the case of *For the Term of his Natural Life* and its narrative offshoots, it is the landscape itself that is characterized as monstrous, yet at the same time the landscape's privations *produce* Pearce's monstrosity by driving him and his fellow convicts to cannibalism.

Les Roberts's work on cinematic cartography engages with "the growing premium attached to the locational properties of the moving image, and the concomitant processes of spatial and temporal navigation—historiographical, ontological, geographical, archaeological, architectural— that these make possible" (68). Roberts seeks to understand "the different ways film maps and film mapping might be understood as geographical productions of knowledge" (69). For example, blank spaces on the map express the limits of "Western panoptic regimes" of power and knowledge and, as figures 3.1 and 3.2 demonstrate, the inner reaches of Tasmania's southwest constitute one of these "unexplored zones of terra incognita"

8. Given that abject matter is simultaneously of the self and not of the self, such as vomit, blood, feces, and other forms of bodily waste, when the Tasmanian forest vomits forth convicts, this is a powerful indication that they are not "of the land" and they do not properly belong to it.

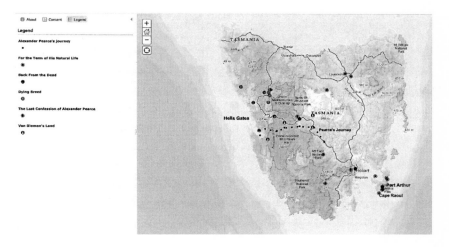

Figure 3.3. Map of shooting locations for films featuring Alexander Pearce's story. Source: Cultural Atlas of Australia.

(Roberts 71). Although figure 3.3 cannot show its exploratory richness and interactive properties, the *Cultural Atlas of Australia* layers different perspectives on and images of place, including information found in historical and contemporary photographs, film footage, and textual extracts from novels and plays that offer insight into evolving perspectives on a locale over time. This is uncommon in maps that show only one dimension of a locale, such as its geography, its history, or its representation in fictional narratives.

In terms of spatial patterns of representation, the *Cultural Atlas* dataset reveals that even though Pearce spent considerable time as an indentured servant in the settled regions of Tasmania between 1820 and 1822, the locations in which his narrative plays out on screen and in print and stage texts are overwhelmingly represented as wild spaces rather than agricultural or urban areas (see figure 3.3). This is partly due to the fact that Tasmania was sparsely settled at the time of Pearce's escape, but in the case of film it is also to do with the logistical difficulties and financial costs of dressing the set to recast present-day Tasmanian urban environments as colonial spaces without power lines, roads, or other evidence of modern infrastructure. Regarding temporal patterns, although

Clarke's novel has repeatedly been adapted and performed on stage, the particularities of Pearce's story have most frequently been singled out for the screen. Following World War II, a film production hiatus pervaded not just Tasmania but the whole Australian film industry, which explains the long gap in screen adaptations between 1927 and the TV miniseries in 1983. In a pattern that typifies Tasmanian cultural narratives, even the contemporary films that imagine Pearce's legacy are set wholly or partly in a much earlier time than when they were shot, and the protagonists are predominantly foreigners—convicts, immigrants, or tourists. This preoccupation with exile, alienation, and Tasmania's harsh colonial legacy dominates the island's cultural landscape, as the case-by-case analysis of these films demonstrates below.

For the Term of His Natural Life

The "picturization" of the novel *For the Term of His Natural Life* in 1927 involved the "importation" of an American director and stars, and the prospect of attracting an international audience raised concerns about publicizing Australia's shameful convict history (Tulloch 306–14). In his exploration of the production context for Dawn's film, Michael Roe points out that in response to fears about tarnishing Australia's image, studio spokespeople determined the film "would diminish aspects of the book which were most 'gruesome'" (39), meaning Pearce's journey became a scenic subplot. While the landscape remained an adversary in the story, the film ultimately functioned as a showcase for the country's attractions. As newspapers reported at the time, "Mr. Dawn has taken the fullest advantage of the glorious scenery which Tasmania undoubtedly offers, and scenically speaking, *For the Term of His Natural Life* on completion should be the best advertisement Tasmania has ever had" ("An Australian Film" 5). Dawn brought with him from America the sensibility of an outsider impressed by the drama of Tasmania's landscapes and sea cliffs, and he obligingly opened his set to the public in support of a tie-in "Come to Tasmania" tourism campaign ("Tasmania Invites" 14).

For the Term of His Natural Life exemplifies colonial Gothic fiction in its depiction of crumbling architecture, awe-inspiring landscapes, an atmosphere of anxiety, and a story involving isolation and the fragmentation of identity: Nobleman Richard Devine is wrongly sentenced to hard labor in the Australian penal colony where, under the assumed name of Rufus Dawes, his path crosses that of fellow convict Matt Gabbett. Unlike his historical counterpart, however, in the novel and in Dawn's film adaptation Gabbett's second escape is from Port Arthur on the Tasman Peninsula rather than Sarah Island in Macquarie Harbour. Large sections of Dawn's film—including the Macquarie Harbour scenes—were shot on the Tasman Peninsula, making Port Arthur the center of gravity for the story even though Pearce himself was never incarcerated there. Longstanding tourist attractions such as the Blowhole and Remarkable Cave feature prominently, the convict railway and Eaglehawk Neck kennels were painstakingly reconstructed, and the location used for Gabbett's recapture was the site of a real sandstone quarry located at Safety Cove. Dawn also filmed part of Gabbett's journey at Russell Falls, although it lies northeast of Pearce's actual route. Clarke's novel sees Gabbett head north from Port Arthur after his second escape, and Dawn shot some footage in the Launceston area at Cataract Gorge (Roe 46) and under the bridge at Corra Linn, where he captured scenes of a hungry Gabbett on the lam ("An Australian Film" 5). Other than a geographically incongruous shot of Gabbett against the striking backdrop of Pulpit Rock at Blackheath in the Blue Mountains of New South Wales and the final prison scenes, which were starkly lit sets constructed in Sydney, many of the scenes set in Tasmania were also shot on the island. The film's Gothic and Expressionist aesthetic derive largely from the cinematic treatment of Gabbett and his journey through Tasmania, particularly the title card with a windswept graveyard bearing the text "For days—Gabbett had promised himself that his companion must sleep—and die." Dawn repeatedly complained of Tasmania's fickle light as he waited for the clouds to clear,[9] so it is likely that the Gothic quality attributed to his film, while also present in the novel, was as much due to inclement weather and slow film stock as to stylistic intention.

Both the novel and Dawn's film version of *For the Term of His Natural Life* represent Gabbett and his fellow inmate, Dawes, being incarcerated on Sarah Island. While at Macquarie Harbour, Dawes is held in solitary

9. At the time of filming, a number of newspapers reported that Dawn was struggling to capture good footage in poor light (see, for instance, Curtis and "An Australian").

confinement on Grummet Rock, a small island near the Sarah Island penitentiary, which is off the shore of the larger prison island of Tasmania, located off the south coast of the greatest of all prison islands, the convict continent of Australia. In "A Phenomenology of Islands" Peter Hay tests the idea that islands are defined by their edges: "Islanders," he writes, "are more aware of and more confronted by the fact of boundaries" (21). This sense of confronting the boundary of the island prison is most prominent in representations of Hell's Gates, the treacherously shallow sea channel that guards the narrow entry to Macquarie Harbour. In convict days the rocks at the harbor mouth were reportedly painted with a line from Dante's Inferno, a narrative of the descent into Hades: "Abandon all hope, ye who enter here." Roslynn Haynes describes it in her extended study of Tasmanian landscape representations in writing, art, and photography:

> [The] landscape enacts and reinforces the repression and punishment meted out by society, brutalising oppressors and oppressed alike. Convicts are constrained not in haunted castles or subterranean vaults, but in a natural prison whose walls are the land itself: first the storm-swept coast at Macquarie Harbour with its Hell's Gates, then the Tasman Peninsula, with its two 'locks' upon the door. (*Tasmanian* 222)

The locks Haynes refers to are geographic features preventing escape from the Port Arthur penitentiary: the Southern Ocean and the narrow, heavily guarded sandbar at Eaglehawk Neck. This "Gothic prison" metaphor is pervasive in representations of the colony, and scholars such as Gerry Turcotte refer to Australia itself as "the dungeon of the world" (10).

Clarke himself never actually visited Macquarie Harbour: his descriptions were based on James Ross's *Van Diemen's Land Anniversary* (Robson 106). The novelist's inventive treatment of the southwest has been augmented in screen adaptations, as is evident in Dawes's attempt to escape by leaping into the roiling sea off Grummet Rock. The real Grummet Rock is a humble affair without spectacular sea cliffs. When making his feature film, Dawn intended to spend a week in Macquarie Harbour shooting scenic footage "in order that every scene should reproduce the correct locale of the story" ("For the Term" 10). However, while scouting for locations, Dawn was struck by the peaceful beauty of the Gordon River

Figure 3.4. Cape Raoul, Tasman Peninsula. Source: Jane Stadler.

and Macquarie Harbour and the innocuous appearance of the harbor mouth, Hell's Gates (see figure 3.5). Reporting that the Gordon's tranquility was incongruent with the brutality of the penal colony and that the hazards of Hell's Gates needed to appear "fearful and repelling" ("Cinematograph" 2), Dawn shot the lumber scenes in New South Wales and chose Cape Raoul's jagged rocky spires (figure 3.4) at the southernmost tip of the Tasman Peninsula to represent Hell's Gates.

Cape Raoul also posed as Hell's Gates in the version of *For the Term of His Natural Life* that was made for television in the 1980s, cementing this falsely fearsome image of the mouth of Macquarie Harbour in the national imaginary. However, much of the television production was in fact shot on the Limestone Coast in South Australia, where the open terrain and the quality of light gives a much more optimistic tone to the story. Indeed, the miniseries was so much a product of the egalitarian spirit and revisionist approach to convict history that characterized the period leading up to Australia's Bicentennial celebrations in 1988 that the ending was

Figure 3.5. Hell's Gates, Macquarie Harbour. Source: Jane Stadler.

changed to have Rufus Dawes happily married to the warden's daughter, Sylvia Vickers, his fortune and good name restored, and the grisly Gabbett storyline was excised.

Dawn also alters the novel's ending so that the unjustly sentenced convict and his sweetheart are last seen on a raft at sea after a storm destroys their ship. A glimmer of hope remains that they will survive their adventures on Tasmania's "fatal shore" and make a home together. This was reportedly a concession to "audience preference for an ending which promised that Rufus and Sylvia would live happily ever after" (Roe 36). Such an ending implies Dawes would be able to overcome class barriers to become a landholder and achieve social justice on the mainland. This might be explained by John Tulloch's thesis that Australians eventually grounded their national identity "in a broadly accepted equalitarian social doctrine" (349). Following the initial opposition between humans and environment in the early days of the colonization of Australia, the landscape came to be seen as generative of identity: "The environmental conditions of the land produce the improvisation, intolerance of conventions and manly independence" and "signify the true Australian" (348).

However, subsequent iterations of Pearce's story were far bloodier and darker as Australia came to more fully recognize the injustices wrought by colonialism.

While figures 3.4 and 3.5 can provide only a small indication of this, the geovisualization of these historic narratives on the *Cultural Atlas of Australia* dramatically illustrates these changing perceptions of the landscape using film stills, textual extracts, and archival and contemporary location photography to document different perspectives on the environment through which Pearce travelled in 1822.

Dying Breed

Like the miniseries that sees Dawes live on past the end of Clarke's novel, the contemporary horror film *Dying Breed* imagines the continuation of Pearce's journey through more accessible terrain in Tasmania's northwest. In *Dying Breed,* the legacy of Alexander Pearce lives on in Tasmania's gloomy forests, misty waterways, and isolated mining townships that harbor inbred descendants of the bloodthirsty convict line. The film represents the sanctuary of the Tarkine wilderness where two endangered species hide: descendants of cannibal convicts and the thylacine—the extinct marsupial commonly known as the Tasmanian tiger. As Catherine Simpson writes:

> Evidently the thylacine and the Sarah Island community "need to stay hidden to survive" as one of the locals puts it, but both species also need fresh "stock" to reproduce, and naïve tourists who wander into their domain are there for the taking/eating/raping. While the narrative link is only hinted at, rather than explicitly portrayed, the thylacine has evidently managed to survive due to its symbiotic relationship with the residents who leave the remains of their victims for the carnivorous thylacine to devour. (49)

In Simpson's interpretation, "outsiders, or foreigners all 'deserve' what they get for committing eco-cultural trespass" in *Dying Breed:* "Meanwhile, provided they have lived in the area long enough to be able to 'read' its signs, and understand its dangers and mythology, local white settler Australians can claim a greater sense of belonging" (50). *Dying Breed* marks the point at which discourses of environmentalism and Gothicism overtly intersect in Tasmanian cinema as the heroine, an environmental scientist, enters the wilderness to search for the thylacine and confront Tasmania's horrific convict history.

Haynes's comment that representations of Tasmania's insular island community feature "references to allegedly inbred, mentally defective individuals" in narratives wherein "the landscape became both symbol and catalyst of psychic and psychological debility" (*Tasmanian* 219) could have inspired the script for *Dying Breed*. The movie begins with a map of Tasmania in which the rivers and arterial roads run red, as though with blood. The action opens on Pearce's second escape from Sarah Island, but instead of giving himself up he leaps into a chasm and is presumed dead. The ensuing story takes place in the present when four travelers, who are initially researching the Tasmanian tiger, go in search of a missing Irishwoman who ran afoul of Pearce's descendants when she visited the backwater town of Sarah, a fictional island community on the Pieman River. Victoria's Dandenong Ranges doubled as Tasmania in some sequences and "township scenes were shot in Coal Creek Village in Korumburra in Gippsland" (Millar 19), but much of the footage is shot in locations that Pearce might have travelled through, had his northbound escape route been successful. After braving the Fatman Barge on the Pieman River crossing at Corinna (where historic graves concealed in the trees on the riverbank feature later in the film), the doomed travelers grope their way through disused mine shafts filmed in the Zeehan Spray Tunnel and stumble upon evidence of foul play at a woodman's hut. Other shooting locations include the Murchison Dam spillway, a misty graveyard of sunken trees at Mackintosh Dam, and near the end of the film a dramatic death scene high on the rail bridge at Bastyan Dam.

While *Dying Breed* liberally deploys the iconography of the horror genre, the filmmakers struggled with the darkness of the Tasmanian landscape in more than metaphorical terms. Thick vegetation, unpredictable weather, and the challenges of maintaining continuity when clouds scuttle across the sun made location shooting expensive and exhausting, frequently necessitating the displacement or substitution of Tasmanian landmarks. In recent years faster film stock and portable equipment have made working on rough terrain with inadequate light more achievable, but contemporary filmmakers still tell extraordinary tales about braving the elements in Tasmania. Regarding the midwinter shoot that took place over a period of ten days when six hundred millimeters (23.6 inches) of rain fell and the crew was battered with 50-miles-per-hour (80-km.-per-hour) winds and sleet, *Dying Breed*'s cinematographer Geoffrey Hall cheerfully notes: "I think we had terrific locations and the fact that we had such incredible weather in terms of rain and mist was just a total plus" (*"Dying Breed* Production Notes" 7). The effect is certainly atmospheric and, as Carly Millar observes, "the sheer beauty of the sweeping vistas and densely canopied woodland make the Tasmanian wilderness the real star of the movie" (19).

The Last Confession of Alexander Pearce

Unlike *Dying Breed* and adaptations of *His Natural Life, Van Diemen's Land,* and *The Last Confession of Alexander Pearce* are loyal to historical records regarding Pearce. Much of the dialogue and voiceover narration is drawn from Pearce's confessions, and these films convey a landscape in which humans are insignificant and cannibalism seems a desperate inevitability. Other than colonial exteriors and prison cells shot in New South Wales, *Last Confession* was filmed in the gentle landscape of button grass plains in Tasmania's Central Lakes District, with King William's Saddle gracing the horizon.

Publicity for the production made much of the fact that locations on Pearce's actual escape route were integral to the film, but these locations were toward the end of Pearce's journey, when he was nearing the settled districts. The filmmakers resorted to shooting mountain footage atop the accessible slopes of Mount Wellington and forest scenery in Tahune near Hobart because it is virtually impossible to get production equipment into the Western Tiers. Other locations on Pearce's route present different logistical difficulties: Loddon Plains where Bodenham was cannibalized has an unpleasant tendency to bog unwary travelers in waist-deep mud, and King William Valley is now inaccessible since being flooded for the Butler's Gorge hydroelectric project in the 1950s. Of necessity many of the film locations are north or east of Pearce's route, though it is likely he did pass near Derwent Bridge, which was the filmmakers' base camp. The set for the Macquarie Harbor penal colony and Huon pine timber works was constructed at a bend in the river near Derwent Bridge, displacing Sarah

Island yet again, and the scenic tourist lookout at Nelson Falls substitutes as a backdrop for the dangerous Franklin River crossing.

Despite being an important narrative setting for all films in the Pearce production cycle, the mountainous terrain of Tasmania's southwest wilderness thus far remains unfilmable, yet thanks to Pearce it is far from being an abstract, unknowable space devoid of value or history. Due to the contemporary transport corridors through which travelers and filmmakers move, the Central Highlands and the Lake District in Tasmania are becoming increasingly familiar and are acquiring what might be termed a misplaced spatial history associated with Pearce. This spatial fabrication of history is most evident in the geovisualized data related to Hell's Gates (discussed above in relation to figures 3.4–3.5), but it is also evident in more subtle ways in these other cinematic images of the Western Tiers and the Franklin-Gordon Wild Rivers region, which are geolocated in relation to Pearce's narrative on the *Cultural Atlas of Australia.*

Van Diemen's Land

Albeit in a limited way facilitated by tourism infrastructure and Forestry Tasmania staff, *Van Diemen's Land* has the distinction of being the first production to actually shoot in Macquarie Harbour itself and to film on the Gordon River where Pearce's journey began. Although some locations such as Nelson Falls also appear in *Last Confession,* the *Van Diemen's Land* aesthetic is quite different, cueing the audience to be as dispirited and overawed as the convicts trekking through the relentless mountainous terrain. When Pearce confides, "I wish meself death," one can well imagine the desperation he felt. The first undercurrents of *Van Diemen's Land*'s chilling sound design feature a low drone as the camera slowly descends into the wilderness along the deep green Gordon River where the trees appear like a dark fortress, the color leached away so the world seems bleak and hopeless. Pearce's Gaelic voiceover describes this desaturated landscape as "the end of the world; a fine prison" and the cinematography reinforces the sense that the inhospitable, rugged wilderness stands sentinel over the remote prison colony. The close shots of tangled branches and the sense of being entrapped is captured by artful cinematography and editing, seamlessly intercutting footage of the convict work party grappling with real Huon pine logs in the freezing waters of Macquarie Harbour with shots of the convicts pelting through the forest near Mariners Falls in the Otway region of Victoria. As the Tasmanian Search and Rescue team discovered, it is impossible to run through the dense undergrowth in Tasmania's Wild Rivers region, hence the geographic place again cedes screen space to a distant location double.[10]

On location on the Gordon River itself, the camera seems to stalk the fugitives in *Van Diemen's Land;* mounted high on a riverboat it glides down into ravines, never quite attaining a vantage point that reveals familiar landmarks or a pathway to freedom. The disembodied voiceover narration, the unsettling score, and the lurking camera convey a disturbing sense that the restless spirits of Pearce and his former companions haunt the landscape. Pearce's confession communicates a strong sense of the despair he and his companions felt in this adversarial landscape when they "arrived at a river they supposed to be Gordon's River in consequence of their being so weak and exhausted durst not cross the river. Here they sat down and being almost famished for the want of food began to intimate to each other that it would be much better for one to be sacrificed as food for the rest than for the whole of them to perish" (12). *Van Diemen's Land* begins and ends with spectral camera movements that suggest an inhospitable landscape, indelibly marked by violence and death and now inhabited by ghosts. The film's director, Jonathan auf der Heide, has said in interviews that Pearce's story was long seen as a stain on Australia's reputation, so it was buried as a grisly subplot of a melodramatic romance in which the "darkness" of Tasmania's wilderness "stemmed from the alienation and fear that the settlers and convicts experienced in the early days of British settlement. . . . I wanted to give it the feel that 'life' wasn't

10. The issue is not so much that a film is shot in an "inauthentic" location far from where the historical narrative actually unfolded, for all cinematic landscapes are but representations and interpretations of place. Rather, here and elsewhere, the question is how the choice of a location double affects the qualitative construction of a sense of place. While the landscape aesthetic is similar, the affective charge of the Otways differs from that of Tasmania's southwest. The more open Victorian location creates space for some light-hearted moments in the film that would not have been possible had the forward momentum of the plot stalled to show convicts slogging through impenetrable scrub.

welcome there and that it was a harsh and brutal character. Pearce would then have to, in order to survive, become like the landscape" (qtd. in Bullock, "Strange" 42).

While *Van Diemen's Land* offers little historical context either before or after Pearce's fateful journey, the very absences in the narrative are indicative of the harsh conditions of the newly colonized land. The film alludes to the colonial land grab mentality as the band of unhappy men ascend to the summit of a mountain and glimpse Frenchman's Cap soon after they escape Macquarie Harbor. They look about themselves in dismay and remark that they are gazing at "all the land they could possibly desire," yet they desire nothing more than to escape from it. Here, one can't help but reflect on another absence for the landscape is depicted as being empty of Aboriginal inhabitants, although this was not the case. This perceived emptiness tacitly reinforces the myth of *terra nullius* and conspires to elide the genocide that occurred when the Aborigines who once lived Tasmania and were eradicated during the Black Line of 1830 in which the military "dispersed" Tasmanian Aborigines in an attempt to remove them from settled areas where they were believed to be a threat to agriculturalists (Clement).

Near the end of their long journey when Pearce and Greenhill emerged from the thickly wooded mountains of the Western Tiers, they came upon beautiful button grass plains that they thought to be a stock run, so they eagerly began searching for a settlement. The location of these plains is most likely near Derwent Bridge in the Central Lakes district. Pearce's confession to Rev. Knopwood reveals that, instead of stockmen and dwellings, they encountered an Aboriginal encampment:

> At the extent of these plains they perceived a smoke, which again raised their spirits to go and see what it was whatever the result would be, on approaching near it they heard the voice of some human beings conversing but could not understand what they said this convinced them they were a Tribe of Black Natives—and they knowing that they were seldom or ever without kangaroo, oppossums [*sic*] or other Beast, made them form a resolution of Rushing them without any hesitation accordingly they got themselves in readiness. The one furnishing himself with a large stick the other with the Axe then both of them crept slyly in ambush until they drew within 20 or 30 yards of them. Then they both rushed on them each exerting his utmost

strength striking several of these unfortunate Blacks some severe blows
which so terrified them that they all immediately dispersed. (Pearce)

This aggressive treatment of Indigenous people was characteristic of colonial attitudes and it reflected the fears and prejudices of the day. Ironically, following their opportunistic attack and the theft of food, Pearce
and Greenhill fled in fear of retribution by the Aborigines: "For although
these Natives are not Cannibals there has been several instances of people being barbarously murdered by them in several parts of the Colony"
(Pearce).

In each subsequent retelling of Pearce's story, the contact with Tasmanian Aborigines that Pearce mentions in his confessions is elided and the
land through which he travels is represented as being empty of inhabitants. During the period in which Pearce traversed Tasmania, members
of the Toogee Indigenous language group lived along the coastline of the
Macquarie Harbour area of Tasmania's southwest and were known to
venture inland along the banks of the Gordon and Franklin Rivers. However, Indigenous people mainly subsisted on seafood, and the dense, dark
forest canopy meant this region did not support enough wildlife or edible
plants to sustain communities away from the coast or watercourses. It is
therefore not surprising that Pearce and his companions did not encounter Aborigines until they neared the eastern settlements. Archaeological
research suggests that Southwestern Tasmanian Pleistocene sites in caves
at limestone outcrops along the Franklin-Gordon waterways have not
had "any human occupation at all in the last 12,000 years" and historical sources show that more recent Aboriginal activity was concentrated
on the coast and was more sporadic on the shores and in the hinterland
of Macquarie Harbour (Allen and Cosgrove 11).

THE GOTHIC LANDSCAPE

Other than the systematic erasure of the land's Indigenous inhabitants,
one of the most evident patterns that is revealed by mapping different
versions of Pearce's story and geovisualizing changing perceptions of the
landscape is the dominance of the Gothic mode of representation. Gothic
fiction has its origins in novels written in England, Ireland, Germany,
and France, followed by the melodramatic stage performances and later

screen productions that adapted many of these novels. While the tradition traveled to colonial outposts and Australia was being settled as the Gothic boom was at its height in the UK, the Gothic mode is widely acknowledged to have emerged in England with the publication of Horace Walpole's *The Castle of Otranto* in 1764. Gothic literature flourished in the 1830s, extending by some accounts to include *Jane Eyre* (1874) and even *Dracula* (1897). In Australia, according to Turcotte, Gothic fiction was "modified to accommodate the climate" (19). Turcotte contends that the Gothic is a "literary mode" that communicates a form of "spiritual malaise":

> [It] emphasizes the horror, uncertainty and desperation of the human experience, often representing the solitariness of that experience through characters trapped in a hostile environment, or pursued by an unspecified or unidentifiable danger. From its inception the Gothic has dealt with fears and themes which are endemic in the colonial experience: isolation, entrapment, fear of pursuit and fear of the unknown. (11)

Before Turcotte's articulation of a nationwide sense of the uncanny Gothic sensibility pervading Australian space, Jim Davidson advanced a convincing argument for Tasmania's pre-eminent Australian Gothic status. It is as though during the period from Australia's convict past to the near-present postcolonial period of reengagement with a haunted and troubled history, Tasmania functioned as the crucible for the nation's unsettled relationship with colonial practices. The continued repetition of Gothic-styled Tasmanian vistas, such as "a myriad of sudden lakes, or the wonderfully overwrought coastline of Tasman Peninsula, with its clefts and pavements and blowholes located exactly where a gothic novelist would want them" (Davidson 310), means that the Gothic not only has become a dominant mode of representation but has provided the lens through which much critical discourse on Tasmanian landscape and culture has been focused. Influential art critic Edward Colless argues the Gothic tradition has been widely used by artists as a way of rendering the Tasmanian landscape familiar by association with the English notion of the picturesque as an aesthetic ideal and with well-worn melodramatic literary and theatrical conventions. Further, as Keryn Stewart and Helen Hopcroft suggest:

Place and spatial concerns resonate through the Tasmanian Gothic sensibility; the landscape is seen as an active element in the gothic narrative, even a quasi-sentient force animated with menace. Tasmania's wild landscapes and grimly picturesque ruins, with their links to the violent and bloody convict past of the island, provide fertile ground for gothic imaginings; artists, writers and critics have long used the island as an imaginative site to play out these concerns.

Haynes claims, "Gothic was first used in relation to Tasmania only in 1976" (*Tasmanian* 219). By 1988 Davidson had developed the idea of the Tasmanian Gothic as a theme or style extending across novels, plays, and films set in an "uncommonly picturesque" landscape haunted by the past (310). Following Davidson, Emily Bullock suggests that "the past is a persistent presence in films about Tasmania, melding with and reinforcing a sense of isolation, menace and melancholy that is so frequently made to appear natural in its landscapes" ("Rumblings" 78). More recently, Carleton has traced the prevalence of the Gothic trope through Australian literary fiction, cinema, and theater. Carleton identifies the "psychological return of the repressed" and the "preoccupation with history's 'haunting' of the present" as core components of the Gothic sensibility, noting that "The Australian landscape and the nation's 'haunted' history—of violent Aboriginal dispossession and early British convict transportation—have long combined to provide an equation where a Gothic reading of Australian culture and space is not only logical, but in certain ways unavoidable" ("Australian" 51). Although Tasmania is the site of a systematic and well-publicized attempted genocide of Aborigines, as noted above, Tasmanian fiction elides racial concerns in favor of convict narratives, whereas the Gothic stories that play out in Australia's North are where issues of racial identity tend to be staged, as demonstrated in chapter 2.

Cinema researchers David Thomas and Gary Gillard link the Gothic's defining features to Sigmund Freud's discussion of the hauntingly familiar, yet disturbingly strange experience of the uncanny and Tzvetan Todorov's account of psychological ambiguity in fantastic narratives wherein narrative structures are distorted by transformations of space and time and by psychological and social decay (36–44). In *Dying Breed,* just as in *For the Term of His Natural Life* and other films in the cycle, the displacement of narrative settings such as Sarah Island and Hell's Gates to shooting locations in more hospitable regions of Tasmania or even other states of Australia could produce what would, in a Gothic interpretation, be termed an "uncanny" landscape that seems at once familiar yet also eerily strange. Ironically, such a reading is limited to "canny" spectators who have personal experience of the locations: for those who have not visited the places in which the story is set, the unsettling slippage between recognition and spatial uncertainty never occurs. Location doubles—like body doubles—are unnoticeable in a well-made film.

The extended narrative cycle examined in this chapter provides ample evidence to corroborate Tuan's claim that "art trains attention and educates sensibility; it prepares one to respond to the character of alien places and situations" ("Place" 162). In choosing a case study set in a region in which historical maps and even contemporary maps provide little detail, we sought to contribute to international work on mapping spatial history by developing digital cartographic methodologies that enable geocritical and historical analysis by systematically examining and geolocating images and textual extracts. This technique has revealed changing perceptions of space over time, documenting the elision and reinforcement of narrative details about place and space that render the landscape an evolving character in the telling and retelling of Pearce's historic narrative. This geovisualization process, which is archived on the *Cultural Atlas of Australia* website and translated into discursive form in this chapter, retains the experiential dimension offered in landscape narratives and images that can often be lost in more traditional applications of GIS and spatial history research methods.

Pearce's tale of convict atrocities cultivates perceptions of the Tasmanian landscape and locates Tasmania in relation to shifting conceptions of national identity. In early Australian cinema, according to Tulloch, "the relationship between man and landscape first appears as purely an oppositional one" as Australian settlers struggle against drought, isolation, bushfires and floods (346). This is evident in Clarke's novel, yet by the time it was made into a feature film in 1927 attitudes were already shifting as Australia began to reflect on its convict past and sought to distance itself from the history of brutality that included Indigenous dispossession and other forms of colonial violence such as convict floggings. Our systematic mapping of representations of the landscape of the past onto southwest Tasmania's rugged topography has revealed recurring patterns of Gothic imagery and the disturbing erasure of the Aboriginal presence in the landscape. We have been able to discern these patterns by geovisualizing the way the land is portrayed in historical documents such as Pearce's confessions and subsequent narrative dramatizations of his story.

In his landmark analysis of nation and narration, Turner contends that "narratives are ultimately produced by culture; thus they generate meanings, take on significances, and assume forms that are *articulations* of the values, beliefs—the ideology—of the culture" (1). Patterns recurring in cultural narratives (such as repeated myths, connotations, characters and symbols, and "formal preferences" such as dominant stylistic choices and genres) reveal "which meanings are most easily articulated within the culture, which meanings are preferred by it, and which are seen to be the most significant for it" (Turner 19). In this sense the recurring elision of Aboriginal Australians from retellings of Pearce's journey narrative that the process of narrative mapping has brought to light is indicative of cultural "disease" regarding colonial history. On one level the absence of Indigenous Australians in every retelling of Pearce's story merely shows that the authors, playwrights, filmmakers, and their narrative protagonists saw the land though European eyes and failed to see either the limited food that grew there or to represent the Aboriginal people that Pearce reports encountering toward the end of his long journey. On another level this perceived emptiness tacitly reinforces the myth of *terra nullius* and conspires to elide the genocide that was to occur in the six years following Peace's death when European settlers eradicated Tasmanian Aborigines.

Drawing together the patterns of Gothic representation and the erasure of Aboriginal Tasmanians, the films in this study evoke a landscape experienced as a place haunted by the cruelties of colonial history.[11] In

11. As historian Maria Tumarkin writes in her analysis of ideas about trauma and survival and their effects on landscapes and communities, Tasmania—particularly Port Arthur and Macquarie Harbour—can function as a site onto which anxieties about colonial savagery and Australia's national origins can be projected and thereby expelled from the mainland imaginary (199).

each of its cinematic instantiations, Pearce's journey is imagined as a de-
bilitating trek through land so inhospitable that the fugitives resort to
cannibalism to avoid starvation, yet the terrain also has the picturesque,
unreal quality of an old oil painting. Auf der Heide states of the locations
he chose for *Van Diemen's Land*: "[They] had to represent Pearce's state
of mind so we could have an insight as to what he's thinking. Each location visually represents the emotion he's experiencing" (qtd. in Bullock, "Strange" 43). The difficult river crossing can be read as entering the
troubled waters of the soul, the sullen sky and creeping mists bespeak a
dark confusion of the mind, the tangled paperbark forest whose peeling
white bark is branded by deep shadows and bleeding sap signals Pearce
is ensnared in a realm of moral turpitude. However, Tasmania is a living
place that cannot be reduced to a metaphor for colonial prisons and the
symbolic use of the land as a screen on which to project the protagonist's
psychic state is not the only way to interpret cinematic landscapes. As
Christopher Tilley writes, "The landscape is continually being encultured,
bringing things into meaning as part of a symbolic process by which human consciousness makes the physical reality of the natural environment
into an intelligible and socialized form. The landscape is redolent with
past actions, it plays a major role in constituting a sense of history and
the past" (67).

To return to the distinction between space and place, if space must be
encultured to become place and if pathways "structure experiences of the
places they link" (Tilley 30), then the story of Pearce's lonely journey plays
an important mediating role, inscribing the untrammeled, uninhabited
southwest corner of Tasmania as a textual space that can be vicariously experienced, valued for its historical, aesthetic, and ecological richness, and
given a place in Australian culture. Yet Pearce's spatial story has proven
difficult to capture on screen and filmmakers have constructed a disori-
enting itinerary piecing his journey together with footage from different
states and regions, resulting in what might be termed an "imaginative
cinematic geography" (Mitchell and Stadler, "Imaginative").

This chapter has approached spatial representation and perception from
a geocritical perspective that moves beyond the analysis of an individual
text or author's treatment of space to "locate places in temporal depth"
across an intertextual, multifocal study of representations of a region or

territory (Westphal, Foreword xiv). As Haynes writes, "The process of re-lating to the Tasmanian landscape imaginatively required a context and the inscription of narratives and art to provide it with cultural resonances" (*Tasmanian* xii). The many screen versions of Pearce's story give insight into both the regional patterns and historical locatedness that Westphal values and the cultural inscription of place that Haynes sees as crucial to enabling people to find their place in the landscape. The cannibal-convict film cycle demonstrates not only how representations of Tasmania are shaped by production logistics, but also that such practical and economic constraints intersect with politically charged sensitivities about place, history, and identity to produce a vicarious narrative experience charac-terized by imaginative and dislocated perceptions of the landscape.

4

MOBILITY AND TRAVEL NARRATIVES

Geovisualizing the Cultural Politics of Belonging to the Land

In 2011 an endearing story about a dog the same color as the dusty red Outback broke box office records to become one of the top ten highest grossing Australian films of all time. The name of the film and its eponymous protagonist, "Red Dog," derive from the reddish brown coat that is characteristic of the Red Cloud Kelpie, a breed of Australian sheep and cattle dog that is widely believed to be part dingo.[1] The tale of Red Dog wandering the country in search of his master eclipsed even well-loved travel narratives such as *The Adventures of Priscilla, Queen of the Desert* (Stephan Elliott, 1994). The perennial popularity of travel narratives and their capacity to dramatize the geopolitical relationship between the land and its people make the genre significant for investigating the nexus between travel, colonialism, and cultural perceptions of place and belonging (see Gilbert and Johnston; Bishop, "Driving"). For Indigenous Australians, the landscape itself is believed to have been created through a kind of travel narrative in that the land takes its form from ancestral beings that traversed the continent during the Dreamtime and marked

---

1. While the origins of the Kelpie breed are not well documented, the name dates back to 1872 when Jack Gleeson chose a pup from the litter of a Collie who was thought to have mated with a dingo. Gleeson named the puppy Kelpie, after a mythological Celtic creature, and she became known as "Gleeson's Kelpie." Her daughter "King's Kelpie" won sheepdog trials and her pups were in great demand, becoming known as "Kelpie's pups" and, thereafter, Kelpies. The breed was distinctive because at least one red puppy was born in each litter, suggestive of the dingo bloodline (Parsons 78; MacLeod).

it with the story of their passage. Contemporary Aborigines use cultural rituals including walkabout, song, dance, and storytelling to honor these ancestral beings who still reside in landmarks such as water holes and rock formations: "The narrated songlines of Australian Indigenous peoples offer an example of the cultural representation of complex and culturally specific forms of spatial cognition and connection between people and place" (Mills). Settler-colonial explorers first traversed the interior of the Australian continent in 1800–1860, charting their journeys in journals and maps. These travelogues were soon supplemented by literary fiction and plays that dramatized exploration and convict transportation, and, by the turn of the century, the "sightseeing" films of early cinema afforded "a way for the less wealthy classes to see what otherwise was only accessible to them in still film through painting or photography" (M. Lefebvre, Introduction xi). Among the earliest travel films of Australia are the tourism narratives and Indigenous mythologies created by Gaston Méliès, brother and business partner of the better-known director George Méliès. For instance, in Gaston Méliès's *Captured by Aborigines* (1913), an Aboriginal elder rescues an English explorer in Queensland from cannibals. By 2014, the top fifty Australian feature films ranked by total gross Australian box office included sixteen travel narratives ("Australian Content"). Excluding fourteen films on the top fifty list that take place overseas, travel narratives represent 44% of the most popular features, including *Mad Max* (George Miller, 1979), *Wolf Creek* (Greg McLean, 2005), *Australia* (Baz Luhrmann, 2008), and *Bran Nue Dae* (Rachel Perkins, 2009). Not only have travel narratives come to occupy a prominent place in Australia's cultural industries, their evolution from the early travelogues and sightseeing films suggests they instantiate a form of storytelling ideally suited to reflecting changing understandings of space and place and especially how exploration, development, and the experience of the "other"—Indigenous peoples, immigrants, and landscapes—shape sociopolitical perceptions and practices.

Using GIS map layers to reveal patterns of colonial and Indigenous cultural activity on the landscape through which the protagonists travel, this chapter takes as its central case study the 2011 film *Red Dog* (Kriv Stenders), which is based on the true story of a dog roaming the transport corridors between mine sites in Australia's northwest Pilbara region in the 1970s. The film depicts Australia's West as a resource-rich space of mobility, and representations of Red Dog's travels highlight the network of economic, geographical, and cultural factors that shape mobility and understandings of place and belonging in Australia's largest, richest, and most sparsely populated state. This chapter uses geovisualization techniques to investigate spatial politics and mobility in *Red Dog* and to reveal complex relationships that are otherwise obscured by the film's deployment of quirky humor, apparently harmless cultural stereotypes, and a feel-good narrative. In particular, we examine tensions between the mining industry, the Pilbara community, and myths of national and regional identity conveyed in cultural narratives, including those of Indigenous Australians and those perpetuated in the western genre. We undertake a pragmatic form of geographical and narrative mapping to reinterpret not just the relationship between cultural politics and geography but also the important role that mobility plays in the narrative of colonial progress and expansion. In the case of *Red Dog,* we use geovisualization as a mode of narrative analysis in order to make visible the complex spatial history that is implicit in the relationship between the story of Red Dog's wanderings and the socioeconomic development of the Pilbara region. We compare the accepted history of Red Dog's travels with the stories and maps that chart his movements, and we investigate the parallel history of the location in which the story takes place by geovisualizing the complex imbrications of the mining industry, the Pilbara community, and myths of national and regional identity conveyed in film.

The film *Red Dog* is based on three books that narrate the true story of an itinerant worker's nomadic dog that was adopted by the mining community of the Pilbara. *Red Dog* was adapted for the screen from a 2001 Louis de Bernières children's novella of the same name. De Bernières in turn borrows heavily from two published historical versions of the true story of Red Dog: Nancy Gillespie's 1983 *Red Dog* and Beverley Duckett's 1993 *Red Dog: The Pilbara Wanderer.* All three books and the film are structured in some ways like an oral history of Red Dog's life, a canine biography told in the form of anecdotes by those who knew him. As the story unfolds, Red Dog's friends take turns recounting how he came to have his own bank account, became a fully-fledged member of the mine workers union, and was loved and cared for by the entire community. The story takes place around Dampier, where Red Dog bonds with John, a Hamersley Iron bus driver. In the film, Red Dog's owner is a traveling bus driver called John Grant in homage to *Wake in Fright* (analyzed in chapter 1), but the real Red Dog belonged to a man called John Stazzonelli and his family. Legend has it that when John failed to come home one day, Red Dog began searching for him far and wide, and while hitchhiking along the mining routes he became known as the "Pilbara Wanderer."

Soon after the film's release, Sarah Burnside, a writer who describes herself as a commentator on the contemporary political landscape, published the article "*Red Dog* Whitewashes the Pilbara." In it she made the point that, despite *Red Dog*'s many enjoyable qualities, the film excludes all trace of the rich Indigenous culture, the numerous sacred sites, and the significant population of Aboriginal Australians living in the Pilbara region. Shortly thereafter, in early 2012, artist and barrister Campbell Thomson took this geopolitical critique further in his incisive response to the film, the poem "Australia Is a Film about a Red Dog," published in the *Overland Literary Journal*:

> Dogs float here with the first boat people to become dingoes
> But *Gadiya* design you to round up stock & name Dampier after a pirate
> In 1861 they invade & kill a big mob of *Yaburara* when a policeman is speared
>
> Hooves pockmark the red earth's skin
> They build a port to take tons of country to Japan.
> Now Rio Tinto sends ships every day to China
> & aims for 333 million tons a year.
>
> Homeless men drive monsters that eat *Marga* ancestors turned to iron
> Ore and don't know why they feel bad in this place.
> ....
> It [*Red Dog*] leaves the *Yaburara* and *Ngarluma* mobs
> On the cutting room floor
> & makes sure Koko as you is a shoo in for best shaggy dog.
> Grant rides his Harley to work after nookie, hits a roo, and skids.
> We don't see the face of the only (dead) native in ninety minutes
> ....
> With WA and the Feds putting up the seed funding
> No surprise it makes mining beautiful

To appreciate Thomson's poem, readers benefit from knowing something about the history of Dampier, which is one of the main locations featured in Red Dog's story. Named after William Dampier, the buccaneering navigator who explored the Western Australian coast in 1699, the industrial port of Dampier and its surrounds were later the site of an altercation between Australian Aborigines and Francis Thomas Gregory's northwest expedition near the Harding River in 1861 (see Palmer, "Petroglyphs" 153). By 1866, the Dampier-Roebourne area had become the administrative center for the far northern reaches of the Swan River Colony and "in 1887, the discovery of gold in the Pilbara led to further inroads into Aboriginal territory" (Vinnicombe 6). The area around Dampier, Roebourne, and Karratha is the country of the Ngarluma people and neighboring groups such as the Yaburara, Indjibundi, and Mardudunira. These Indigenous groups are the custodians of land and the rich rock art and petroglyph galleries in the region,[2] which are considered to be the work of the Margas:

> The Margas were Dream Time ancestral figures who, according to the mythology of the area, formulated the teachings and social patterns that were followed by the tribe. They gave the food sources and taught that certain principles should be obeyed. Their law was as indestructible as the rock that now bears the teachings. (Palmer, "Petroglyphs" 155)

Thomson's poem references this rich Indigenous cultural history, and it not only forges strong associations between Australian Aborigines, native animals, and a contemporary underclass—the disenfranchised "boat people" seeking political asylum on Australian shores—it also makes a link between the Red Dog of the film and the native red dogs (dingoes) that were introduced to Australia by Aborigines. The Aboriginal belief that

2. "The Dampier Archipelago and associated Burrup Peninsula, located on the Indian Ocean coast of Western Australia's Pilbara region about 1550 km north of Perth, has long been known as the locale of a prodigious distribution of Aboriginal petroglyphs. The density of motifs and the range of subject matter, techniques and patination qualify this body of art as among the richest expressions of pre-literate documentation in the world. The Dampier Archipelago, comprising some forty-two rocky islands and islets, is the visible component of a relatively recently drowned landmass, the shorelines of which stabilised about 6000 years ago. Formerly known as Dampier Island, the 'Burrup Peninsula' is the largest landmass in the archipelago. This projection of land, approximately 27 km long and 5 km wide, is an artificial peninsula associated with recent industrial development" (Vinnicombe 3).

time is flexible or elastic enables dogs that were introduced to Australia some three thousand to four thousand years ago to be present in Dreamtime creation myths alongside native animals, often taking the place of the Tasmanian tiger, or thylacine, a carnivorous canine marsupial with tiger-like stripes that is widely represented in Pilbara rock art (see Parker 122, 140).[3] To an even greater extent than Burnside's article, Thomson's poem addresses tensions between Indigenous cosmological perceptions of the land and Western capitalist views of the land as a resource to be stocked with and eroded by hard-hoofed livestock, mined of its ore, and otherwise exploited for commercial gain. Thomson also critiques the aesthetic, narrative, and political choices made by the filmmakers—particularly the exclusion of members of the Yaburara and Ngarluma Indigenous language groups who have lived in the Pilbara for at least thirty thousand years. Indeed, viewers of the film *Red Dog* might be forgiven for perceiving the Pilbara to be a space devoid of Aboriginal people or cultural history prior to Dampier's arrival.

Commentators such as Thomson and Burnside stoked a heated debate about the award-winning and commercially successful film, the lucrative Pilbara mining industry that provided substantial funding for the film production, and the disadvantage and disenfranchisement of the Indigenous people living in the district. Why, critics asked, might an upbeat family film about a dog roaming the Pilbara in the 1970s be expected to engage with the cultural and environmental costs of mining, and why should it represent Aborigines, a group that makes up less than 2.5% of the Australian population?[4] With the aid of GIS and other geovi-

3. In Caroline Bird and Sylvia Hallam's "A Review of Archaeology and Rock Art in the Dampier Archipelago" (2006), it is documented that "about twelve depictions thought to be of thylacines, or Tasmanian tigers, have now been recorded in the Dampier Archipelago. Thylacines are believed to have been extinct for some 3000 years on the Australian mainland," and these depictions are dated at approximately eighteen thousand to twelve thousand years old (18). As Vinnicombe in her documentation of the Dampier Rock Art notes, "Dog-like creatures with legs of equal length and sharply pointed ears are occasionally shown. Some of these have stripes across the body, and may depict the Thylacine. It is, however, often difficult to assign this identification with certainty, although a large and imposing juxtaposition of male and female images on Angel Island, with striped bodies and upturned tails thickened at the base, are undeniable contenders to the 'Thylacine' claim" (51).

4. For population statistics, see Australian Bureau of Statistics ("Census Data").

sualization strategies that locate Red Dog's tale and his travels in relation to the Pilbara's geopolitical history, we address these very questions. In doing so, we engage with longstanding debates about colonialism, Indigeneity, and contested relationships with the Australian land, and we test Jane Mills's assertion that "just as cartographic knowledge has been intimately bound to the exploitative exercise of colonial power, so too has the history of cinema."

GEOVISUALIZATION, NARRATIVE, AND MOBILITY

Where narrative representations of maps, landscapes, and journeys provide epistemological and ontological insights about the cultural and political geography of a place and its inhabitants, geovisualization techniques can illuminate narrative representations of place and space and foreground spatial politics. However, a static map representation of narrative locations may also have the unwelcome effect of effacing or eliding mobility and temporality within the narrative—subordinating the journey to its locations and foregrounding space at the expense of temporal passage. As we will demonstrate is the case with *Red Dog,* many films, books, poems, and plays contain within them journeys and narrative landscapes that are not substitutes for the real, geographical world but that have the potential to yield valuable insights about how that geographical reality is perceived, understood, and experienced over time. Like maps and other geovisualization techniques, these cultural narratives are not just representations; they are also generative—productive of meanings, social relationships, and subject positions.

Cinema's capacity to represent a mobile gaze roving inquisitively, attentively, or contemplatively over the landscape has both ontological and epistemological interest as it reveals much about the ways in which the world is seen and experienced, even as the borders of the screen provide a reminder that a great deal is excluded from our perceptual frame. In their analysis of mobility, geography, and film, Tim Cresswell and Deborah Dixon state that while the study of landscape is "built around observation from a fixed point of a static scene, film viewing involves the observer taking a mobile view on a mobile world"; in consequence, cinematic landscapes resist fixity and the act of viewing film can be understood as a "kinaesthetic experience" of place and emplacement (4–5). The kinesthetic experience of landscape is particularly prominent in *Red Dog* because the film uses music, lyrics, and a lively audiovisual tempo to celebrate living and working on the land as it presents a montage of locations that include the red desert, the vivid azure ocean, and mammoth iron ore mining machinery, much like home movie footage or snapshots taken on the course of a journey. As Mike Crang points out, there are many parallels between a camera's viewfinder, the cinema screen, and the windshield of a car, to the extent that the cinema spectator often functions as virtual double for a passenger seated in a car (20). In *Red Dog*, the vehicle-mounted traveling shots that roam across the landscape synthesize technologies of vision and mobility to the extent that Jeffrey Ruoff argues that cinema can be considered "as a mode of transportation" (8). *Red Dog* exemplifies the ways in which journey films use traveling shots to produce spatial experience, thereby coming to function as audiovisual vehicles for constructing and touring the locations they represent.

Teamed with the geovisualization techniques of interactive cartography, cultural narratives produce a different way of being in and knowing the land by engaging with and moving through it. Digital cartography generates a novel form of spatial knowledge, just as previous modes of mapping and representing place gave rise to different modes such as the objective, ordered, controlled vision of space offered when viewing a map compared to the embodied, affective experience of a place at ground level or the Indigenous cosmological connection to land and to the past. As film historian Tom Gunning observes in his work on the cinema of attractions, since its inception film has documented and produced new experiences of spatial perception and movement, allowing audiences to see *how* we see the landscape as well as enabling us to see new things and to see in new ways mediated by technologies of transport and cinematography. Because the advent of cinema coincided with the development of mechanized transport and the emergence of a class who travelled for leisure (M. Lefebvre, Introduction xi; Horne), early travel films contributed to modernity's technological and cultural mediation of space and time. According to David B. Clarke and Marcus A. Doel, cinema brought with it a shift in the way landscapes were perceived in Western art and narratives, changing from "picturesque" modes of perception that offered the illusion of mastery and completion to a more "panoramic" mode of perception, which locates the viewing subject in the middle of an active process of vision and exploration (218). We take up these ideas from scholars such as Gunning, Rouff, Crang, and Clarke and Doel to demonstrate the significance of the film *Red Dog* in shaping how the Australian landscape is viewed and, in turn, how the film's roving, panoramic "dog's eye view" frames and even distorts perceptions of the Pilbara and its spatial history.

CARTOGRAPHY, CINEMA, AND TRAVEL NARRATIVES

While narrated representations of travel and landscape offer important experiential dimensions, we complement this with cartographic techniques to reveal the history of previous surveys, journeys, and events that might go unrecognized in the glossy celluloid image or, as Thomson's poem suggests, be discarded in the editing room. This is why qualitative GIS and interactive mapping techniques that offer multiple narratives and perspectives over time are powerful ways of understanding spatial history and interpreting the cultural significance of narratives and the spaces in which they take place. This does not mean that we advocate a return to the imperial view of the land that traditional cartography has been associated with.[5] Just as cartographic technologies such as the sextant aided navigation and facilitated the carving up of space into the gridlines and territorial boundaries familiar on modern maps, and just as technologies of cinema and transport produced new perspectives on the world and journeys within it, contemporary developments in digital technology and GIS have enabled a different way of seeing and engaging with the land. In her work on cartographic metaphors in literature, Peta Mitchell argues that in parallel with contemporary ways of conceptualizing and narrating space, place, and mobility, technological developments have fostered the emergence of a "new, more affective, ontological, and embodied cartographic epistemology" (*Cartographic* 3). With the popular uptake of interactive digital cartography in which people can toggle between a

5. As noted in our introduction to this volume, scholars such as Peta Mitchell (*Cartographic*), Gillian Rose, Ross Gibson (*South*), and Denis Cosgrove have argued that, as Euclidean geometry came to organize the conception and representation of the land and the ways it was surveyed, mapped, bounded, and owned, the European concept of landscape became associated with Renaissance conceptions of space and with capitalist or imperial appropriation and ownership of that space.

conventional mapped view, a satellite view embellished with photographs and annotated place marks, and panoramic street view, there is a sense in which reading the map and journeying have become, to an extent, one and the same process. While reading a novel or watching a film or a play is a journey through diegetic space and hence a kind of map-making endeavor, engagement with spatial narratives plotted on an interactive map that allows virtual movement through its story-world constitutes a similar kind of journey.

Like Ruoff, who asserts that cinema is a form of transportation, Tom Conley, whose particular research interest is maps in films, argues that films themselves can be considered a form of cartography: "Films *are* maps insofar as each medium can be defined as a form of what cartographers call 'locational imaging'. . . in its first shots a film establishes a geography with which every spectator is asked to contend" (*Cartographic Cinema* 2). Conley sees maps as being connected to questions of ontology and history (and to this we add epistemology) in that "a map in a movie begs and baits us to ponder the fact that *who we are* or whomever we believe ourselves to be depends, whether or not our locus is fixed or moving, on often unconscious perceptions about *where* we come from and may be going" (*Cartographic Cinema* 3). Film's exercise of power and ideology differs from that of mapmaking; nevertheless, Conley's point that films geovisualize narrative worlds and construct ways for audiences to navigate through them and "produce space through the act of perception" (*Cartographic Cinema* 20) is pertinent to spatial humanities research into how cultural narratives layer meanings on the geographic landscape and how digital cartography might represent this terrain.

METHODOLOGY

One characteristic of cinema that makes its capacity for geovisualization distinctive is its experiential quality, which derives in large part from the use of the moving image and multiple points of view that literally animate the landscape. Bodenhamer has noted the value of animated maps "in helping to understand movement as a basic characteristic of human existence" ("Beyond" 9). Indeed, the film *Red Dog* contains an animated map of Red Dog's travels, superimposed on a montage sequence of him running through the landscape, jumping on a plane, and catching other forms of transportation. This map shows his journeys along the major highways up and down the coast of Western Australia and as far northeast as Darwin in the Northern Territory. Developing a methodology that might be considered a form of qualitative GIS, we transferred the routes identified in the animated cinematic map of Red Dog's travels onto a map detailing the shooting locations and narrative settings drawn from the film and its literary and historical source texts; however, since the information that maps and films leave out is also meaningful, we have used GIS to overlay and interpret information about mine sites and sacred Aboriginal sites in the region.

In their pioneering work on GIS methodologies for humanities research, Phil Jones and James Evans write, "Qualitative GIS seeks to take a different kind of approach to data collection, analysis and visualisation. The aim is to look at *how* individuals understand space and what the impacts of these understandings are for the production of sociospatial relations" (93). Instead of using oral histories or interviews to access sociospatial relations and conceptions of space, which is Jones and Evans's "spatial transcript" technique for advancing understandings of "the ways that space and mobilities are co-constructed" (92), our qualitative use of GIS interrogates different cultural narratives that are located in the same place and compares the intersecting and divergent perspectives found in these narratives with the kinds of spatial data that can be harvested by the GIS software system and other databases and archives.

In addition to reviewing land rights claims and associated literature relevant to the *Red Dog* narrative location dataset, our methodology involved locating and downloading relevant datasets from Geoscience Australia, Department of Mines and Petroleum (Western Australia), Department of Aboriginal Affairs (Western Australia), Department of Environment (Federal Government), and the National Native Title Tribunal (Federal Government). We replaced multiple points that overlapped or clustered too densely in areas of the map with a single location point to avoid cluttering the map and to increase map clarity. For example, in figures 4.1 and 4.3, the paw print icons that represent locations that Red Dog traveled to in the film or in one of the books that narrate his journeys may be located at the midpoint between two locations or the centroid of multiple locations in areas where Red Dog had a lot of activity, such as around

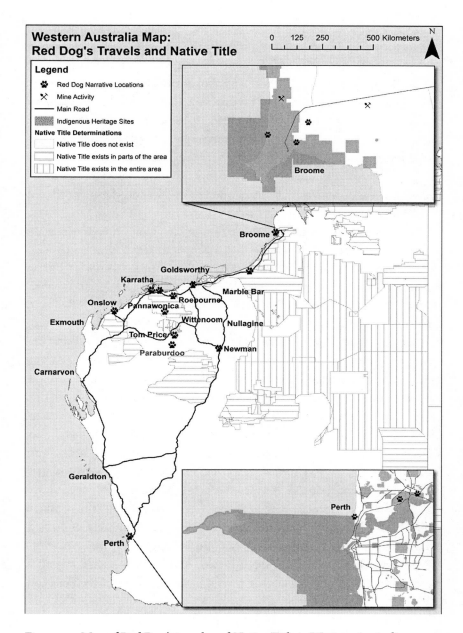

Figure 4.1. Map of Red Dog's travels and Native Title in Western Australia.
Source: Jane Stadler and Luke Houghton.

Dampier. Focusing on the Pilbara region in Western Australia where Red Dog lived, we added transport data layers to show the roads and rail networks that he frequented, and we included a data layer showing operating mines and mining activity (marked by shovel and pick axe icons in figure 4.3) to show the mine sites that he is known to have visited or would have had access to via this transport network. To avoid clutter and to increase clarity, the mining activity icons represent either a single mine or multiple mines located in the immediate area surrounding the icon. Indigenous data layers were also implemented to document Indigenous Heritage Sites and Native Title Determinations clipped to region and these are shown as shaded polygon layers.

To provide some context for the extent of Red Dog's travels, the state of Western Australia shown in figure 4.1 covers an area five times the size of Texas. Its eastern regions are desert, its west coast is bounded by the Indian Ocean, and its northernmost landscapes are dramatic, monsoonal, resource-rich, and remote. The state's economic and cultural hub lies in the arable land of the southwest, near the capital city of Perth, and a transient population of mine workers (known as fly-in-fly-out or FIFO workers), small Aboriginal communities, and isolated sheep and cattle stations characterize the sparsely populated northern areas. The Pilbara region through which Red Dog roamed has a population density of less than one person per 3.86 square miles (10 sq. km.). Situated just below the Kimberley region, which starred in Luhrmann's film *Australia*, the Pilbara is, as its regional council suggests, "Australia's paradox": rich in both natural and Indigenous heritage and mineral resources, it struggles between competing needs for preservation and development. Mining, and particularly iron ore, dominates the Pilbara economy to the extent that "the primary production of Western Australia accounts for approximately one-third of national merchandise exports" (Pick, Butler, and Dayaram 519).[6]

Mapping patterns of cultural production and narrative distribution in Western Australia reveals that this disproportionate relationship between

6. According to Pick, Butler, and Dayaram, the Pilbara "is one of the major sources of [national merchandise] exports producing 55 per cent of the state's major export commodities (minerals and energy) and accounting for virtually all crude oil, petroleum condensate, liquefied natural gas and natural gas production. The region is also the production centre for 97 per cent of national iron ore output" (519).

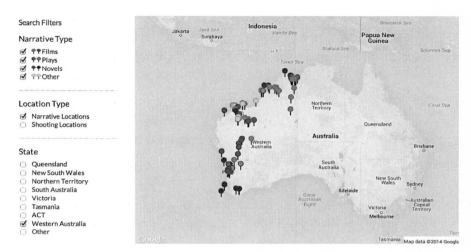

Figure 4.2. Map of films, plays, and novels set in Western Australia.
Source: Cultural Atlas of Australia.

the Pilbara and less prosperous but more populous neighboring regions
also extends to cultural representation (see figure 4.2). The northwest
of Western Australia—incorporating both the Pilbara and the Kimberley
regions—exerts a magnetic pull in Australian literature, film, and theater. Narratives such as *Dirt Music* (Tim Winton, 2001), *Bran Nue Dae*
(Rachel Perkins's 2009 film, based on Jimmy Chi's 1991 play), *Japanese
Story* (Sue Brooks, 2003), *Mad Bastards* (Brendan Fletcher, 2010), and
Rabbit-Proof Fence (Phillip Noyce's 2002 film, based on Doris Pilkington
Garimara's 1996 novel, *Follow the Rabbit-Proof Fence*) reveal distinctive
patterns of movement from the state's populous south toward its remote
and inhospitable north, a dominant spatial trajectory that has until now
gone unremarked in the scholarly literature. These travel narratives feature south-to-north trajectories that travel some one and a half thousand
miles from Perth into the far north. Disproportionate representations
of the northwest indicate that the Kimberley and Pilbara regions occupy
a significant place in the cultural imaginary. Indeed, nearly all of the narratives mentioned above focus on Indigenous belonging and narratives
of dispossession, yet *Red Dog* does not. While the film of *Red Dog* and its
source texts elide the Indigenous presence in the area, qualitative GIS and
an analysis of spatial history and narrative tropes reveal that, as we argue

below, Red Dog may be seen to function as a substitutive metonymic signifier of Indigeneity. By virtue of the association between Kelpies and dingoes and Red Dog's nomadic and friendly nature (a "dog for every-one"), he functions to confer a raceless (nonhuman) yet Indigenized sense of belonging to the Pilbara.

WESTERNS, SPATIAL EXPLORATION,

AND COLONIAL DEVELOPMENT

As a spatial story, the meaning of *Red Dog*'s narrative is framed and filtered by generic conventions that mobilize a set of expectations and assump-tions that tacitly legitimate particular forms of inclusion and exclusion. Here again the Western Australian setting is distinctive, for *Red Dog* shares what might be termed—following Ludwig Wittgenstein (1978) and, after him, genre theorists such as John Cawelti (1999)—a "family resemblance" to the western genre. Like the subgenre of "mining west-erns"[7] with which it is affiliated, *Red Dog* reworks staple elements of the western—namely, spatial exploration, use of the land and its resources, frontier communities, and the tension between "civilizing forces" and "wild" or "natural" impulses. Like the frontier narratives of the Australian North discussed in chapter 2, *Red Dog*'s representation of the Australian West as an "unsettled" and "uncivilized" frontier space ripe for expansion and progress, its emphasis on mobility, and its appropriation of structural, iconographic and ideological characteristics of the western genre bring to light fresh perspectives on the western as a mode of spatial storytelling at the same time as it offers insight into the story of the Pilbara.

Although the American West is well theorized as a space that is cen-tral to narratives of national identity, Australian westerns and the place of the West in Australian films have received relatively little scholarly attention. According to Peter Limbrick's perceptive study of Australian westerns, the omission of Indigenous people from westerns is not uncom-mon: "Many American westerns had, by the advent of sound, removed Indians entirely from the diegesis, their presence instead encoded into the

---

7. See Robin L. Murray and Joseph K. Heumann's ecocritical analysis of mining westerns including such films as *The Treasure of Sierra Madre* (John Huston, 1948) in their article, "Mining Westerns."

many spatialized conflicts between white settlers and the land, between East or West, or between different white ethnicities and their claims to various parts of land" (87). *Red Dog* does represent a strong spatialized distinction between Australia's urban centers and the North West, and the story focuses on a variety of "white ethnicities" in the Pilbara mining community. As the character Vanno (Arthur Angel), a homesick Italian miner, says, "From all the countries they come, for the money, for the work. From Poland, New Zealand, Ireland, Greece, Latvia, America, even Melbourne." Here the city of Melbourne in eastern Australia figures as a foreign country in relation to the Pilbara. The multicultural community includes people from across the nation and all over the world, yet there are no Aborigines, despite the fact that a demographic study titled *Indigenous People and the Pilbara Mining Boom* states that in 1981, which is when the earliest reliable census of Indigenous residents was performed—just two years after Red Dog's death—Aborigines made up nearly 10% of the Pilbara population (Taylor and Scambary 15). By the time the film *Red Dog* was in pre-production, this figure had risen to 15%, making the Pilbara the region with the third-highest population density of people with Indigenous backgrounds in Western Australia (Dept. of Aboriginal Affairs). The film is not a documentary and casting cannot be expected to provide proportional representation of every demographic, but the omission of Aborigines obscures their place in the Pilbara narrative and the myth of the West that it constructs. Even though disputes about resource acquisition and land use are excluded from the frame, the spatial history of the Pilbara is central to Red Dog's story and to establishing the film's "family resemblance" to the western genre. It is this aspect to which we now turn.

As ecomedia scholar Pat Brereton has explained, spatial exploration is central to the western genre's structure:

> The uses and abuses of landscape provide the feeding ground for much narrative construction and visual exposition. While there is often little explicit reference to the geo-politics of ecology, the genre nevertheless addresses the right of the human species to own and control the landscape, together with what this means for social organization. (35)[8]

8. A similar point about the centrality of the genre's setting is made in Deborah Carmichael's 2006 anthology *The Landscape of Hollywood Westerns*.

In *Red Dog* the mining infrastructure visibly dominates virtually every aspect of the narrative, but the significance to the story of living in a frontier community and working on the land is articulated most clearly in the scene in which the miners discuss the values that define the Pilbara and spontaneously join together in singing a number by a band fittingly called The Dingoes. At this point in the story the mining community rejects its colonial heritage by refusing to erect a statue of the English explorer William Dampier, for whom the town of Dampier was named and who is disparagingly referred to as "a pirate" in Thomson's poem. Instead, the community votes for a statue to commemorate Red Dog, arguing that he "represents the Pilbara in all of us." The bronze statue of Red Dog referred to in the film was in fact erected in 1980 and still stands at the entrance to Dampier.

A rowdy chorus of the song "Way out West" functions to celebrate the mining community following this proclamation that Red Dog embodies the character of the Pilbara:

> Way out West where the rain don't fall
> Got a job with a company digging for ore[9]
> Just to make some change
> Living and working on the land.

The centrality of setting to defining the western genre and the character of the people who live "way out west" is so crucial that media geographer Stefan Zimmermann refers to westerns as a "geographical film genre"[10] defined by components including "the rural setting, the importance of landscape, and the immediacy of social commentary" (136).[11]

---

9. With permission from The Dingoes, the filmmakers altered the lyrics from "Got a job with a company drilling for oil" to "digging for ore." According to a note on the film's soundtrack CD, the band prefers the new lyrics because they capture a sense of place.

10. Limbrick identifies the western as a genre in which "space and landscape are central narrative concerns" (88). Edward Buscombe has also researched the history of landscape in the western genre in "Inventing Monument Valley."

11. Zimmermann traces the Australian western's origins to bushranger films, claiming *The Story of the Kelly Gang* (Charles Tait, 1906) marked "the beginning of the cinematic Western genre"; he goes on to argue that significant elements of the Kelly myth and of Australian national identity are "based upon a Western narrative" (139). By

In her discussion of conflict between native American Indians' notions of emplacement versus the settler-colonial concept of land as property in westerns, Cynthia-Lou Coleman observes that "place is infused with multiple meanings: one view emerging from the deeply interwoven relationship of community to location, and another marked by legal contract and ownership of a commodity. The construction of place that unfolds in cinema aptly illustrates the deep division between these epistemologies" (279). If the film *Red Dog* is understood to function in some respects like an Australian western, it appears that Hamersley Iron is positioned in the settler colonial role—it is Hamersley that is said to "own" the town of Dampier, and it is Hamersley that commissions the statue of William Dampier. According to the logic of the binary oppositions that structure the western genre,[12] this subtly functions to *indigenize* the multicultural mineworkers and their mascot, Red Dog. Red Dog is explicitly affiliated with nomadic Aborigines when he is described as "going walkabout" (de Bernières 9).[13] Thus, Red Dog is implicitly aligned with both the mining community and Indigenous culture even though, as we have noted above and as Thomson points out in his poem, Aborigines are not present in the narrative.

Limbrick claims that in the Australian western *Eureka Stockade* (Harry Watt, 1949), native animals "do the metonymic work of standing in for both the Australian bush and for the invisible Indigenous humans" (87). Since Red Dog's wandering habits are compared with the tradition of "walkabout" and since he also physically resembles the closest thing to an Australian native dog, the ochre-colored dingo, he has a strong affiliation with inhabitants of the Pilbara that predate Western settlement by

contrast, Bill Routt argues Australian bushranger films developed somewhat earlier than and, initially, quite independently of American westerns. In this sense they should not be considered a derivative genre, though Routt does acknowledge the relationship of more recent bushranger films such as *Mad Dog Morgan* (Philippe Mora, 1976) to classic westerns. See also Grayson Cooke's "Whither the Australian Western?"

12. Structural accounts of the western frequently note the opposition of civilization and savagery, culture and nature, colonizers and colonized peoples. See, for instance, influential research by Jim Kitses and Will Wright.

13. Similarly, Parker argues, "Like Aborigines, dingoes are semi-nomadic" (164).

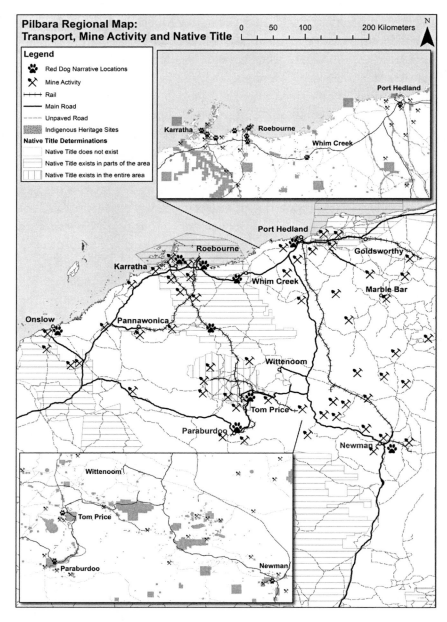

Figure 4.3. Map of Red Dog locations, Native Title, and mine activity in the Pilbara region. Source: Jane Stadler and Luke Houghton.

many thousands of years.[14] According to Merryl Ann Parker, the figure of the roaming wild dog is important in Aboriginal cosmology and in the northwest of Western Australia the myth of the dingo is a travel story that involves chasing an emu over a large tract of country (150–56). The dingoes "act as Dreaming 'surveyors' for the Walmadjeri people, trotting around the Balgo area, locating, describing and naming the water sources, compiling a meticulous myth/map" (Parker 156).

As documented in figure 4.3 and noted in the introduction to this chapter, the Dampier region in the Pilbara has one of the richest petroglyph sites in Australia and is of considerable cultural heritage significance: "According to the local Aboriginal belief system, petroglyphs are permanent signs left by Ancestral beings. As the initiators of Aboriginal Law, these Ancestral beings left designs in the rocks as records both of their own existence and as evidence of the Law they formulated" (Vinnicombe 13). In the Roebourne and Port Hedland region, "the petroglyphs were but a small part of an extensive mythical travel line"; furthermore, as noted in the research Kingsley Palmer conducted during Red Dog's lifetime, the art is believed to have been created not by humans but by ancestors in the Dreamtime to educate or inform people in later years ("Myth" 42). Perhaps not coincidentally, one of Palmer's Indigenous informants was a "dogger," meaning that he baited and trapped dingoes profession-

---

14. According to the Western Australian Dingo Association: "Today the dingo's resting place is known as dog rock. The emu can still be seen lying on its stomach if you visit Meekatharra at a place known as Gabinintha or Yagoongoo. Sometimes when the wildflowers bloom in red and yellow you can see the emu's fat and blood below Yagoongoo hill. But most of the emu's fat turned into gold and was named Kulkulli. Kulkulli has been mined of its gold now, but that is the place where the giant dingo travelled leaving behind the emu's fat." The Warrigal is a mythical shapeshifting dingo creature that takes human-dog form and is known by different names in various language groups. There are over 50 dingo myths originating in the Western Desert (see *Dingo Makes Us Human* [2000] and *Wild Dog Dreaming* [2011] by Deborah Bird Rose, and Ronald Berndt and Catherine Berndt's *The Speaking Land* [1989]). According to Parker, "The dingo played an important role in ancient Aboriginal myths. It appeared in creative [creation] myths as a Dreaming ancestor, giving birth to the first people making rivers and scratching out waterholes. In social myths it taught people how to live harmoniously within their own group and with strangers. It had a role in warning myths, advising people to treat its wildness with caution and respect. Finally it dealt with death, rejecting an offer of eternal life for itself and all its human descendants" (133).

ally to prevent depredation of stock on stations in the Pilbara region. In this instance the informant's knowledge of sacred Aboriginal sites maps directly onto his knowledge of the prevalence and movement of dingoes throughout the region: "Informant C. Kurima [was] born at Deepdale Station, and moved to nearby stations where he worked until 1953 when he became a Government dogger. He now works at this job, which takes him to remote places in the bush, and during his extensive travels he has come across many Aboriginal sites" (Palmer, "Petroglyphs" 159). Disturbingly, a contemporaneous report "Water and the Indigenous People in the Pilbara" asserts that in the era of the Native Welfare Act, Aborigines had to obtain a license to gain citizenship rights or even to drink in bars and public places, and this was often referred to in derogatory terms as "a dog license" (Barber and Jackson 33). Such prejudices may go some way to explaining the exclusion of Indigenous people from the various versions of the Red Dog story. While native animals function as a totemic "stand in" for Indigenous people and the "dog license" acts as a derogatory form of exclusion in ways that are specific to the Pilbara, these issues can be understood in relation to the displacement of Indigenous peoples that is characteristic of westerns and they are linked to the logic of colonial expansion and development that marks the genre.

As Enzo Virili, project engineer for Dampier Salt between 1972 and 1976, notes, the 1960s was the beginning of "an intense time of industrial development in the region" and prior to this time, "few white men had ever set foot on the islands of the Dampier Archipelago" (6).[15] The Western Australian government signed an export agreement with Japan when Dampier was developed as a port, at which point the "tide of development could not be turned" despite growing awareness of the mythological significance of the rock art in the region (Virili 6). As Patricia Vinnicombe's research shows, "in 1966 Hamersley Iron Pty Ltd commenced iron ore

15. Virili sought to preserve the rock art but his reports were edited and his recommendations were not taken up, according to Vinnicombe (7). Dampier Island is now known as the Burrup Peninsula and is connected to the mainland by a bridge and covered by roads serving the Dampier Salt solar operation. These are the same haulage roads on which Red Dog used to hitchhike, as seen in the film. These haulage roads from Dampier Saltworks damaged historical Aboriginal middens and cut through areas of Indigenous cultural significance (Virili 17).

production at Mt Tom Price and exported its first shipment of iron ore to Japan. To support mining interests, Dampier township was developed on the Burrup and in 1967, the Dampier solar salt fields were established there as a result of increased demand for industrial salt by the Japanese chemical industry" (6). Vinnicombe goes on to indicate that the Indigenous rock art sites remained largely undisturbed until the mid-1960s but by the 1970s vandals had destroyed or defaced Aboriginal art galleries at numerous sites, including the Rio Tinto Gorge and the Dampier power station site (7).

When mineral exploration began in the region in 1971, the dingo myth was unsuccessfully invoked to prevent mining and development that would affect sacred sites (Parker 167). Ironically, the dingo's most important role in the Indigenous mythology of the region "is as a model or a benchmark for the care of the environment" (Parker 133). As figure 4.3 demonstrates, Red Dog retraces the steps of the mythical dingo, most probably visiting some of the sacred sites on the dingo Dreaming trail that have now been overwritten by mine sites. In 1978, plans to mine natural gas off the North West Shelf of the Western Australian coast resulted in a detailed environmental assessment and survey work by the Department of Aboriginal Sites being carried out on behalf of Woodside Petroleum Development Pty Ltd. (Vinnicombe 8). Numerous sacred sites were found at Searipple Passage at the northern end of the Peninsula, so Woodside decided on Withnell Bay/King Bay further south as the site for the gas treatment plant. However, the Withnell/King Bay region was also rich in cultural significance to the Aboriginal people, and as the development progressed, "720 sites were documented in the preferred southern lease area. Of these, 349 were destroyed to make way for development, 56 were partially destroyed and the remaining 315 sites that were on the periphery of the construction areas remained preserved in situ" (Vinnicombe 8).

We have argued that by bridging the divide between nature and culture through his habit of "going walkabout" (de Bernières 9) and his affinity with the land and its peoples, Red Dog connects different factions of the Pilbara community and occupies an apparently neutral ideological position that provides a comfortable point of identification as he traverses a landscape dominated by the mining industry. In terms of the relationship between cultural narratives, capital, and geography, the story of Red

Dog, his entire history, is bound to mining and is occasioned by it. Red Dog was born at Paraburdoo within a year of the town's establishment by Hamersley Iron; he then moved to Hamersley Iron's port town of Dampier—again within a year of its establishment. This relationship between the story of Red Dog and the story of mining in the Pilbara is further compounded by the fact that Rio Tinto, the asset manager of Hamersley Iron, was a major sponsor of the *Red Dog* film production. In 1952 Australian mining magnate Lang Hancock was forced by poor visibility to fly low over the Hamersley Ranges just north of Paraburdoo, where the Tom Price mine would later be built. In telling his "discovery" story, Hancock said he noticed that walls of a gorge "looked to [him] to be solid iron" and, from the "rusty looking colour of it," appeared to be "oxidised iron" (McRobert). At the time, Hancock's hands were tied because the Australian Government had placed an embargo on all iron ore exports. It took a full decade for Hancock to lobby for this embargo to be lifted so he could begin to mine the area. Hancock brought in Rio Tinto in the early 1960s to form what would become Hamersley Iron. In the mid-1960s, the Western Australian government signed an export agreement with Japan, and the Dampier Archipelago was developed as a port despite growing awareness of the significance of Indigenous culture and rock art in the region:

> In 1966 Hamersley Iron Pty Ltd commenced iron ore production at Mt Tom Price and exported its first shipment of iron ore to Japan. To support mining interests, Dampier township was developed on the Burrup Peninsula and in 1967, the Dampier solar salt fields were established there as a result of increased demand for industrial salt by the Japanese chemical industry. (Vinnicombe 6)

Although questions have been raised about whether the film *Red Dog* was a puff-piece for the mining industry at a time when debates about carbon trading and mining super taxes figured prominently in the media, most critics have tended toward accepting that the film is not intentional propaganda. The film's producer, Nelson Woss, has stated in interviews that the film could not have been made in Australia and in Pilbara locations without the financial and infrastructural support of Rio Tinto. In Woss's account, it was he who did the courting, persuading Rio Tinto that it was a movie about a much-loved dog and not about the mining industry, but that it "would show the rest of the country what they were doing"

(Maddox). However, what the film *Red Dog* shows of the activities of the mining industry in the Pilbara is only a small part of the overall picture. For example, in addition to the known violation of Indigenous sacred sites on the Dampier Peninsula and surrounding land, Aboriginal heritage research and consultation showed that Hancock Prospecting's major Hope Downs mining project infringed on the Malea Indigenous rock shelter 75 kilometers northwest of Newman in Western Australia, which "was found to contain a significant depth of cultural deposit" (Edwards and Murphy 44). Carbon dating of artifacts excavated from this site show "evidence for the presence of Aboriginal groups in the Pilbara Uplands between 17,900 and 9870 BP" (Edwards and Murphy 45).

In *Spaces of Capital,* geographer David Harvey seeks to understand "the dialectical relationship between forms of geographical knowledge and socioeconomic and ecological development" (209). As Harvey has claimed, and as this chapter has demonstrated, the media and other industries such as tourism produce geographical knowledge in that they function as institutions that actively create, teach, and perpetuate geographical discourses (*Spaces* 209).[16] In the case of *Red Dog,* the mining industry has been complicit in this production of geographical knowledge, too, and the economic interests of filmmakers and mining magnates have influenced how the land and its populace are represented. In his analysis of the relationship between resources, population, and ideology, Harvey makes the point that "a critical geography might go so far as to challenge forms of political-economic power, marked by hyper-development, spiraling social inequalities, and multiple signs of environmental degradation" (Harvey, *Spaces* 208). Here, our geocritical analysis of contemporary narratives has attempted to perform some of the work that Harvey advocates in his "critical geography" approach by tracing how political and economic power travels through the production of cultural texts and the geographical knowledge they convey. Our analysis has found that, despite the wealth generated by the resources of the land, the influx of industry supported by neo-liberal policy has had a dramatic effect on Pilbara communities.

16. As Tilley points out, "To understand a landscape truly it must be felt, but to convey some of this feeling to others it has to be talked about, recounted, or written and depicted" (31).

As David Pick and his colleagues have pointed out, "rather than reaping the benefits of the wealth being generated in the region," many residents of the Pilbara, and particularly its Indigenous residents, "experience social breakdown and unmet social needs, and the local democratic institutions are weak and ineffective" (Pick, Butler, and Dayaram 516).

This complex relationship between the Red Dog story, its production as a film, and the iron-ore mining industry of the Pilbara is, we argue, nowhere more evident than in the depiction of mobility. All the trips Red Dog takes are linked to the mining industry: hitching rides on ore trains and ships, on Hamersley Iron buses, and in or on the utility vehicles, cars, motorcycles, planes, and caravans of workers associated with the mining towns.

Another aspect of *Red Dog*'s depiction of mobility that speaks to current debates about transient FIFO workers in the resource sector and the impact this has on isolated, regional communities. In a passage that contains the sole, past-tense, acknowledgment of Australian Aborigines in his novel, de Bernières describes the impact of mining on Dampier's demography:

> The town was so full of lonely men. There had been a few aborigines and even fewer white people there before the iron ore companies and the salt company had moved in, but just recently a massive and rapid development had begun to take place. New docks were constructed, new roads, new houses for the workers, a new railway and a new airport. In order to build all this hundreds of men had arrived from all corners of the world, bringing nothing with them but their physical strength, their optimism and their memories of distant homes. (21)

The Pilbara population is characteristically transient, which is in part due to the weather and the remote location. The film highlights a number of different levels of mobility. The most dominant level is that of Red Dog's travels, but there is also the mobility of an itinerant, largely migrant mining workforce, along with the mechanized transport represented in the film. Less immediately apparent but very much a part of the film's emphasis on mobility is the mobility of the spectator's gaze, which is facilitated by technologies and vehicles that are not seen in the film. Film audiences vicariously experience the mobility of Red Dog and, like Red Dog himself, the audience's movement through the Pilbara is in turn facilitated by industry. *Red Dog* and 2003's *Japanese Story* are two films that directly represent travel linked to the resources boom. Increasingly, the Western Australian mining industry is funding films set in the Pilbara and Kimberley regions, such as 2010's *Mad Bastards,* and 2012's *Satellite Boy,* both of which foreground contemporary Indigenous issues. The vehicle-mounted traveling shots that feature so prominently in *Red Dog* synthesize technologies of vision and technologies of transportation to the extent that, as Ruoff has argued in relation to journey films more generally, the film functions as an audiovisual vehicle for constructing and touring space. In this sense cinema produces spatial experience even as it showcases time, space, and motion. *Red Dog* transports the audience to the locations presented on screen; similarly, trains, planes, cars, boats, and helicopters can be understood as modes of representation because audiences and travelers have become so habituated to viewing landscapes framed by the windscreen of a moving vehicle.[17]

Woss, *Red Dog*'s producer, was at pains not to be seen as part of the FIFO problem, stating that he really wanted to embed the production in the Pilbara region and work with "the companies that were part of the story" (Bodey). The Kimberley and the Pilbara populations are typically highly mobile, in part due to the weather and the remote location. Transience and community have coexisted in the region dating back to nomadic Aboriginal life (walkabout) and the establishment of seasonal settler-colonial stock routes (shearers and drovers were less likely to live in the region than to travel through it in mustering season). As Britta Kuhlenbeck observes of the Pilbara landscape:

> Historical remnants or ghost towns are an index of transition or, perhaps, transience. They serve as a reminder of the ephemeral nature of human dwellings and human beings. Perhaps the "transient" architecture (dongas, portable homes, caravans) and itinerant attitude of miners working in the Pilbara today are an acknowledgment of this history. (48)

These traditional, industrial, and touristic travel practices produce geographical discourses in ways that supplement the spatial narratives of maps, novels, and films for, as Harvey notes, the state, supranational in-

17. The authors are grateful to John Edmond for the reference to Jeffrey Ruoff and for discussions of this point.

stitutions, commerce and corporations, educational institutions, research, and also media and tourism industries are prolific sources of geographic knowledge and the "aesthetic and emotive" impact of the landscape discourses that such industries generate is based on highly selective images and narratives of the environment (*Spaces* 215–16). In information produced by these industries, "commercial requirements introduce a bias towards the immediate, the spectacular, the aesthetically acceptable" (Harvey, *Spaces* 216), which is one reason that the slow-moving and unattractive process of territorial disputes and Native Title claims do not appear even in narratives such as Red Dog that are concerned with the mining industry and the way the land shapes and is shaped by the residents of the Pilbara.

In his influential research on emotional geographies, John Urry argues that the concept of landscape "emphasises leisure, relaxation and the visual consumption of place especially by those 'touring'" (77). While this neglects the importance of other dimensions of and gazes at landscape such as exploration, military strategy, or private ownership of real estate boasting city views or ocean vistas, it does capture an important aspect noted in scholarly literature on travel narratives, which is the transformation of landscape into a spectacle and a commodity (see Wulff). Urry's work about the centrality of visuality and mediated or virtual mobility to the experience of place has important implications for an assessment of the role film plays in the emotional associations with the Pilbara landscape and the concept of belonging. The experience of being caught between immobility in the cinema and vicarious mobility within the screen space is similar to what Susan Best terms the "traveller's sensibility, or mode of being 'between locations,'" which "allows a particular kind of emplacement—what Edward Casey calls 'dwelling on route, that is dwelling-as-wandering'" (67). As we have demonstrated, travel films such as *Red Dog* can aid outsiders to come to terms with the Australian landscape and find their place within it by following the protagonists' travels through the strange land and GIS technologies can play a vital role in geovisualizing these narrative journeys and locating them in the landscape. As Urry puts it, "It seems that almost all places are 'toured' and the pleasures of place derive at least in part from the emotions involved in visual consumption of place" (82). Following Urry, we note that the chief conduit for the affective charge of the film is the spectacle of the landscape itself, although perceptions of landscape are communicated through dynamic traveling shots underscored by music, lyrics, and maps that tell the story of the land and also by the spectator's "Indigenized" affiliation with the nomadic protagonist who tours this landscape and belongs to it—Red Dog.

To conclude, the journeys figuring within cultural narratives can be understood as the "discursive articulation of a spatializing practice" (Tilley 32). *Red Dog* exemplifies in its story, its production, and its history, the interpenetration of culture, capital, and geography. As Harvey has claimed and as our analysis has shown, the media, the narrative arts, and the cultural industries more broadly produce geographical knowledge (*Spaces* 209). Mapping Red Dog's story renders these spatial histories and cultural relationships more visible, revealing the nation's troubled cultural and geographic landscape. *Red Dog* provides a complex and interesting perspective on the relationships between mobility, industry, and human and natural resources in Australia's West from the 1970s to the present. The film's production is bound up with the Pilbara mining industry, and reflective of an increasing investment by the resources sector in the cultural sector. *Red Dog* is, this chapter has argued, in many ways the exemplary text to show just how intertwined the mining and cultural industries are becoming, for the history of Red Dog tracks so closely the history of mining in the Pilbara and illustrates so vividly the mobilities that characterize the Australian West.

This chapter has contended that mapping cultural narratives onto the physical landscape can make visible, in cultural and geopolitical terms, the imprint of settler colonialism on the Australian land and its people. We have examined this spatial history as it is expressed through the geographic and social mobility that travel narratives record, and by using GIS map layers, Indigenous land claims data, and census information to document the corresponding changes to the landscape—the trade and transport corridors, fences, settlements, mine sites, and power lines that "make colonial expansion visible" (Banivanua Mar and Edmonds 2). In doing so, we have shown that mapping travel narratives is a powerful way of revealing the ongoing process of cultural inscription of the landscape. Colonization entails the "textualization" of the land, which "occurred in large part by way of the systematic mapping and naming—by explorers and geographers of these 'new' territories—of landforms, waterways, and white townships" (Mitchell, *Cartographic* 58). This process rests on the assumption that the land being explored is a "terra nullius," a territory that belongs to no one and is conceptualized as a tabula rasa, a blank slate with no names, pathways, maps, social groups, or geocultural formations of its own. This misconception and misappropriation of the Australian landscape has had enduring political ramifications that can be traced in what popular cultural texts such as *Red Dog* elide, as Thomson pointedly notes in his poem "Australia Is a Film about a Red Dog."

5

TERRA INCOGNITA

Mapping the Uncertain and the Unknown

The concept of terra incognita—unknown land—occupies a significant place in the Australian spatial imaginary. The notion that an antipodean landmass—a "great south land"—lay undiscovered (by the West, at least) in the unmapped emptiness below the known world fired the imaginations of philosophers, geographers, and explorers for some two thousand years before Europeans first made landfall on Australian coasts. According to Paul Arthur:

> The concept of the antipodes was born out of an ancient geographical theory of balance. A giant southern continent (one far larger than the Australian landmass) featured in the classical imagination as early as the fifth century BC. Greek thinkers, including Pythagoras, Aristotle, and later Pomponius Mela and Ptolemy, supported the belief that the earth was spherical and that a great south land must exist to balance those of the northern hemisphere. These were theories that formed a basis for Renaissance geographical thought. ("Antipodean" 1864)

Integral to the Renaissance concept of terra incognita was the "rediscovery" of Ptolemy's second-century *Cosmographia,* or *Geography,* in the early fifteenth century.[1] The *Geography,* which hypothesized the existence of a southern continent, had been lost to the West for over a thousand years. Its translation into Latin in 1409 added further impetus to the fifteenth-

1. See Mitchell, *Cartographic* 34–36.

century Voyages of Discovery that sought to fill in the blank spaces on the world map, which were by now being labeled *terra incognita*.

As Bronwen Douglas explains, "The idea of an antipodean *terra incognita* took on new life during the fifteenth-century Renaissance with the publication of old maps in novel printed formats. So, on the *mappa mundi* produced for the 1482 edition of Ptolemy's *Cosmographia*, a landlocked 'Indian Sea' is enclosed to the south by '*terra incognita*'" (181). Moreover, following the "making-known" of the New World in the late fifteenth century, only one significant terra incognita remained,[2] and, as William J. Lines writes, "During the sixteenth and seventeenth centuries Renaissance cartographers drew the land boundaries for a continent in the south temperate zone and affixed the name *Terra Australis Incognita*—the unknown south land" (15). Invoking spatial theory as a tool for rereading Australian history in order to better understand the ways in which the nation represents itself to itself, John O'Carroll goes some way to tracing the etiology of conceptions of the Australian landmass before European settlement in 1788. O'Carroll identifies a number of "problematic cultural imaginings" that characterized early European thought and were projected onto the continent's physical and symbolic landscape, which was variously imagined—"as 'arse-ended,' as land upside-down, as bad experience, as paradisal tourist space, as site of an identity crisis" (13).

Before Australia was encountered as spatial reality, it was not only imagined, as we have argued throughout this book, it was imaginatively configured as something of a utopian space. The concept of utopia (and of island utopias, specifically) can be traced to Thomas More, whose "Platonic" work was, in turn "inspired formally by ancient Greek philosophy and politics" (O'Carroll 21). More's Platonism, according to O'Carroll, constructs a "geography of encirclement" that is "profoundly binary in character and [that] makes the island both the ground of reality on the one

2. In his 1507 map, Martin Waldseemüller was the first to label the newly mapped New World with the name "America." By 1513, however, in his *Tabula terre nova*, Waldseemüller had replaced "America" with "Terra Incognita," most likely, as Seymour I. Schwartz puts it, because he had "gained an appreciation that Columbus rather than Vespucci was the true discoverer of the South American continent" (Schwartz 273; cf. Douglas 184).

hand, and its speculative paradise on the other" (21). When Renaissance cartographers conjoined the notions of *terra incognita* and *terra australis,*[3] they began a search for a continent to which they were already attributing a "host of signifiers: oddity, difference, distance, paradise" configured in binary terms, and they were thus imagining into being and transferring to the actual colony once it was founded "a two thousand year history" (O'Carroll 23). Since *terra australis incognita* had been dichotomously imagined as utopian space, and as strange and dangerous space, when it was finally "discovered" by Europeans it was a crushing disappointment (barren, hot, infertile, inhospitable), yet it was also filled with strange plants and animals that confirmed its oddness and "topsy-turviness."

In the introduction to this book we charted the spatial history of Australia as it has been explored by academics in the fields of literary geography and film geography and those engaged in spatial enquiry in Australian literary, film, and theater studies. Subsequent chapters have investigated how authors, filmmakers, and playwrights have imagined Australia's landscape and brought it into being in narrative fiction, populating the unknown land with stories. As Ross Gibson argues, the focus on landscape in the nation's narrative fiction can be understood to arise from the fact that Australia is only recently colonized and storytelling is a way of making the land "ours," staking a claim:

> Every plot of earth, every spoke of Spinifex hasn't accrued a story, hasn't yet become a sign in the arbitrary system of meaning which is history. To white sensibility most of Australia is empty space, devoid of inhabitants, architecture, artefacts. It hasn't been incorporated into the symbolic order, except as a signifier of emptiness, a *tabula rasa*, a sublime structuring void louring over all Australian culture. ("Camera" 210–11)

Our final chapter speaks to this history, recognizing that *terra incognita* has become a trope in itself in Australian narrative fiction, as exemplified by stories that take place in the "louring void" of the Northern Terri-

---

3. Referring to unknown lands as "incognita" goes back further than the phrase "terra australis." Douglas identifies a map from c. 940 that "depicts a southern continent annotated as: '*Deserta terra vicina solida ardore incognita nobis*' ('a deserted neighbouring land, hardened by heat, unknown to us')" (181–82). The earliest mention of "terra australis" on a map is thought to be in 1523, after the Magellanic voyages (Douglas 186).

tory's central deserts and that bring central Australia into being within the broader cultural imaginary. Australia's geography may now be mapped, under surveillance by satellites, and rendered navigable by GIS, yet the continent's cultural narratives contain ongoing and contemporary manifestations of terra incognita and this, in turn, presents certain cartographic challenges to the narrative geographer.

This chapter tackles the technical and conceptual difficulties and the spatial politics of mapping fictionally uncertain spaces. Barbara Piatti's and Anne-Kathrin Reuschel's work with the *Literary Atlas of Europe* identifies the problems inherent in mapping totally imaginary settings, regions with nebulous boundaries and unlocalized or generic spaces—stories that are set "somewhere" but not some *place*. Sometimes there is a reason why authors seek ambiguity and anonymity for the places they represent.[4] They therefore create symbolic and metonymic spaces that the reader or viewer has to decode and which the geocritic or cultural cartographer then has to approximate or guess at in order to map. In this chapter, we explore these digital mapping challenges in relation to key Australian mythic or symbolic spaces depicted in representative films and plays. The "Dead Heart" is one such broad mythic terrain that has been evoked sufficiently frequently across all three narrative forms over time as to constitute a national geographic imaginary landscape located in the Central Australian desert. How do you map a mythic landscape? What are its boundaries? In order to achieve this we will begin by examining contemporary scholarly

---

4. In the Australian example, Thea Astley uses some references to real places such as Cooktown and Townsville in Far North Queensland in her novel *It's Raining in Mango* (1989), but other towns—such as the eponymous one, which is a substitute for the real rainforest town of Kuranda—are anonymized. Cairns becomes Reeftown, and Mareeba becomes Tobaccotown, reflecting their predominant agricultural-geophysical associations. The novel draws on a lot of historical research, but the towns' titles remain as largely metonymic signifiers of their chief reasons for existing—they become "imagined landscapes" in a very literal sense. In Xavier Herbert's novel *Capricornia* (1938), a similar regime of place name substitution takes place, but names here are less tethered to metonymic references. Whilst the name "Batman" makes political sense for Melbourne— John Batman was an historical figure in colonial Melbourne—"Port Zodiac" is a more prosaic substitute for Port Darwin, as the Northern Territory's capital was then known. Perhaps in both authors' cases anonymity allows for more liberal fictionalization of events that take place in small settlements in novels where the lines between historical veracity and fictive example sometimes blur.

readings of Australian desert space (in general) and Central Australia (in particular) to set up a critical framework for reading the films *The Adventures of Priscilla, Queen of the Desert* (Stephan Elliott, 1994) and *Samson and Delilah* (Warwick Thornton, 2009) and plays *Still Angela* (Jenny Kemp, 2002), *Namatjira* (Scott Rankin, 2011) and *Head Full of Love* (Alana Valentine, 2012).

In chapter 2, we discussed the mythic properties and cultural functions of the Australian "Deep North," drawing parallels to similar marginalized zones or, as David R. Jansson would describe them, "internal orients" in Canada and the United States in order to demonstrate how a cultural atlas can produce results that may surprise the humanities scholar in terms of depth and breadth of representation. In the first part of this chapter, we pick up again on this notion of national myth-making and the mapping of iconic landscapes and regions, but this time we do so in order to explore some of the challenges inherent in naming a space a "cultural landscape" and to point out the tensions inherent in marrying (in this case) Indigenous and non-Indigenous ways of knowing (and troping) iconic Australian space.[5]

One of the critical concepts that will be foundational to this chapter and its discussion of the tensions between Western and Indigenous ways of conceptualizing, naming, using, and mapping land is Ken Gelder and Jane Jacobs's notion of an "uncanny" Australia. According to Gelder and Jacobs, postcolonialism is frequently coupled with an underlying anxiety that erupts at critical points at which the nation feels itself to be under threat from a perceived hostile Indigenous other that seeks to contest

---

5. By *non-Indigenous* we refer here to the majority population, acknowledging that terms such as *white, European,* and *Western* are inadequate to describe the cultural diversity of Australian settler communities over the two hundred and twenty-plus years of colonial and postcolonial occupation, excluding as they do the Asian and Pacific Island demographics that have always composed substantial proportions of the Australian population. When we do default to these sorts of standard descriptors of majority population, we do so with an awareness of their limitations. The Australian Bureau of Statistics estimates that in 2011 there were 669,881 Aboriginal people living in Australia, representing just 3 percent of the total population of 21,670,143 ("Estimates"). The most common non-Indigenous ancestries in this census period were English 25.9 percent, Irish 7.5 percent, Scottish 6.4 percent, and Italian 3.3 percent. Interestingly, 25.4 percent of those surveyed in the nationwide audit in 2011 expressed their ancestry as "Australian."

(white) Australian access to and occupation of space and place. In their 1995 article, "Uncanny Australia," Gelder and Jacobs cite the 1992 Australian High Court decision resulting in the Native Title Act 1993—or the Mabo decision, as it became known—as one key recent instance of such an intensification of national anxiety. Gelder and Jacobs explain:

> *Terra nullius,* the founding fantasy of modern Australian nationhood, was rejected by this ruling and Aborigines were given the opportunity to make claims over a much wider range of lands than had previously been provided for under existing land rights legislation. The rejection of *terra nullius* was certainly read by some as the moment when *all* (or at least, "too much") of Australia might become available for Aboriginal reclamation. (150)[6]

Gelder and Jacobs use the Freudian psychoanalytic term *uncanny* to account for this broad cultural anxiety of having something familiar (one's home, one's land, one's sense of self as it is defined in connection with this spatial attachment) being rendered suddenly simultaneously *un*familiar (by virtue of it belonging, or being claimed by, the other). An "uncanny Australia," then, according to Gelder and Jacobs's logic, is one that operates simultaneously as "ours" and "theirs" yet which resists "conventional, colonial distinctions between self and other, here and there, mine and yours" (151). The nation's homogeneity is subsequently troubled by a range of complex postcolonial narratives in which simplistic binary definitions of, and relations to, space and place are challenged by the reality of dynamic multicultural co-existence and co-occupation. We turn now to a discussion of a key metonymic cultural landscape—the Australian "Center."

A HISTORY OF AUSTRALIAN DESERT SPACE
AND THE NATION'S CENTER

"In the 1920s and 1930s," Michael Cathcart writes, "if you had asked white Australians what geographical feature lay at the *Centre* of Australia, no

---

6. See also Gelder and Jacobs's elaboration of this topic in their 1998 book, *Uncanny Australia.*

7. For those unfamiliar with Australian geography, Ayers Rock is a huge red sandstone rock formation named for Sir Henry Ayers and later reverting to its indigenous

coast-dweller would have replied Ayers Rock [Uluru]" (214).[7] Lake Eyre was, in fact, long considered the continent's geophysical and symbolic Center. Cathcart cites this act of national figurative (mis)placement as having its origins in earlier vanquished longings for an inland sea. J. W. Gregory coined the phrase "Dead Heart" in 1906 to describe the Lake Eyre basin, the nomenclature sealing what Cathcart describes as "the disappointment of a great colonial dream. Lake Eyre was a withered parody of Sturt's 'inland sea.' It was a surrender to 'the death-like silence' which had so appalled explorers and settlers in the second half of the nineteenth century" (J. Gregory, qtd. in Cathcart 214).

Roslynn Haynes (*Seeking*) and Libby Robin ("Accounting"; *How*) concur with the notion of disappointment being a kind of founding (European) trope of Central Australian desert space. By combining this disappointment with the nation's central "emptiness"—as perpetuated by the foundational national *terra nullius* principle—Australia's inland became a symbol of European failure to conquer and inscribe its internal territory in the same system of Western values as it had on the southern and eastern littoral fringes. As Robin puts it:

> The empty interior of Australia awaited wisdom from its seafaring cities for much of the colonial, pastoral past. Its "emptiness" was essential to the *terra nullius* myth. And apart from the country adjacent to the coast and the ports—the "inside country," the desert country of the Outback was beyond the nation's pastoral identity. ("Accounting" 3–4)[8]

This inability on the part of Anglo-Celtic Australia to successfully utilize or cultivate (much less populate) the arid interior contributed significantly to the founding trope of disappointment motivating the construction of the "Empty Center" myth, and stands in stark contrast to, say, the westward push of the United States' early colonial settlement process. Where the great, fertile Mississippi River and its tributaries cut a swathe

name, Uluru. It is located some 200 miles/330 kilometers southwest of Alice Springs; Lake Eyre (known as Kati Thanda to the Indigenous population) is a 5,903-square-mile/9,500-kilometer-squared salt lake located below sea level in the northern reaches of South Australia. Both lie considerably south of the geographic center of the continent—though Uluru is considerably closer to the mark than Lake Eyre.

8. See also Robin's *How a Continent Created a Nation*.

through the heart of what was to become the United States of America, fantasies of a life-sustaining inland sea came to naught in Australia's case. The "Dead Heart" symbolism arguably disguised a sense of masculinist embarrassment at having failed to conquer the nation's vast inland spaces. Writers and explorers, and a tranche of other contributors to national myth-making praxis—artists, politicians, missionaries, pastoralists, and bush dwellers—in the late nineteenth century painted an increasingly bleak national perception of the arid interior as sterile and lifeless, and of being *unable* to sustain the kind of colonial ventures the nation had in mind. As Christy Collis writes, faced with the crisis of "imperial spatial incompetence . . . and with what their limited vision saw as the semiotic void of the interior, exploration writers constructed the desert as almost entirely empty. If they couldn't understand or conquer it, this was because there was simply nothing there" (40). This deft discursive maneuver helped, according to Collis, to "alleviate the threat of failure for the explorers, [and] it also served the purpose of erasing the facts of Aboriginal ownership and presence" (40).

This symbolic depiction of the "Empty Center" held sway until the turn of the twentieth century when, according to Robin, mineral and natural resource survey practice acted as a galvanizing trigger for modified cartographic representations of Australian spaces along bio-geographical lines ("Accounting"). The arid interior's troping began to shift in the 1920s, transforming from "Dead Heart" to "Red Center," when returning Australian troops from the First World War began to identify with desert spaces, and turned to Australian deserts for metaphorical as well as metaphysical edification. As Robin points out, the Center "became a place of pilgrimage for some—a place to exorcise some of the horrors of war for others. The war inspired a 'wanderlust.' A place 'one thousand miles from the sea' became a challenge, even 'the real thing'" (W. B. Brown, qtd. in Robin, "Accounting" 7). The "Red Center" was becoming the "essential heart of the nation," troped now in images of opportunity rather than disappointment and failure, upon which "grand dreams for Australia could be inscribed" (Robin, "Accounting" 7). There was a resurgence of interest in the Center from the 1920s to the 1950s that Robin traces in part to the (discursive as well as sociological) pioneering work of John Flynn, or "Flynn of the Inland," as writer Ion Idriess coined him, with his famed "desert rhetoric"

(Robin, "Accounting" 8) popularizing the Center in the national gaze. Haynes concurs and points out:

> During the 1930s and '40s the Australian desert was discovered by painters. Aridity became interestingly different and a red landscape was suddenly beautiful; its simple shapes and lines were seen to provide ready-made Modernist studies; and vastness and monotony provoked artists to devise new forms of composition. (*Seeking* 5)

We see here the rise of a European/Anglo-Celtic romanticization and spiritualization of the Center that was to remain a dominant trope assigned to the space for the remainder of the century, and arguably still into the present day, though we will explore ways in which Indigenous creative responses to place challenge this view.

Whether "Empty," "Dead," or "Red," though—and regardless of resurgent interest in the Center, or of totalizing spatial myths that erased or marginalized Aboriginal presence and occupation of inland (and, of course, the whole of) Australia—Central Australia was, even at this time, according to Tom Griffiths, "also the land of another culture":

> It was where "tribal" Aborigines lived. . . . Travelling to the centre was to travel differently. One went "walkabout" in Australian culture to become liminal, or to escape. . . . So travelling to the centre was a release and a pilgrimage; it was also an exploration of Aboriginality, or at least one's personal experience of it. (179)

Travel writing in the 1940s and 1950s underwent something of a domestic generic explosion, foremost among the popular proponents of which was Frank Clune (see, for example, his *The Red Heart: Sagas of Centralia*). Just as Griffiths argues that "travelling to the heart of the continent was a journey through time" (179), so too Cathcart claims that Clune's influential populist representations of the Center strove to (actively mis-)construct Aboriginal culture—and particularly their relationship to "Oolera" (Uluru)—as being simultaneously ancient and present, yet somehow discontinuously fractured: as belonging *to the past* even while he described their contemporary relationship with the region. As Cathcart puts it:

> In any case, if Clune had his way, the Rock was about to become a whiteman's symbol. It was Ayer's Rock (and not Lake Eyre), he declared, which was located in the *centre* of Australia. It was, he told readers of *Walkabout*,

'in the heart of the continent'. . . in the 'Red Heart of the Country'. . . and in
'our Centre.' And critical to this centrality was its Aboriginality—its provenance as 'Oolera.' He wrote of it as if it were an Australian Stonehenge—a
rocky enigma where one could still sense the magic even though the Druids
had departed. (216)

By the end of the century, a 180-degree turn has occurred in terms of mainstream Australian imagining of the Center where, to quote Haynes, what
was once "execrated for its failure to provide an inland sea" has now become "the most exported image of Australia: in tourist offices around the
world Uluru vies with Sydney Opera House as *the* icon of the continent"
(*Seeking* 3). Haynes provides a summary analysis of Central Australia at
the turn of the twenty-first century that opens up key questions for our
own reading of contemporary film and theater production in the present
era. Eco-tours to the Center—"especially those featuring an 'Aboriginal
experience'"—have now provided a traveling experience that, according
to Haynes, contains a moral imperative: a "residual glow of virtue" (*Seeking* 6). Haynes writes:

> Travelling in the desert, even within the comfort cocoon of an aircondi-
> tioned bus and with five-star overnight accommodation, suggests a satisfy-
> ing element of self-renunciation, of anti-materialism, perhaps spiritual
> rebirth. New Age cults and the lucrative market in Aboriginal artefacts are
> drawn as if by a magnet to Alice Springs, capital of desert land, and to its
> internationally famous icon, Uluru. (*Seeking* 6)

It is to this contemporary magnetic center of spiritual rebirth and intercultural exchange that we now turn our attention as we read the Center as
a unique regional site of Australian identity-formation through the work
of prominent contemporary film and theater-makers.

CONTEMPORARY REPRESENTATION OF THE
CENTER ON STAGE AND SCREEN

The first text we discuss here is Elliott's 1994 film, *The Adventures of Priscilla, Queen of the Desert*. The film has become something of a cult classic
over time: it has achieved further recognition internationally via its stage
musical iteration, *Priscilla, Queen of the Desert* (2006), and, in Australia,
via a reality-television talent quest, *I Will Survive* (2012). David Carter

sums up the myriad ways in which *Priscilla* can and has been interpreted by film critics and academic scholars since its 1994 debut, and he is worth quoting at length here by way of authoritative round-up of scholarly opinion:

> The argument about the film could be twisted in a number of ways: either that it overturns the old Australian legends by its high camp journey into the centre or that it confirms them because the only women who make it are really white men after all. (That isn't true, of course, for there's a successful white businesswoman and a transsexual at the film's centre.) Or it might be that the desert is still the forbidding but alluring place that demands to be conquered by white men even if they can only go there in disguise. Doubtless the film calls up all the layered meanings which the culture has already attached, variously and vicariously, to masculinity, Aboriginality, land, journeys into the centre, being lost in the desert and so on. (94)[9]

Carter navigates here the field of feminist, queer, postcolonial, and critical race and whiteness theories that typically apply to analysis of the film. The corollary effect of this range of perspectives tends to result in an interrogation of the ways in which the traditional Australian "bush legend"[10] is queered by this infiltration of white, masculinist space by the deviant (transsexual/bisexual/homosexual) other; and thence to a reading of the film's clumsy appropriation of Indigenous iconography—and people—as the central protagonists convert the desert people to disco mid-journey and then use Aboriginal motifs as part of their drag-act design in the Convention Centre in Alice Springs at the film's end. When read through the prism of whiteness theory, the film's racial politics are

---

9. Other significant scholarly analysis of the film includes Philip Brophy's monograph *The Adventures of Priscilla, Queen of the Desert;* Damian Riggs's *Priscilla, (White) Queen of the Desert;* Alan McKee's "How to Tell the Difference"; Pamela Robertson's "The Adventures of Priscilla in Oz"; and Allen James Thomas's "Camping Outback."

10. The "bush legend" is what theater historian and critic John McCallum refers to as incorporating a "romanticised" and "sentimental" view of the bush as being the "real" Australia, in which qualities of "maleness" and "mateship" are central and valorized above others ("The 'Doll'"). In this sense, the "bush legend" might be seen to operate as a specific space-myth: it actively promulgates interpretations of Australianness, constituting particular qualities in particular spaces as being authentic at the expense of others. It serves a cultural function, in other words, privileging (presumably white, youthful) maleness as being somehow quintessentially Australian.

placed within a longer tradition of cultural representation of Central Australia where, according to Hilary Harris, "European encounters with the
desert" are set against "the larger contemporary crisis of western nations
as the *keepers* of civilisation versus Middle Eastern nations as the literal
and metaphoric *deserts* of civilisation" (100). Harris quotes Pamela Robertson to argue that "the Indigenous characters in *Priscilla*, while diegetically celebrated, are nevertheless inscriptions of an Aboriginality typical
of a racially supremacist white Australian imagination" (qtd. in H. Harris
100). Although the film putatively offers an inclusive image of queers and
Aborigines celebrating their otherness together to an Indigenous-disco
mash-up of Gloria Gaynor's "I Will Survive," Robertson concludes that
ultimately *Priscilla* offers "no insight into Aboriginal culture" and that its
"Aboriginal characters are not so much united with the drag queens but
existing *for* them" (qtd. in H. Harris 101). There is little arguing with this
sentiment; the film's racial politics are ham-fisted at best. Hilary Harris's
more absolutist reading of the film, however, suggests some kind of cultural supremacist agenda to the project as she concludes that "*Priscilla*
offers a commodified, dehistoricised 'image' of tradition, and yokes it to
the film's larger project of consolidating white racial power (in the form
of national belonging) for queers with white skin and white culture" (102).

David Carter's view is more nuanced. Dubious Aboriginal (and, it must
be said, Filipina) representation notwithstanding, Carter argues that inscriptions of landscape offer a third way of reading the film (between the
queer/feminist or postcolonial/whiteness theoretical positions outlined
above). Carter subscribes to the view that rather than colonizing the Cen-
ter/Desert in the myriad metaphoric ways discussed above, the characters
are finding something "best described as 'homely'" in the landscape, but
not calling it home (94). They do not settle or conquer the landscape. They
"comment on the space that 'never ends' and decide to turn for 'home,' but
the desert landscapes have been more than anything else *welcoming* to
them" (Carter 94). Carter seems to be suggesting here that the film resists
collapsing itself into late twentieth-century schema of the Center as site
of quasi-spiritual (white) questing; that is, the characters may embark on
their journey to the Center to search for meaning or belonging, but they
don't find it there.

Of particular interest to our own reading of imagined landscapes is Carter's suggestion that the film reads the Red Center as *hybrid space*. While he acknowledges that the "Red Center" landscape "is there in all its sublime spaciousness (it is often accompanied by opera)," he goes on to say, "it is no longer there as the mythic or mysterious centre which must be pierced, the forbidding other against which identity (masculine and national) will be registered or else the self dissolved" (94). The result for Carter is a hybrid rendering of mythical Central Australian desert space, where cultures are put in conversation with one another—or "where exotic and familiar, primeval and modern, traditional and trashy, Aboriginal and non-Aboriginal, Aboriginal and Abba are put into plausible, unpredictable, low-key relationships to each other (low-key despite the high camp)" (94). It is a version of Gelder and Jacobs's uncanny being articulated here as the queer meets the hypermasculine, white meets black—or to use "the film's language," we witness the clashing of "cocks in frocks on rocks, the extremes of nature and culture which these juxtapositions invoke" but they "neither clash nor synthesise" (Carter 94). Again, this is an argument that whiteness theory contests. No amount of mediation is going to bring David Carter's, Pamela Robertson's, and Hilary Harris's views into alignment. It is our own contention here that this schism in ways of reading the film and its cultural codes in relation to the Center actually produces a critical state of unsettlement that mirrors Joanne Tompkins's wider argument about contested ways of knowing, using, and—most important in a theatrical context—representing Australian space (as discussed in chapter 2). We are not, however, ultimately convinced that the film resists constructing the Center as a site of white spiritual questing, nor that this cultural usage of Central Australian desert space has been exhausted. It is, after all, while standing upon Carmichael Crag in Kings Canyon (see figure 5.1) and gazing at the sublime landscape in Watarrka National Park that Bernadette (Terence Stamp) seems to contemplate her future and her decision to romantically approach Bob (Bill Hunter). Ironically, the characters climbing Kings Canyon (and finding their place in the desert and perhaps performing queer conquest?) was meant to be shot atop Uluru, but sensitivity to the significance to Aboriginal people precluded it. In this very particular cultural context, Uluru cannot be of spiritual significance

Figure 5.1. Carmichael Crag in Kings Canyon/Watarrka National Park.
Source: Stephen Carleton.

to both kinds of people in the same way—as fine a demonstration of the
Gelder and Jacobs uncanny as any.

The characters in *Priscilla* may not find home here, but they do discover
that Sydney *is* home as a result of their metaphysical encounter with the
Center. Having been jaded and spent by the rigors of Sydney's parochial
queer rat race, the characters' stocks are recharged by their desert encounter. They return home fundamentally altered but refreshed. While
the Center may be homely-but-not-home—uncannily Australian—the
critical analysis surrounding the film produces more unsettlement than
does its diegesis. It is an important film for this very reason, brokering as it
does a representation of the Center that challenges some normative myths
surrounding the region, but arguably perpetuating others.

In Jenny Kemp's contemporary performance piece *Still Angela,* we
again witness a Caucasian character's spiritual journey to the Center. This
time it is a Melbourne woman's Ghan train journey to Alice Springs that

represents metonymically a larger questing for selfhood within a floundering relationship.[11] Kemp's oeuvre has been widely read as a feminist Australian theater intervention (see Fensham, "Making") and more recently as an example of the postdramatic turn in contemporary performance studies (see Hamilton). In this analysis, we focus on Kemp's depiction of geography and space.

At home, in Melbourne, Angela is performed by four different actors representing her fractured selves.[12] Rather than employing narrative drama to interrogate Angela's marriage or her midlife crisis, Kemp uses dance phrases, image montages, and stream-of-consciousness textual sequences to explore the character's psychological perspective. We listen to a list of objects and actions of domesticity, for instance, or watch an anthropomorphized chess game that seems to represent both images of war and of the "danger of movement" when stasis seems to be the prevailing domestic paradigm. Snippets of text hint that this may be a "battle of the sexes" as Angela ponders whether to marry or not to marry (Kemp). To escape the stifling sense of domestic, suburban entrapment—perhaps at first psychologically rather than physically—one version of Angela declares that "there is a picture on the wall of a desert," and suddenly we are on the train, with video-projected images of travel through red desert landscapes accompanying the choreography onstage. The train is configured as mobile domestic space, while a voiceover equates the metonymic desert space outside as an extension of Angela's own psyche: it is the Outback, the "dead heart." Angela takes a walk at Finke River, which is one of the largest rivers in the Northern Territory, and ends up in a Gothic childhood garden—a dream sequence or memory of a childhood train journey in which a character referred to as "Nurse" sends her off on an unnamed excursion that marks some kind of crucial or scarring rite of passage.

11. The Ghan is the North–South railway line that now runs from Adelaide through Alice Springs to Darwin. The Alice Springs–Darwin leg only opened in 2004 and had been almost a century in the planning. The original line, which ended in Alice Springs, was opened in 1929. According to the company's own website, "Originally the Afghan Express, the name The Ghan was inspired by the pioneering Afghan cameleers who blazed a permanent trail into the Red Centre of Australia over 150 years ago" ("Ghan").

12. In the original production of *Still Angela,* the four Angelas were played by Margaret Mills, Natasha Herbert, Lucy Taylor, and Felicity MacDonald.

In a second train sequence later in the piece, the return journey is equated with appetite (references to meat, wine, cream) and sexual adventure ("to be inside your own erotic rhythm," the adult Angela declares). This time rather than desert images, the video montage represents a cultivated rural landscape, a town's cemetery that lies perhaps on the outskirts of Adelaide. On the train she meets a man who has just come from the desert. It is a potentially erotic encounter with a like soul who is also moving across the country in search of orientation. Upon arrival from the epic, symbolic train journey Angela concludes that she is "nowhere. And everywhere." Still in the chair she began the piece in; still Angela (Kemp).

In a postperformance interview, Kemp describes the desert as the underworld, and the journey itself as being about making a transition from being in a relationship with another person to a relationship with self. Reading the text through a feminist lens, Fensham argues that by "allowing female actors to signify the many different facets of an imaginative life, Kemp creates an opening for women, and men, to reconstruct their daily lives" ("Making" 61). This piece in particular "asks what happens when a middle-aged woman constrained by a long term relationship sits down in her chair. From the stillness, she journeys with her various others, including her earlier selves, into the Australian desert in search of autonomy and integration" (Fensham, "Making" 61). In this sense, the piece aligns with descriptions by scholars such as Robin and Haynes (*Seeking*) of the Center as a site of white spiritual questing. It is a deracinated landscape in Kemp's piece; a symbolic space that triggers associations (of other childhood journeys, of emptiness and death-of-heart), while the train journey itself represents the personal passage from stasis to movement, accompanied by the separate associations (of appetite, of sexual rhythm) that this engenders.

It is interesting to note here that the journey into the Center is accompanied by images of red desert and emptiness, and transports Angela into a mythic or dream world aligned with her own childhood. To be fair to Kemp's vision and theatrical modus operandi, all space is configured as mythical or symbolic space in her hands—including the suburban home, the kitchen, and the kitchen chair. The Central Australian desert is not represented here as the site of the mythic-symbolic in contrast to the metropolitan center as the site of the real. In Kemp's imaginative world, all space is equally symbolic in its theatrical representation. It is the particular range of signifiers associated with the Center that is of interest in this equation. The journey *to* the Center is a lonely one into the emptiness of the self, and into the past; the journey *from* the Center is marked by awakening of appetite (both physiological and sexual) and is accompanied by images of outer suburbia—a return, in a sense, to the built environment and the prospect of a reintegrated self that has been altered somehow by the sojourn into the desert. It is on the journey home that Angela meets a potential suitor referred to generically as "the Man," a kindred spirit.

Kemp resists collapsing the text into a trite black–white schema that casts the Center as site of Aboriginal mysticism. We do not see the Gelder and Jacobs "uncanny" or the intercultural tensions of Tompkins's "unsettled" Australia at play in this personal journey to the Center because we do not encounter Indigeneity. But as an example of a Caucasian encounter with the Central Australian desert space as mythical terrain, we do see here a perpetuation of non-Indigenous ways of knowing the Australian inland that align with late twentieth-century literary, filmic, and theatrical tropes established in the preceding decades of this play's 2002 premiere. The Center is ultimately perhaps configured here as personal mythic space, and it is the journey itself rather than the destination that informs the central character's realization of self.

If we can read Kemp's text as a "white" way of reading landscape and metaphor in the Center (and, again, this is not an observation designed to perpetuate hierarchies of perception in which one cultural perspective is honored as more valid or valuable than another), then by way of complete contrast, we can read Warwick Thornton's film *Samson and Delilah* as an Indigenous representation of the same region.

Thornton's driving vision and autonomy not only embosses the film with his own unique vision in this logistical sense, it also endows the project with a degree of influence and Thornton himself (as an Indigenous, Alice Springs–born filmmaker) with an authority to represent the de-

picted community that raises the stakes enormously. There is a risk that
the film is conscripted to say all things to all Indigenous audiences, or to
be some kind of defining barometer about the current state of Indigenous
health, reconciliation, or youth culture. As Thornton himself cautions:

> You have to be careful. People might need to hear about the next step in
> reconciliation. But is this the right film to do that? [As unflinching as it is in
> its portrayal of social problems such as petrol sniffing and domestic violence
> within Central Australian Aboriginal communities.] You have to be careful
> about what you bring and you need. *Samson and Delilah* is this beautiful
> journey of these two children, and it's bloody hard. But this film isn't the
> defining next step in reconciliation. And it's dangerous for people to have to,
> or want to, need that. (qtd. in Redwood 34)

Bearing that caveat in mind, we offer here a focused reading of the film
that concentrates on its depiction of urban Central Australian space—
Alice Springs as city space in the desert—by way of contrast to this (and
other) films' depiction of the Center as mythic terrain or sublime landscape.[13] We do so in order to discuss ways in which the film engages with
notions of the "uncanny" and the "unsettled," but also to provide an alternative view of the region that resists quasi-spiritual mythologizing of the
Central Australian Outback/dead/red/heart.

The first and most important factor to raise in debunking myths
of Central Australian emptiness is that this is a landscape that has been
inhabited by Aboriginal communities for millennia and by the 28,500
people who currently live in Alice Springs.[14] Although drawing on biblical
parable in its title, and often being read as a modern-day Romeo and Juliet
story in its promotional materials and critical review, *Samson and Delilah*
is essentially a social realist investigation of Indigenous youth in Central Australia—more akin to the gritty realist films of Mike Leigh than

13. Wim Wenders's *Until the End of the World* (1991), Nicolas Roeg's *Walkabout* (1971),
James Trainor's *Journey Out of Darkness* (1967), and even Fred Schepisi's *Evil Angels* (1988)
could be included in this list.

14. These 2011 figures are drawn from census data presented in a report by Pawinee
Yuhun, Andrew Taylor, and James Winter. Yuhun and colleagues state that 20.2 percent
of this population is Indigenous and 19.9 percent were born overseas, with the largest
percentages of overseas-born people coming from the United Kingdon, the United States,
and New Zealand, respectively.

Baz Luhrmann's customary pastiche, in that sense. Indeed, Bruce Isaacs reads it as a political text and states that "against Luhrmann's mythologising of the Australian 'frontier' [in *Australia*] (which is not of itself a bad thing—Hollywood made some of its greatest films about its own mythical frontiers), *Samson and Delilah* returns to the here and now, depicting communities and lives that express a contemporary reality" (15). Philip Batty goes a step further and commends Thornton's willingness to push beyond "correct line" approaches to Indigenous concerns. Batty states of *Samson and Delilah,* as in other short films by Thornton:

> The contradictions and seemingly intractable problems of contemporary Aboriginal life are examined with a fearlessness that not only incorporates humour and irony, but avoids soapbox politics and easy answers. Thornton's willingness to take on topics that few others have wanted to touch—Aboriginal alcoholism, substance abuse, domestic violence—gives his work an independence of vision that few, if any, other films on Aboriginal Australia, have matched. (167)

In the central characters' disenfranchisement, Isaacs (like Batty) reads Indigenous communities' "collective suffering" into the text; the film's urban setting is strategically important in conveying this sense of alienation. Samson and Delilah live in a country outstation west of Alice Springs (filmed in the abandoned community of Jay Creek) in conditions of economic and physical deprivation. Both young characters are finding life there untenable and, after Delilah's grandmother dies and Samson has an altercation with his brother, they take the community's car and steal away to Alice Springs. They are effectively experiencing a self-imposed exile from their home communities and enter Alice Springs as outsiders. Isaacs argues that in the urban landscape of the "Centralian capital" (as Alice Springs is sometimes colloquially referred to), "they are forced to confront a new world of shopping centers (from which Samson and Delilah must ultimately steal to feed themselves) and street side cafes, where White Australia lives in relative opulence" (16). It is an uncaring or indifferent white Australia that greets the pair (presumably this description of non-Indigenous characters as "white" includes European and other international tourists; Alice Springs, like all Australian cities, is never entirely white, if whiteness is reduced to Anglo-Celtic ethnicity. See the statistics referred to in note 5). We never hear these characters speak; we view them through Samson's and Delilah's eyes, from the outside looking in. They are indifferent consumers who will not buy Delilah's art.[15]

The spaces that Samson and Delilah occupy in Alice Springs, then, are interstitial; the two sleep under the bridge in the dry Todd River bed, they wander through shopping arcades that link the busy mall with the shopping centers, they reconvene in car parks. As Isaacs argues:

> There is something shocking in Thornton's vision of this country away from Samson and Delilah's own community. While their own community can't seem to provide them with what they are looking for, in the township of Alice Springs two Indigenous teenagers are regarded by white Australia with suspicion. Indigenous art and myth function as commodities here, sold to tourists and locals, one presumes, as an example of exoticism. But Indigenous people are not listened to, or spoken to, and thus not understood. (Isaacs 16)

While viewing Alice Springs through Thornton's lens and Samson's and Delilah's eyes produces a version of the Center that accords with Robin's, Haynes's, and David Carter's readings of it as a consumerist or touristic milieu in which Indigenous life—and art—is commodified and exoticized for capitalistic consumption, the film distances itself from such practices. It is "white" Australia that exists in the "fishbowl" here; urban and touristic consumption of Indigenous cosmology is placed in uncanny and unsettled parallel to Indigenous occupation of space. "White" Australia drives over the bridge that "black" Australia sleeps under; we see "white" eyes refusing to meet the gaze of "black" disenfranchisement and despair. The two worlds abut each other—they even *collide* in the terrible moment when Delilah, disoriented by hunger and the effects of petrol sniffing, is struck by the passing car—but they never synthesize.

What makes this filmic rendering of the "uncanny" (Central) Australia different to *Priscilla* and the suite of films constituting a tradition before it is that this is the first time we have witnessed the Center through an Indigenous director's lens. The positioning of protagonists and witnesses is in-

---

15. Prior to her grandmother's death, Delilah helped her grandmother paint and sell traditional Aboriginal dot paintings to an opportunistic Caucasian art dealer who sold them for an exorbitant profit in Alice Springs.

verted or even subverted here, and the depiction of landscape, even in this urban environment, is different. Gone are the sweeping vistas and eerie or quasi-metaphysical long shots of the MacDonnell Ranges or other iconic geographical markers (Uluru, Standley Chasm, Ormiston Gorge, Emily Gap, Simpson's Gap—all used in films such as *Jedda* [Charles Chauvel, 1955] and *The Overlanders* [Harry Watt, 1946]). *Samson and Delilah* contains long shots of Alice Springs's Stott Terrace Bridge filmed *from* the crag-top in nearby Olive Pink nature reserve, but we are viewing the township from this vantage point rather than vice versa. This is neither a Gothic desert nor one in which the sublime is being conscripted to activate white longing or anxiety. It is as though we are arriving here at a cultural representation of the Center—both its urban space and its landscape—in the twenty-first century that aligns with Haynes's assertion that the desert is an active agent that "has begun to liberate Australian landscape and consciousness from its subservience to European dominance" (*Seeking* 6). Haynes is still arguing here that the Center has become marketable in its "silence, immensity, and ancientness," and in its Aboriginality too. And yet with Thornton's texturing of the same region, and his ironic rendering of European/Anglo/White onlookers as hapless or indifferent witnesses of *real* Indigenous people (as against the art or the handicrafts that they produce), there is a rendering of the Center here that transforms it one stage further than the postcolonial space that Haynes is describing it as. There is an element of self-reflexivity layered onto the representation in this instance, as the film (via the filmmaker) demonstrates an Indigenous perspective that *alludes* to these ways in which the dominant culture commodifies Aboriginality in the Center.

MAPPING THE CENTER

Having analyzed the Center as mythic space using key creative texts as the source to mount the case for a contemporary tradition, how do we then *map* this space? Which version of Center do we use? The Indigenous or the non-Indigenous? And what do these different ways of mapping even mean?

Christopher Tilley provides useful summary analysis of different ways in which Indigenous and non-Indigenous people conceptualize and represent Australian landscapes, which in turn highlights the problems in-

Figure 5.2. Marsupial Mole rock formation, Uluru. Source: Stephen Carleton.

herent in mapping such uncanny space. If the two (let's broadly refer to them as Western and Indigenous) ways of conceptualizing space are so vastly different, then the mapping process is equally fraught with the perils of misrepresentation.

To help the cultural outsider understand Australian Aboriginal cosmologies and spatial practices, Tilley writes, "The Aboriginal landscape is one replete with highly elaborate totemic geography linking together place and people. Formed in the Dreamtime, the landscape provides an ancestral map for human activity" (38). The landscape, in other words, is encountered and understood as a living map that, as well as helping people to navigate, also provides cultural memory and knowledge linking prehistory with the present. In this cosmological equation, the earth "came into being as a result of the actions of the ancestors. These ancestors continue to exist in spirit form, and in the era of creation they travelled the earth, and in their doings created topographical features" (Tilley 40).

In specific relation to Uluru, and to connect its Aboriginal ontologies with that of the Western association with it outlined earlier in this chapter, Tilley draws on the anthropological research of Ronald Berndt

(1972) and Charles Mountford (1965) to point out about local creation mythology:

> Uluru was created by ten ancestral beings: the south face with its crevices and alluvial fans bears the marks of the battle between poisonous snakes and carpet snakes, and lizards; wallabies created the northern face and the marsupial mole created holes and caves. . . . The landscape is thus represented in myth and represents the myth. (43–47)

As well as being an account of Uluru's creation, these stories provide an immemorial map for the monolith itself, as the battle sites and animals comprise physical features of the rock that can still be used to navigate the site today (see figure 5.2).

When it comes to mapping larger topographies, Tilley notes that Aboriginal art can often be used as a geovisual navigation tool or to augment spatial knowledge and history:[16]

> Depictions of the landscape in Australian Aboriginal art are notable for the bird's-eye view they adopt, a decentred perspective in which numerous points have equal value. Sacred sites and ancestral tracks linking them become laid out as on a map, but these "maps" have much more in common with the sensuous places of medieval "cartography" than they do with a Euclidean geometric space of modern cartographic representation. . . . Rock paintings and dot paintings draw out the spirits and replenish the land. (51)

Tilley goes on to explain that Aboriginal art of this kind often refers to the land's topographic features and also to the mythological entities and events of the Dreamtime, creating a visual record of Dreamtime narratives as well as a map of an area of land (51). To invoke the Gelder and Jacobs "uncanny" again, then, when these Indigenous ways of knowing and mapping landscape are placed over the top of Western cartographic mapping systems that measure topographies along lines of longitude and latitude (that in turn draw in Euclidian geometric traditions), two completely different ways of represent the same spaces occur. Attempts to map "Aboriginal Australia" onto a Euclidian geovisual template are not

16. See also Eric Michaels, who notes that "all traditionally based Aboriginal paintings" are "pages of an atlas, maps that describe as a whole the Australian landscape" (58–59) and Peta Mitchell, *Cartographic* (91–93).

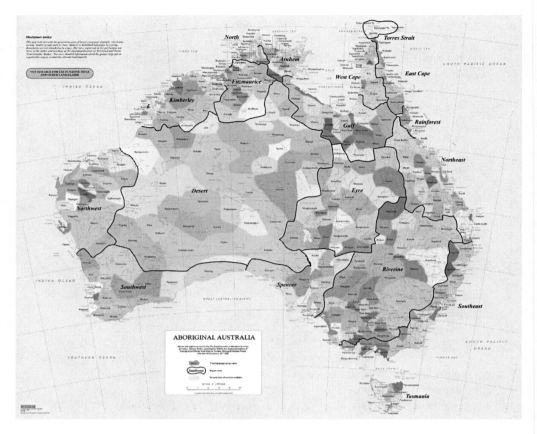

Figure 5.3. Map of Aboriginal language groups in Australia. Source: David R. Horton, creator, © Aboriginal Studies Press, AIATSIS and Auslig/Sinclair, Knight, Merz, 1996.

This map is just one representation of many other map sources that are available for Aboriginal Australia. Using published resources available between 1988 and 1994, this map attempts to represent all the language, social, or nation groups of the Indigenous people of Australia. It indicates only the general location of larger groupings of people, which may include smaller groups such as clans, dialects, or individual languages in a group. Boundaries are not intended to be exact. This map is not suitable for use in Native Title and other land claims. No reproduction allowed without permission.

uncommon, and can be used to indicate the geographical distribution of, say, Indigenous languages or homelands. David Horton's 1996 map of "Aboriginal Australia" is one such example of the latter (see figure 5.3).

To return to our original questions about the difficulties inherent in mapping mythic zones or imagined space, such as the Red/Dead Cen-

Figure 5.4. Stott Terrace Bridge, Alice Springs. Source: Stephen Carleton.

ter—whether that is a zone whose creative conceptualization has been generated in narratives by an Aboriginal Australian, a non-Aboriginal Australian, or a visitor from another culture altogether—the challenges become quite pragmatic ones. In assembling data for this chapter and for the *Cultural Atlas of Australia,* we found that we could quite easily identify shooting locations, say, for Thornton's *Samson and Delilah.*

The Stott Terrace Bridge over the Todd River is the bridge under which Samson and Delilah sleep during their time in Alice Springs (see figures 5.4 and 5.5). The bridge and the nature reserve that surrounds it are geophysical locations that can be located, photographed and mapped along concrete spatial coordinates.

What happens, though, when we want to represent a broader conceptual zone such as Jenny Kemp's "the empty heart"? Identifying the Ghan train station in Alice Springs is an easy enough task. But geovisualizing a mythic zone is a task well beyond the capabilities of the atlas map and its technical features. Barbara Piatti and her colleagues discuss similar challenges that faced the team working on the *Literary Atlas of Europe.* As they explain, some narrative spaces lack definite borders:

Figure 5.5. Stott Terrace Bridge and Olive Pink nature reserve, Alice Springs.
Source: Stephen Carleton.

> Usually, cartography works with hard boundaries to show the edges of
> phenomenon mapped. A place, or the limits of one element mapped can be
> accurately described. But, when mapping literature, a "soft" boundary might
> be more appropriate, whereby less accurate definitions about where exactly
> the "edge" of a world of a particular piece of literature ends. (182)

Anne-Kathrin Reuschel elaborates on some of the solutions this team
found when it came to visualising "spatial uncertainty." Drawing on existing research by Jörg Trau and Lorenz Hurni and Alan M. MacEachran,
Reuschel lists a number of solutions that include deploying "'colour hue',
'colour saturation', 'colour value', 'texture' and 'size'" to apply a "'contour
crispness' that provides 'fuzzy shapes' to depict an area" (299). Reuschel
writes that this endeavor "is implemented by area-filling the depicted geometry so that the fill fades as distance from the centre increases" (300).
In the Kemp example, then, the train station in Alice Springs might act
as "ground zero" for the center of the Center, and a fuzzy image would
span out from there into the surrounding landscape, growing fainter until it reached a nominal geographical perimeter. Alternatively, Reuschel

suggests that "settings and projects places can be depicted as polygons (e.g., regions, such as a valley, a suburb or the countryside)" that can take on idiosyncratic shapes to fill particular topographical regions or zones (300). In this case, the cartographer still has to identify hard boundaries where they may not exist. The solution in this instance is to assign a specific radius that is then "transformed into 'fuzzy points'" (300). Fictional locations depicted as polygons keep their shape through the blur and are visually defined with a fuzzy contour to acknowledge the nebulousness of their boundaries.[17]

Reuschel (after Piatti et al.) comes to the rather sobering conclusion that these solutions are not going to service all literary (and in our case, filmic or theatrical) texts and their invocation of imagined landscapes. "Fictional places that could not be classed into one of the defined references to reality or those that could not be grasped with coordinates remain uncategorized or even unvisualised," she writes, before concluding that "It may even happen that whole fictional texts remain unmappable" (Reuschel 307). Perhaps the Red Center or the Dead Heart or the Empty Heart as the Australian Center has variously been troped is one such zone that defies concrete mapping and geovisualization. Whereas the American South can be mapped along political contours—specific state boundaries that delineate conceptual zones such as North and South—and the Canadian North (as discussed in chapter 2) can be separated along a line of latitude dividing provinces from territories, in the Australian example mythic zones such as the Center, the North, and the Never-Never remain vague, and "uncannily" so when competing Indigenous cosmological concepts are added to the mapping equation.

Setting aside the question of mapping now, and returning to the notion of the "uncanny" Australian center, this notion of competing perspectives of real and imagined spaces—indigenous and non-Indigenous creative responses to specific landscapes and regions—are being challenged by contemporary stage works that embrace a shared approach to storytelling. Recent Australian plays *Namatjira* by Scott Rankin (created with the Namatjira family) and *Head Full of Love* by Alana Valentine (directed

17. See Reuschel for illustrations of these blurry zones and polygon geometries (300).

by Indigenous artist Wesley Enoch) are in and of themselves examples of intercultural collaborations that would appear to mark something of a trend in contemporary theater representing the Center. Both are 2010 productions; both have toured nationally. And both depict the Center (Hermannsburg and Alice Springs, respectively, as well as outlying communities in the Alice region) through a combination of Indigenous and non-Indigenous eyes. In their diegeses, they are each preoccupied with this notion of "white" and "black" ways of knowing the land colliding and falling into conversation. *Namatjira* explores, among other things, the effects of "white" culture's attention—fame and money—on the artist; *Head Full of Love* explores an unlikely friendship between a middle-aged (Caucasian) Sydney woman and a similarly aged Indigenous woman. They bond over beanies—the weaving of which becomes a metaphor for intercultural integration.

By happy accident, while we were undertaking field research in the region for *Namatjira, Priscilla,* and *Samson and Delilah* for this chapter, the Alice Springs Beanie Festival was in full swing at the Araluen Arts Centre. The festival provides an income for Arrernte, Pitjantjatjara, Luritja, and other desert women, and in fact the *Head Full of Love* theater season is used as a fundraiser for kidney dialysis machines for communities of the region. Having assumed the festival was primarily a forum to showcase and sell local Aboriginal women's design, we were surprised to see local Indigenous handicrafts restricted to a single table. The rest of the room in the Araluen Centre was festooned with an array of wonderful designs by women from all over Australia—mostly, if names and faces in the crowd were anything to go by, Anglo-Celtic. This is not to summarily dismiss the festival or its agenda as having usurped that of its indigenous participants (though one does wonder); rather, it is to register misapprehension and surprise at the weighting of representation. We were also surprised to witness the comfortable attendance of a cross-dressing male shopper in silver knee-high boots, matching synthetic body suit, and makeup. It turns out an anniversary *Priscilla* pilgrimage was taking place, with Alice Springs its final stage. For an uncanny and unsettling moment in the Araluen Arts Centre in July 2012, several of the texts discussed in this article were converging in the one time and place; it was as though the Beanie Festival was the unintentional conduit for the range of cultural ways of "knowing"

Alice Springs and Central Australian desert space, one that extends beyond white appropriation or Indigenous authenticity and into the surreal,
or at least the unexpected.

In relation to environmental practice, Robin points out that one of the
key catchphrases being used to trope contemporary Australian desert
space management, and subsequently to trope the Center itself, is "desert
knowledge" ("Accounting"). There is an implicit assumption of Aboriginal consultation couched within the term that suggests mutual benefit
to be derived from combined black and white approaches to arid zone
spatial-management practices, and to the way in which "country" itself is
regarded. As Robin puts it:

> The new term "desert knowledge" embraces both the physical and the moral
> in the arid country. . . ."Desert knowledge" is explicitly cultural. It considers
> both local indigenous knowledge and western science in relation to country
> that is sparse in population, but is clearly very different from other deserts.
> Australians need ways of thinking about our inland that are neither cringe
> nor strut, but do acknowledge difference. ("Accounting" 21)

A hardline postcolonial or whiteness theory reading of our experience
of the Beanie Festival would still conclude that Indigenous agency is being
colonized by white Australian consumerism and cultural tourism. While
that may be true of the event itself, one gets the sense here of something
more genuinely intercultural taking place in the hands of Australian filmmakers and theater-makers.

CONCLUSION

This chapter has addressed some of the uncertainties of narrative mapping and has engaged with the significance of spaces that encompass cultural meanings that in some ways exceed their geographic parameters; the
book as a whole has worked through a number of different ways in which
the Australian landscape has been imagined, narrated, and remediated. It
has also examined various approaches to interpreting patterns of spatial
representation using digital cartography and geovisualization techniques
to move between close readings of texts (traditional textual analysis) and
distant readings of patterns of spatial data mapped on the *Cultural Atlas
of Australia* and drawn from other sources. An important aspect of the

geocritical research method that we have implemented throughout the book is the layering and clustering of different perspectives on place and narrative to create a multifaceted understanding of how Australia's people—including scholars, creators and consumers of cultural narratives, early settlers, outsiders, and Indigenous Australians—have come to perceive particular regions over time and across various media forms.

In the introductory chapter, we articulated the ways in which scholarly studies of narrative space have tended to divide along disciplinary lines. Despite their common focus and shared body of theoretical work, humanities-based studies of space and place in literature, film, and theater have, broadly speaking, been established as discrete subfields with very few studies treating more than one narrative form. We also identified a lack of dialogue between these humanities-based approaches to space and narrative and their counterparts within geography: namely, the subfields of literary geography and film geography, which again rarely engage with one another. Narrative geovisualization projects also tend to reflect the same medium- and disciplinary-specific focus; that is, the field has been dominated by an array of digital literary-mapping projects and film-mapping projects, but rarely, if ever, a mapping project that examines the representation of space, place, and landscape across a range of narrative forms. In *Imagined Landscapes* we have begun the work of articulating the connections between the discipline-specific and medium-specific insights offered within the spatial humanities.

When we set about mapping the translation of spatial representation across media forms, *Wake in Fright* presented peculiar cartographic challenges because it is one of the few critically acclaimed Australian texts to have a strong presence on the page, the screen, and the stage. As chapter 1 demonstrates, different media adaptations handle space in quite different ways. While theater stages and performs spatiality in concrete, physical terms it also conjures locations through the use of metonymic and allusive mise-en-scène in suggestive, abstract ways. For instance, the theater audience can experience a strong sense of emplacement as they gather around the set of an Outback homestead's broad veranda, but even though they may be close enough to see the red dust on the corrugated iron and chip at the paint peeling off the woodwork, the homestead may not be located in any state of Australia. Instead, it might represent the liminal space where the bush and the town meet—a nowhere and anywhere space of possibility and encounter where the land shapes its people and the people shape the landscape.

Literary texts, by contrast, build settings with words rather than props and plywood, so they are able to feature a wider variety of narrative locations that can be elaborated in descriptive detail that in turn can bring places to life with, potentially, a higher degree of specificity. In literary texts, locations can often be georeferenced according to landmarks, place names, or measures of time and distance that are given in the narrative. Along with this level of detail, novels also have the capacity to rewrite the landscape in inventive and geographically impossible ways that may evoke subjective or symbolic renderings of space, whereas cinema often enacts geovisualization in very literal ways by showing locations, maps, and road signs.

When a narrative is filmed, each scene must realize its setting in the studio or on location, and these narrative settings may correspond to or be far distant from the geographic places named or conjured in the script. Plotting shooting locations in relation to narrative settings complicates the question of how the imagined geography of a narrative relates to the geospace and we addressed this issue in relation to mapping fictional places in chapter 2, mythic space in chapter 3, using cinematic location doubles and charting historical spaces in chapter 4, and tracing the parallels between subjective journeys to the self and physical journeys to central Australia in this final chapter.

Broadly speaking, the patterns of representation discerned in the course of mapping Australian cultural narratives and plotting different perspectives on the places and events occurring in those narratives accord with existing research on discrete texts and genres in Australian literary, film, and theater studies. For example, we have identified barren cultural spaces on the map, such as the central and south-eastern reaches of Western Australia where few, if any, noteworthy narratives are set or shot. While this apparent *terra nullius* or terra incognita is a cartographic and cultural void that reflects both the selective processes of cultural mapping and, to an extent, the imperial view of a cartographic endeavor that does not record Indigenous oral traditions, it also corresponds to the very low population density of these remote, inaccessible areas. However, other equally sparsely populated areas such as the Pilbara and Kimberley regions of northwestern Australia and the inhospitable deserts of central Australia feature disproportionately high narrative concentrations.[18] Using GIS to layer the narrative map with information about regional demography and land use, one might speculate that the resources boom is related to the cluster of texts set in the northwest, yet the unprecedented levels of development in the mining industry in Western Australia also affect the Kalgoorlie-Boulder district in the southwest goldfields, where few narratives take place.

Examining the patterns of representation more closely using a geocritical approach, we were able to identify recurring instances in which the far north and northwest of the nation have come to occupy the narrative imaginary as a place of interracial encounter and a frontier zone in which the nation's anxieties about incursions by neighboring Asian nations and unsettled relations with Indigenous Australians play out, as demonstrated in chapter 2. Chapters 3 and 4 noted that while there are significant narratives featuring Indigenous protagonists and issues set in Tasmania (for example, Beth Roberts's novel *Manganinnie,* which was adapted for film by John Honey), New South Wales (Fred Schepisi's *The Chant of Jimmie Blacksmith*), South Australia (Rachel Perkins's *One Night the Moon*), and Central Australia (Thornton's *Samson and Delilah*), the largest concentration by far is in the North and Northwest, as exemplified by texts such as *(Follow the) Rabbit-Proof Fence* (Pilkington Garimara; Noyce), *Australia* (Luhrmann), *Bran Nue Dae* (Chi; Perkins), and *Jedda* (Chauvel), as well as the series of texts that document and dramatize the story of Indigenous resistance leader Jandamarra (Idriess; Mudrooroo; Torres; Hawke). As discussed in chapter 3, this belies the fact that Tasmania was the site of the nation's most notorious and systematic colonial genocide, known variously as the Black Line, the Black Drive, or the Black War of 1830, when settlers systematically scoured the settled areas of the island state to

18. The Pilbara has a population density of less than 2.6 inhabitants per square mile (i.e., less than one person per square kilometer) and the Kimberley and the Goldfields regions share a population density of less than 0.26 inhabitants per square mile (i.e., less than 0.1 person per square kilometer), according to 2013 figures provided by the Australian Bureau of Statistics ("Western Australia").

eradicate Tasmanian Aborigines because they were perceived as a threat to Europeans and their livestock. With the exception of *Manganinnie* (B. Roberts; Honey), Tasmanian narratives have largely effaced this disturbing history and have, instead, concentrated on revisiting and reimagining the convict past. Compared to other states, Tasmanian narratives are overwhelmingly concerned with the return of repressed historical trauma, showing that the convict stain persists and the state has become emblematic of the penal colony's harsh history.

As noted in chapter 4, Tasmania's connection with the colonial past is unsurprising given that its verdant landscape is reminiscent of the United Kingdom and particularly the haunted forests, Gothic mountains, and dramatic coastlines of Scotland and Ireland. Indeed, the Gothic is another narrative mode that this spatial humanities mapping endeavor has illuminated. However, while Tasmania may be the site most strongly associated with convict history, it is not the only crucible of the Gothic. We have identified several different zones in which the Gothic operates to express European perceptions of the landscape as "un-home-like" (*unheimlich* or uncanny): chapter 1 reveals the Gothic through an outsider's perspective on the sun-blasted desert landscape of Outback New South Wales and chapter 2 traces Gothic tropes across the Tropical North.

In mapping approximately two hundred Australian narratives and examining a variety of perspectives on these spatial stories and the places they represent, we have built on and extended the insights afforded by preexisting studies of individual texts to situate these perspectives within a network of intertexts and influences for which landscape and location provide the coordinates of meaning-making. This geocritical mapping of the nation's cultural topography is necessarily incomplete as new perspectives and new texts, or fresh perspectives on old texts continue to accrue; nevertheless, we hope that the representational tropes and analytic techniques detailed in this book are indicative of the richness of this evolving field and contribute new ways of engaging with Australian narrative fiction and the land within which it is set.

WORKS CITED

ABS (Australian Bureau of Statistics). *Census of the Commonwealth of Australia 1954.* Vol. 1, pt. 1. *Analysis of Population in Local Government Areas.* Commonwealth of Australia, 1954. Print.

———. *Census of the Commonwealth of Australia 1954.* Vol. 1, pt. 5. *Population and Occupied Dwellings in Localities with a Population of 50 Persons or More.* Commonwealth of Australia, 1954. Print.

———. "Census Data." 2011. Web. 10 Oct. 2014. http://www.censusdata.abs.gov.au/census_services/getproduct/census/2011/quickstat/0.

———. "Estimates of Aboriginal and Torres Strait Islander Australians, June 2011." June 2011. Web. 11 Oct. 2014. http://www.abs.gov.au/ausstats/abs@.nsf/mf/3238.0.55.001.

———. "Western Australia: Regional Population Growth, Australia, 2012–13." 3 Apr. 2014. Web. 12 Oct. 2014. http://www.abs.gov.au/ausstats/abs@.nsf/Products/3218.0~2012-13~Main+Features~Western+Australia?OpenDocument.

Allen, Jim, and Richard Cosgrove. "Background History of the Southern Forests Archaeological Project." *Report of the Southern Forests Archaeological Project: Volume 1.* Ed. Jim Allen. Melbourne: La Trobe University, 1996. 3–17. Print.

Aiken, Charles S. "Faulkner's Yoknapatawpha County: Geographical Fact into Fiction." *Geographical Review* 67 (1977): 1–21. Print.

———. "Faulkner's Yoknapatawpha County: A Place in the American South." *Geographical Review* 69 (1979): 331–48. Print.

Aitken, Stuart C., and Leo E. Zonn, eds. "Weir(d) Sex: Representation of Gender–Environment Relations in Peter Weir's *Picnic at Hanging Rock* and *Gallipoli*." *Environment and Planning D: Society and Space* 11.2 (1993): 191–212. Print.

———. *Place, Power, Situation, and Spectacle: A Geography of Film.* Lanham, Md.: Rowman and Littlefield, 1994. Print.

"An Australian Film." *Examiner* 28 Sep. 1926: 5. *Trove.* Web. 13 Apr. 2014. http://nla.gov.au/nla.news-article51365386.

Anderson, Joel, dir. *Lake Mungo.* 2008. DVD.

Arthur, Paul Longley. "Fantasies of the Antipodes." Barcan and Buchanan, *Imagining* 37–46. Print.

———. "Antipodean Myths of Australian Identity." *History Compass* 5/6 (2007): 1862–78.

Ash, Kathryn. *Flutter.* Brisbane: Playlab, 2004. Print.

Ash, Kathryn, Stephen Carleton, Gail Evans, and Anne Harris. *Surviving Jonah Salt.* Brisbane: Playlab, 2004. Print.

Astley, Thea. *It's Raining in Mango.* Ringwood, Vic.: Penguin. 1989.

auf der Heide, Jonathan, dir. *Hell's Gates.* 2007. Short film.

———, dir. *Van Diemen's Land.* 2009. DVD.

AusStage Mapping. Web. 1 Jan. 2014. http://www.ausstage.edu.au/pages/map/#tabs-3.

AustLit. Web. 1 Jan. 2014. http://www.austlit.edu.au.

Australian Cinemas Map. Web. 1 June 2014. http://auscinemas.flinders.edu.au.

"Australian Content Box Office." *Screen Australia* Jan. 2014. Web. 10 Oct. 2014. http://www.screenaustralia.gov.au/research/statistics/boxofficeaustraliatop100.aspx.

Banivanua Mar, Tracey, and Penelope Edmonds. "Introduction: Making Space in Settler Colonies." *Making Settler Colonial Space: Perspectives on Race, Place, and Identity.* Ed. Tracey Banivanua Mar and Penelope Edmonds. Basingstoke: Palgrave Macmillan, 2010. 1–24. Print.

Barber, Marcus, and Sue Jackson. *Water and the Indigenous People in the Pilbara, Western Australia: A Preliminary Study.* CSIRO: Water for a Healthy Country, 2011. 1–94. Print.

Barcan, Ruth, and Ian Buchanan, eds. *Imagining Australian Space: Cultural Studies and Spatial Inquiry.* Perth: U of Western Australia P, 1999. Print.

———. "Introduction: Imagining Space." Barcan and Buchanan, *Imagining* 7–11. Print.

Batty, Philip. "Another Country: The World of *Samson and Delilah.*" *Metro* 161 (2009): 164–69. Print.

Baynton, Barbara. *Bush Studies.* London: Duckworth, 1902. Print.

Beattie, Stuart, dir. *Tomorrow When the War Began.* 2010. DVD.

Beeton, Susan. *DVD-Induced Tourism.* Clevedon: Channel View, 2005. Print.

Bennett, Bruce. *An Australian Compass: Essays on Place and Direction in Australian Literature.* Fremantle: Fremantle Arts Centre P, 1991. Print.

Beresford, Michael. *Tiptoe* [2000]. Hanger Collection of Australian Playscripts, Fryer Library, University of Queensland, St. Lucia, 2008. Print.

Berndt, Ronald. "The Walmadjeri and Gugadja." *Hunters and Gatherers Today: A Socioeconomic Study of Eleven Such Cultures in the Twentieth Century.* Ed. M. G. Bicchieri. New York: Holt, Rinehart, and Winston, 1972. 177–216.

Berndt, Ronald, and Catherine Berndt. *The Speaking Land: Myth and Story in Aboriginal Australia.* Ringwood, Vic.: Penguin, 1989. Print.

Best, Susan. "Emplacement and Infinity." *Uncertain Ground: Essays between Art and Nature.* Ed. Martin Thomas. Sydney: Art Gallery of New South Wales P, 1999. 61–75. Print.

Betzien, Angela. *Children of the Black Skirt.* Brisbane: Playlab, 2005. Print.

Birch, Anna, and Joanne Tompkins, eds. *Performing Site-Specific Theatre: Politics, Place, Practice.* New York: Palgrave Macmillan, 2012. Print.

Birch, B. P. "Wessex, Hardy, and the Nature Novelists." *Transactions of the Institute of British Geographers* 6.3 (1981): 348–58. Print.

Bird, Caroline, and Sylvia Hallam. *A Review of Archaeology and Rock Art in the Dampier Archipelago: A Report Prepared for the National Trust of Australia (WA)*. 2006. Web. 1 Aug. 2013. http://www.burrup.org.au/2006-10-20%20Technical%20Report%20Final%20draft%202.pdf.

Bishop, Peter. "Driving Around: The Unsettling of Australia." *Studies in Travel Writing* 2.1 (1998): 144–63. Print.

———. "Gathering the Land: The Alice Springs to Darwin Rail Corridor." *Environment and Planning D: Society and Space* 20 (2002): 295–317. Print.

Blackwell, Greg. "Broken Hill's Emergency Water Trains." *Australian Railway History* 62.886 (2011): 6–25. Print.

———. "*Wake in Fright*'s 'Tiboonda': Where Is the Movie Location?" *Australian Railway History* 62.886 (2011): 3–5. Print.

Blanchot, Maurice. *The Space of Literature*. Trans. Ann Smock. Lincoln: U of Nebraska P, 1982. Print. Originally published as *L'espace littéraire*. Paris: Gallimard, 1955.

Bleszynski, Nick. *Bloodlust: The Unsavoury Tale of Alexander Pearce, the Convict Cannibal*. North Sydney, N.S.W.: William Heinemann, 2008. Print.

Bodenhamer, David J. "The Potential of Spatial Humanities." Bodenhamer, Corrigan, and T. Harris, *Spatial Humanities* 14–30. Print.

———. "Beyond GIS: Geospatial Technologies and the Future of History." von Lünen and Travis, *History and GIS* 1–15. Print.

Bodenhamer, David J., John Corrigan, and Trevor M. Harris, eds. *The Spatial Humanities: GIS and the Future of Humanities Scholarship*. Bloomington: Indiana UP, 2010. Print.

———. Introduction. Bodenhamer, Corrigan, and T. Harris, *Spatial Humanities* vii–xv. Print.

Bodey, Michael. "Red Centre of Attention." *Australian* 30 July 2011. Web. 17 Aug. 2012. http://www.theaustralian.com.au/arts/red-centre-of-attention/story-e6frg8n6-1226102201333.

Bolter, Jay David, and Richard Grusin. *Remediation: Understanding New Media*. Cambridge, Mass.: MIT P, 1999. Print.

Bordwell, David. "Camera Movement and Cinematic Space." *Ciné-Tracts* 1.2 (1977): 19–25. Print.

Bovell, Andrew. *Holy Day*. Sydney: Currency, 2001. Print.

Bradbury, Malcolm, ed. *The Atlas of Literature*. London: De Agostini, 1996. Print.

Branigan, Edward. "The Spectator and the Film Space—Two Theories." *Screen* 22.1 (1981): 55–78. Print.

Brereton, Pat. *Hollywood Utopia: Ecology in Contemporary American Cinema*. Bristol: Intellect, 2005. Print.

Brewster, Anne. "The Stolen Generations: Rites of Passage; Doris Pilkington interviewed by Anne Brewster." *Journal of Commonwealth Literature* 42.1 (2007): 143–59. Print.

Brooks, Sue, dir. *Japanese Story*. 2003. DVD.

Brophy, Philip. *The Adventures of Priscilla, Queen of the Desert*. Sydney: Currency, 2008. Print.

Brosseau, Marc. "Geography's Literature." *Progress in Human Geography* 18.3 (1994): 333–53. Print.

Buckingham, William R., and Samuel F. Dennis, Jr. "Cartographies of Participation: How the Changing Nature of Cartography Has Opened Community and Cartographer Collaboration." *Cartographic Perspectives* 64 (2009): 55–61. Print.

Buckley, Anthony. *Wake in Fright* Call Sheets. Box 27 (Title no. 623381). Buckley, Anthony: Production Papers, to 2002, National Film and Sound Archive, Canberra, ACT, Australia.

———. *Behind a Velvet Light Trap: A Filmmaker's Journey from Cinesound to Cannes.* Prahran, Vic.: Hardie Grant, 2009. Print.

Bullock, Emily. "Strange Silence in *Van Diemen's Land:* An Interview with Jonathan auf der Heide, Director of *Van Diemen's Land.*" *Metro* 162 (2009): 40–43. Print.

———. "Rumblings from Australia's Deep South: Tasmanian Gothic On-screen." *Studies in Australasian Cinema* 5.1 (2011): 71–80. Print.

Bulson, Eric. *Novels, Maps, Modernity: The Spatial Imagination, 1850–2000.* New York: Routledge, 2007. Print.

Burnside, Sarah. "Red Dog Whitewashes the Pilbara." *New Matilda* 16 Aug. 2011. Web. http://newmatilda.com/2011/08/16/red-dog-whitewashes-pilbara.

Buscombe, Edward. "Inventing Monument Valley: Nineteenth-Century Landscape Photography and the Western Film." *Fugitive Images: From Photography to Video.* Ed. Patrice Petro. Bloomington: Indiana UP, 1995. 87–108. Print.

Butler, Mary Anne. *Half Way There.* 2009. Unpublished playscript. Print.

Callahan, David. *Rainforest Narratives: The Work of Janette Turner Hospital.* St. Lucia: U of Queensland P, 2009. Print.

Caputo, Raffaele. "*Wake in Fright:* An Interview with Ted Kotcheff." *Senses of Cinema* 51 (2009). Web. http://sensesofcinema.com/2009/feature-articles/ted-kotcheff-interview/.

Caquard, Sébastien. "Foreshadowing Contemporary Digital Cartography: A Historical Review of Cinematic Maps in Films." *Cartographic Journal* 46.1 (2009): 46–55. Print.

———. "Cartography I: Mapping Narrative Cartography." *Progress in Human Geography* 37.1 (2013): 135–44. Print.

Caquard, Sébastien, and Jean-Pierre Fiset. "How Can We Map Stories? A Cybercartographic Application for Narrative Cartography." *Journal of Maps* 10.1 (2014): 18–25. Print.

Caquard, Sébastien, and D. R. Fraser Taylor. "What Is Cinematic Cartography?" *Cartographic Journal* 46.1 (2009): 5–8. Print.

Caquard, Sébastien, and Benjamin Wright. "Challenging the Digital Cartographic Continuity System: Lessons from Cinema." *Cartography and Art.* Ed. William Cartwright, Georg Gartner, and Antje Lehn. Berlin: Springer, 2009. 193–206. Print.

Carceres, Letitia. "Director's Notes." *Children of the Black Skirt* Real TV. Web. 24 Sep. 2014 http://www.childrenoftheblackskirt.com/?page_id=15.

Carleton, Stephen. *Constance Drinkwater and the Final Days of Somerset.* Brisbane: Playlab, 2006. Print.

———. "Darwin as the Frontier Capital: Theatrical Depictions of City Space in the North." *Australasian Drama Studies* 52 (2008): 52–68. Print.

———. "Staging the North: Finding, Imagining, and Performing an Australian 'Deep North.'" Diss. University of Queensland, 2008. Print.

———. "Cinema and the Australian North: Tracking and Troping Regionally Distinct Landscapes Via Baz Luhrmann's *Australia.*" *Metro* 163 (2009): 50–55. Print.

———. "Australian Gothic Theatre and the Northern Turn." *Australian Literary Studies* 27.2 (2012): 51–67. Print.

Carmichael, Deborah, ed. *The Landscape of Hollywood Westerns: Ecocriticism in an American Film Genre*. Salt Lake City: U of Utah P, 2006. Print.

Carr, Simon. *The Boys Are Back in Town*. London: Hutchinson, 2000. Print.

Carter, David. "Cocks in Frocks: Landscape and Nation in the 1990s." *Journal of Australian Studies* 49 (1996): 89–96. Print.

Carter, Paul. *The Road to Botany Bay: An Essay in Spatial History*. London: Faber and Faber, 1987. Print.

Cartwright, William, Michael P. Peterson, and Georg Gartner, eds. *Multimedia Cartography*. 2nd ed. Berlin: Springer, 2007. Print.

Casey, Edward. *Getting Back into Place: Toward a Renewed Understanding of the Place-World*. Bloomington: Indiana UP, 1993. Print.

Cathcart, Michael. "Uluru." *Words for Country: Landscape and Language in Australia*. Sydney: U of New South Wales P, 2002. Print.

Cawelti, John. *The Six-Gun Mystique Sequel*. Bowling Green, Ohio: Bowling Green State U Popular P, 1999. Print.

Cerwonka, Allaine. *Native to the Nation: Disciplining Landscapes and Bodies in Australia*. Minneapolis: U of Minnesota P, 2004. Print.

Chatman, Seymour. *Story and Discourse: Narrative Structure in Fiction and Film*. Ithaca, N.Y.: Cornell UP, 1978. Print.

Chaudhuri, Una. *Staging Place: The Geography of Modern Drama*. Ann Arbor: U of Michigan P, 2002. Print.

Chaudhuri, Una, and Elinor Fuchs, eds. *Land/Scape/Theater*. Ann Arbor: U of Michigan P, 2000. Print.

Chauvel, Charles, dir. *Jedda*. 1955. DVD.

Chi, Jimmy. *Bran Nue Dae: A Musical Journey*. Sydney: Currency, 1991. Print.

"Cinematograph Party Visit to West Coast." *Mercury* 27 Sep. 1926: 4. Print.

Clarke, David B., and Marcus A. Doel. "From Flatlands to Vernacular Relativity: The Genesis of Early English Screenscapes." *Landscape and Film*. Ed. Martin Lefebvre. New York: Routledge, 2006. 213–45.

Clarke, Marcus. *His Natural Life*. London: Richard Bentley and Son, 1878. Web. 25 Nov. 2013. http://purl.library.usyd.edu.au/setis/id/clahisn.

Clement, Nicholas. *The Black War: Fear, Sex, and Resistance in Tasmania*. St. Lucia: U of Queensland P, 2014. Print.

Clune, Frank. *The Red Heart: Sagas of Centralia*. Melbourne: Hawthorn P. 1944. Print.

Coleman, Cynthia-Lou. "Framing Cinematic Indians within the Social Construction of Place." *American Studies* 46.3/4 (2005): 275–93.

Colless, Edward. "Tasmanian Grotesque." *The Error of My Ways: Selected Writing 1981–1994*. Brisbane: Institute of Modern Art, 1995 [1994]. 147–51. Print.

Collins, Felicity. "After the Apology: Re-framing Violence and Suffering in *First Australians, Australia,* and *Samson and Delilah*." *Continuum: Journal of Media and Cultural Studies* 24.1 (2010): 65–77. Print.

Collins, Felicity, and Therese Davis. *Australian Cinema after Mabo*. Cambridge: Cambridge UP, 2004. Print.

Collins, Paul. *Hell's Gates: The Terrible Journey of Alexander Pearce, Van Diemen's Land Cannibal.* South Yarra: Hardie Grant, 2002. Print.

Collis, Christy. "Exploring Emptiness: Producing Australian Desert Space." *Beyond the Divide* 2.1 (1999): 38–48. Print.

Conley, Tom. *The Self-Made Map: Cartographic Writing in Early Modern France.* Minneapolis: U of Minnesota P, 1996. Print.

———. *Cartographic Cinema.* Minneapolis: U of Minnesota P, 2007. Print.

Cook, Kenneth. *Wake in Fright.* Melbourne: Text, 2009 [1961]. Print.

Cooke, Grayson. "Whither the Australian Western? Performing Genre and the Archive in *Outback and Beyond.*" *Transformations* 24 (2014). Web. 6 Apr. 2015. http://www .transformationsjournal.org/journal/24/03.shtml.

Cooper, David, and Ian N. Gregory. "Mapping the English Lake District: A Literary GIS." *Transactions of the Institute of British Geographers* 36 (2011): 89–108. Print.

Cosgrove, Denis. *Apollo's Eye: A Cartographic Genealogy of the Earth in the Western Imagination.* Baltimore, Md.: Johns Hopkins UP, 2003. Print.

Crampton, Jeremy W. "Maps 2.0: Map Mashups and New Spatial Media." *Mapping: A Critical Introduction to Cartography and GIS.* Malden: Blackwell, 2010. 25–38. Print.

Crampton, Jeremy. W., et al. "Beyond the Geotag: Situating 'Big Data' and Leveraging the Potential of the Geoweb." *Cartography and Geographic Information Science* 40.2 (2013): 130–39. Print.

Crang, Mike. "Rethinking the Observer: Film, Mobility, and the Construction of the Subject." *Engaging Film: Geographies of Mobility and Identity.* Ed. Tim Cresswell and Deborah Dixon. Lanham, Md.: Rowman and Littlefield, 2002. 13–31. Print.

Cranston, C. A., and Robert Zeller, eds. *The Littoral Zone: Australian Contexts and Their Writers.* Amsterdam: Rodopi, 2007. Print.

Craven, Allison. "Tropical Gothic: *Radiance* Revisited." *e-tropic: Electronic Journal of Studies in the Tropics* 7 (2008). Web. 09 Oct. 2014. http://www.jcu.edu.au/etropic/ET7 /CravenRadiance.htm.

———. "Paradise Post-National: Landscape, Location, and Senses of Place in Films Set in Queensland." *Metro* 166 (2010): 108–113. Print.

Cresswell, Tim, and Deborah Dixon, eds. *Engaging Film: Geographies of Mobility and Identity.* Lanham, Md.: Rowman and Littlefield, 2002. Print.

Cultural Atlas of Australia. Web. 1 Jan. 2014. http://www.australian-cultural-atlas.info.

Cummings, J. B. *Bart: My Life.* Sydney: Pan Macmillan, 2009. Print.

Cunningham, Stuart. *Featuring Australia: The Cinema of Charles Chauvel.* Sydney: Allen and Unwin, 1991. Print.

Curran, John, dir. *Praise.* 1998. DVD.

———, dir. *Tracks.* 2013. DVD

Curtis, Percy. "'On Location' with Australia's Movie Colony." *Sunday Times* 26 September 1926. *Trove.* Web. 11 Feb. 2014: 10. http://nla.gov.au/nla.news-article58249879.

Cybercartographic Atlas of Canadian Cinema. Web. 12 July 2014. http://atlascineproject .wordpress.com.

Darian-Smith, Kate, Liz Gunner, and Sarah Nuttall, eds. *Text, Theory, Space: Land, Literature, and History in South Africa and Australia.* London: Routledge, 2005. Print.

Davidson, Jim. "Tasmanian Gothic." *Meanjin* 48.2 (1988): 307–24. Print.

Davis, Jack. *Kullark: The Dreamers.* Sydney: Currency, 1982. Print.

Davis, Richard. "Introduction: Transforming the Frontier in Contemporary Australia." *Dislocating the Frontier: Essaying the Mystique of the Outback.* Ed. Deborah Bird Rose and Richard Davis. Canberra: ANU E P, 2005. 7–22. Print.

Dawn, Norman, dir. *For the Term of His Natural Life.* 1927. DVD.

DeBats, Donald A., and Ian Gregory. "Introduction to Historical GIS and the Study of Urban History." *Social Science History* 35.4 (2011): 455–63. Print.

de Berg, Hazel. "Kenneth Cook Interviewed by Hazel de Berg." 1972. Sound recording. Web. http://nla.gov.au/nla.oh-vn624025.

de Bernières, Louis. *Red Dog.* North Sydney: Vintage, 2001. Print.

de Certeau, Michel. *The Practice of Everyday Life* [1974]. Trans. S. Rendall. Berkeley: U of California P, 1984. Print.

de Heer, Rolf, dir. *The Tracker.* 2002. DVD.

———, dir. *Ten Canoes.* 2006. DVD.

Department of Aboriginal Affairs. "Pilbara." *Government of Western Australia, DAA.* 23 May 2013. Web. 10 Oct. 14. http://www.daa.wa.gov.au/en/About-DAA/Regions/Region-Pilbara/.

Digital Literary Atlas of Ireland, 1922–1949. Web. 12 July 2014. http://www.tcd.ie/trinity longroomhub/digital-atlas/.

Douglas, Bronwen. "Terra Australis to Oceania." *Journal of Pacific History* 45.2 (2010): 179–210.

Dowdall, Barrie, dir. *Exile in Hell.* 2007. TV.

Drucker, Johanna. "Humanistic Theory and Digital Scholarship." *Debates in the Digital Humanities.* Ed. Matthew K. Gold. Minneapolis: U of Minnesota P, 2012. 85–95. Print.

Duckett, Beverley. *Red Dog: The Pilbara Wanderer.* Karratha, W.A.: B. Duckett, 1993. Print.

Dunstone, Bill. "'Another Planet': Landscape as Metaphor in Western Australian Theatre." *European Relations: Essays for Helen Watson-Williams.* Ed. Bruce Bennett and John Hay. Perth: U of Western Australia P, 1985. 67–79. Print.

Dwyer, Jody, dir. *Dying Breed.* 2008. DVD.

"*Dying Breed* Production Notes." 2008. 1–13. Web. 15 Nov. 2011. http://thecia.com.au/reviews/d/images/dying-breed-production-notes.rtf

Edwards, Kevin, and Angela Murphy, "A Preliminary Report on Archaeological Investigations at Malea Rockshelter, Pilbara Region, Western Australia." *Australian Archaeology* 56 (2003): 44–46. Print.

Eklund, Erik. "The Margin as a Centre: Memory and Identity in Broken Hill and Mount Isa." *Outside Country: Histories of Inland Australia.* Ed. Alan Mayne and Stephen Atkinson. Adelaide: Wakefield, 2011. 311–30. Print.

Elliott, Brian. "Clarke, Marcus Andrew Hislop (1846–1881)." *Australian Dictionary of Biography,* National Centre of Biography, Australian National University. Web. 17 Sep. 2014. http://adb.anu.edu.au/biography/clarke-marcus-andrew-hislop-3225/text4859.

Elliott, Stephan, dir. *The Adventures of Priscilla, Queen of the Desert.* 1994. DVD.

Faiman, Peter, dir. *Crocodile Dundee*. 1986. DVD.

Farman, Jason. "Mapping the Digital Empire: Google Earth and the Process of Postmodern Cartography." *New Media and Society* 12.6 (2010): 869–88. Print.

Fensham, Rachel. "Making a Mythopoetic Theatre: Jenny Kemp as Director of an Imaginary Future-Past-Present." *Australasian Drama Studies* 44 (2004): 52–64. Print.

———. "Trajectories of the 'Dead Heart': Performing the Poetics of (Australian) Space." *New Theatre Quarterly* 24.1 (2008): 3–13. Print.

Ferrier, Elizabeth. "Mapping the Local in the Unreal City." *Island Magazine* 41 (1989): 65–69. Print.

"Film Producers Visit Bourke." *Western Herald* 7 Mar. 1969: 1. Print.

Flannery, Tim. Introduction. *Watkin Tench's 1788* by Watkin Tench. Melbourne: Text, 1996. Print.

Fletcher, Brendan, dir. *Mad Bastards*. 2010. DVD.

"For the Term of His Natural Life." *Mercury* 8 Sep. 1926: 11. Web. 12 Aug. 2014. http://nla .gov.au/nla.news-article29457893.

Fotheringham, Richard. *Australian Plays for the Colonial Stage, 1834–1899*. St. Lucia: U of Queensland P, 2006.

Frank, Joseph. "Spatial Form in Modern Literature." *Sewanee Review* 53 (1945): 221–40; 433–56; 643–53. Print.

Galvin, Peter. "The Making of *Wake in Fright*." 2009. SBS. Web. http://www.sbs.com.au /movies/article/2009/06/01/making-wake-fright-part-one.

Ganter, Regina. "Turning the Map Upside Down." *History Compass* 4.1 (2006): 26–35. Print.

Gelder, Ken. "Postcolonial Gothic." *The Handbook of the Gothic*. 2nd ed. Ed. Marie Mulvey-Roberts. New York: New York UP, 2009. 306–307. Print.

Gelder, Ken, and Jane M. Jacobs. "Uncanny Australia." *UTS Review* 1.2 (1995): 150–69. Print.

———. *Uncanny Australia: Sacredness and Identity in a Postcolonial Nation*. Melbourne: Melbourne UP, 1998.

Genoni, Paul. *Subverting the Empire: Explorers and Exploration in Australian Fiction*. Altona: Common Ground, 2004. Print.

"Ghan History, The." *Great Southern Rail*. 2014. Web. 11 Oct. 2014. http://www.great southernrail.com.au/site/the_ghan/history.jsp

Gibson, Chris, Chris Brennan-Horley, and Andrew Warren. "Geographic Information Technologies for Cultural Research: Cultural Mapping and the Prospects of Colliding Epistemologies." *Cultural Trends* 19.4 (2010): 325–48. Print.

Gibson, Ross. *South of the West: Postcolonialism and the Narrative Construction of Australia*. Bloomington: Indiana UP, 1992. Print.

———. "Camera Natura: Landscape in Australian Feature Film" [1983]. *Australian Cultural Studies: A Reader*. Ed. John Frow and Meaghan Morris. Sydney: Allen and Unwin, 1993. 209–21. Print.

Gilbert, Helen. *Sightlines: Race, Gender, and Nation in Contemporary Australian Theatre*. Ann Arbor: U of Michigan P, 1998. Print.

Gilbert, Helen, and Anna Johnston, eds. *In Transit: Travel, Text, Empire*. New York: Peter Lang, 2002. Print.

Gilbert, Helen, and Jacqueline Lo. *Performance and Cosmopolitics: Cross-Cultural Transactions in Australasia.* Basingstoke: Palgrave Macmillan, 2007. Print.

Gilbert, Helen, and Joanne Tompkins. *Postcolonial Drama: Theory, Practice, Politics.* London: Routledge, 1996. Print.

Gillespie, Nancy. *Red Dog.* Dampier, W.A.: N. Gillespie, 1983. Print.

Goddu, Teresa A. "American Gothic." *The Routledge Gothic Companion.* Ed. Catherine Spooner and Emma McEvoy. London: Routledge, 2007. 63–72. Print.

Godfrey, Craig, dir. *Back from the Dead.* 1996. DVD.

GoGwilt, Christopher. *The Invention of the West: Joseph Conrad and the Double-Mapping of Europe and Empire.* Stanford: Stanford UP, 1995. Print.

Going to the Show: Documenting the American South. Web. 12 July 2014. http://docsouth .unc.edu/gtts/.

Goldsmith, Ben, Susan Ward, and Tom O'Regan. *Local Hollywood: Global Film Production and the Gold Coast.* St. Lucia: U of Queensland P, 2010. Print.

Grace, Sherrill E. Introduction. *Staging the North: Twelve Canadian Plays.* Toronto: Playwrights Canada, 1999. Print.

———. *Canada and the Idea of North.* Montreal: McGill-Queen's UP, 2001.

Gregory, Derek. *Geographical Imaginations.* Cambridge, Mass.: Blackwell, 1994. Print.

Gregory, Ian. *A Place in History.* Oxford: Oxbow, 2003. Print.

———. *Historical GIS: Technologies, Methodologies, and Scholarship.* Cambridge: Cambridge UP. 2007. Print.

Gregory, Ian, and Alistair Geddes. "Introduction: From Historical GIS to Spatial Humanities; Deepening Scholarship and Broadening Technology." *Toward Spatial Humanities: Historical GIS and Spatial History.* Ed. Derek Gregory and Alistair Geddes. Bloomington: Indiana UP, 2014. ix–xix. Print.

Gregory, John Walter. *The Dead Heart of Australia: A Journey around Lake Eyre in the Summer of 1901–1902, with Some Account of the Lake Eyre Basin and the Flowing Wells of Central Australia* [1906]. New York Public Library: John Murray, 2007. Print.

Grehan, Helena. *Mapping Cultural Identity in Contemporary Australian Performance.* Brussels: Peter Lang, 2001. Print.

Griffiths, Tom. "Journeys to the Centre." *Hunters and Collectors: The Antiquarian Imagination in Australia.* Cambridge: Cambridge UP, 1996. Print.

Grossetti, Adam. *Mano Nera: Blood, Sweat, and Fear in the North Queensland Canefields.* Brisbane: Playlab, 2005. Print.

Gullón, Ricardo. "On Space in the Novel." *Critical Inquiry* 2.1 (1975): 11–28. Print.

Gunning, Tom. "The Cinema of Attractions: Early Film, Its Spectator, and the Avant-garde." *Early Cinema: Space, Frame, Narrative.* Ed. Thomas Elsaesser. London: British Film Institute, 1990. 63–70. Print.

Haklay, Mordechai. "Neogeography and the Delusion of Democratisation." *Environment and Planning* A 45.1 (2013): 55–69. Print.

Hale, Alan [Kenneth Cook]. *Vantage to the Gale.* Sydney: Horwitz, 1963. Print.

Hallam, Julia. "Film, Space, and Place: Researching a City in Film." *New Review of Film and Television Studies* 8.3 (2010): 277–96. Print.

———. "Mapping, Memory, and the City: Archives, Databases, and Film Historiography." *European Journal of Cultural Studies* 14.3 (2011): 355–72. Print.

———. "Civic Visions: Mapping the 'City' Film 1900–1960." *Culture, Theory, and Critique* 53.1 (2012): 37–58. Print.

Hallam, Julia, and Les Roberts, eds. *Locating the Moving Image: New Approaches to Film and Place.* Bloomington: Indiana UP, 2013. Print.

Hamilton, Margaret. *Transfigured Stages: Major Practitioners and Theatre Aesthetics in Australia.* Amsterdam: Rodopi, 2011. Print.

Hannam, Ken, dir. *Sunday Too Far Away.* 1975. DVD.

Harley, J. B. "Deconstructing the Map." *Cartographica* 26.2 (1989): 1–20.

Harper, Graeme. "A Version of Beauty and Terror: Australian Cinematic Landscapes." Harper and Rayner, *Cinema and Landscape* 242–54. Print.

Harper, Graeme, and Jonathan Rayner, eds. *Cinema and Landscape.* Bristol: Intellect, 2010. Print.

Harris, Hilary. "Desert Training for Whites: Australian Road Movies." *Journal of Australian Studies* 86 (2006): 99–110. Print.

Harris, Trevor M., Susan Bergeron, and Jesse L. Rouse. "Humanities GIS: Place, Spatial Storytelling, and Immersive Visualization in the Humanities." *Geohumanities: Art, History, Text at the Edge of Place.* Ed. Michael Dear, et al. Abingdon, Oxon: Routledge, 2011. 226–40. Print.

Harris, Trevor M., John Corrigan, and David J. Bodenhamer. "Challenges for the Spatial Humanities: Toward a Research Agenda." Bodenhamer, Corrigan, and T. Harris, *Spatial Humanities* 167–76. Print.

Harvey, David. *The Condition of Postmodernity: An Enquiry into the Origins of Cultural Change.* Cambridge, Mass.: Blackwell, 1989. Print.

———. *Spaces of Capital: Towards a Critical Geography.* Edinburgh: Edinburgh UP, 2001. Print.

Hassall, Linda. *Post Office Rose.* In *Independent Brisbane: Four Plays.* Brisbane: Playlab, 2008: 103–70. Print.

Hawke, Steve. *Jandamarra.* Playscript. 2008. Print.

Hay, Peter. "A Phenomenology of Islands." *Island Studies Journal* 1.1 (2006): 19–42. Print.

Haynes, Roslynn. *Seeking the Centre: The Australian Desert in Literature, Art, and Film.* Cambridge: Cambridge UP, 1998. Print.

———. *Tasmanian Visions: Landscapes in Writing, Art, and Photography.* Sandy Bay, Tas.: Polymath, 2006. Print.

Heath, Stephen. "Narrative Space." *Screen* 17.3 (1976): 68–112. Print.

Herbert, Xavier. *Capricornia* [1938]. Sydney: Angus and Robertson, 1975. Print.

Hickie, Amanda. "Diversity at Heart of Design Success: Philip Hickie, 1927–2012." *Sydney Morning Herald* 21 December 2012: 20. Print.

Hicks, Scott, dir. *The Boys Are Back.* 2009. DVD.

Hillcoat, John, dir. *The Proposition.* 2005. DVD.

Hitchcock, Tim. "Academic History Writing and the Headache of Big Data," *Historyonics* 30 Jan. 2012. Web. 18 Jul. 2014. http://historyonics.blogspot.co.uk/2012/01/academic -history-writing-and-headache.html.

Hones, Sheila. "Literary Geography: Setting and Narrative Space." *Social and Cultural Geography* 12.7 (2011): 685–99. Print.

———. *Literary Geographies: Narrative Space in "Let the Great World Spin."* New York: Palgrave Macmillan, 2014. Print.

Honey, John, dir. *Manganinnie.* 1980. DVD.

Hope, Jeanette. *Unincorporated Area of New South Wales Heritage Study.* Sydney: Department of Natural Resources and Heritage Office, 2006. Print.

Horne, Julia. *The Pursuit of Wonder: How Australia's Landscape Was Explored, Nature Discovered, and Tourism Unleashed.* Carlton, Vic.: Miegunyah, 2005. Print.

Horton, David. "Map of Aboriginal Language Groups in Australia." Aboriginal Studies Press, AIATSIS and Auslig/Sinclair, Knight, Merz, 1996. Map.

Hospital, Janette Turner. *Oyster.* London: Virago, 1996. Print.

Huggan, Graham. "Decolonizing the Map: Post-colonialism, Post-structuralism and the Cartographic Connection." *ARIEL* 20.4 (1989): 115–31. Print.

———. *Territorial Disputes: Maps and Mapping Strategies in Contemporary Canadian and Australian Fiction.* Toronto: U of Toronto P, 1994. Print.

Hughes, Robert. *The Fatal Shore: A History of the Transportation of Convicts to Australia, 1787–1868.* London: Harvill, 1987. Print.

Hutcheon, Linda. *A Theory of Adaptation.* New York: Routledge, 2006. Print.

Idriess, Ion L. *Outlaws of the Leopold.* Sydney: Angus and Robertson, 1952. Print.

Irons, Tim. "Will We Remember Them?" *Australian Screen Online.* 2009. Web. http://aso.gov.au/news/2009/11/13/will-we-remember-them/.

I Will Survive. Network Ten. Fremantle Media, 2012. Television.

Isaacs, Bruce. "Screening 'Australia': *Samson and Delilah.*" *Screen Education* 54 (2009): 12–17. Print.

Ivin, Glendyn, dir. *Last Ride.* 2009. DVD.

Jameson, Fredric. *Postmodernism; or, The Cultural Logic of Late Capitalism.* Durham, N.C.: Duke UP, 1991. Print.

Jansson, David R. "Internal Orientalism in America: W. J. Cash's *The Mind of the South* and the Spatial Construction of American National Identity." *Political Geography* 22.3 (2003): 293–316. Print.

Johnson, Stephen, dir. *Yolngu Boy.* 2001. DVD.

Jones, Phil, and James Evans "The Spatial Transcript: Analysing Mobilities through Qualitative GIS." *Area* 44.1 (2012): 92–99. Print.

Kemp, Jenny. *Still Angela.* South Fremantle: Hush Performing Arts Library, 2002. DVD.

Killeen, Jarlath. "Irish Gothic: A Theoretical Introduction." *Irish Journal of Gothic and Horror Studies* 1 (2006). Web. 12 Oct. 2014. http://irishgothichorrorjournal.homestead.com/jarlath.html.

Kitses, Jim. *Horizons West.* London: Thames and Hudson, 1969. Print.

Klenotic, Jeffrey. "Putting Cinema History on the Map: Using GIS to Explore the Spatiality of Cinema." *Explorations in New Cinema History: Approaches and Case Studies.* Ed. Richard Maltby, Daniel Biltereyst, and Philippe Meers. Chichester: Blackwell, 2011. 58–84. Print.

Knowles, Anne. *Past Time, Past Place.* Redlands, Calif.: ESRI P, 2002. Print.

———, ed. *Placing History: How Maps, Spatial Data, and GIS Are Changing Historical Scholarship.* Redlands, Calif.: ESRI P, 2008. Print.

Kossew, Sue. *Writing Woman, Writing Place: Contemporary Australian and South African Fiction*. London: Routledge, 2004. Print.

Kotcheff, Ted, dir. *Wake in Fright*. 1971. DVD.

Kuhlenbeck, Britta. *Re-writing Spatiality: The Production of Space in the Pilbara Region in Western Australia*. Berlin: LIT Verlag Münster, 2011. Print.

Lambert, Anthony. "(Re)Producing Country: Mapping Multiple Australian Spaces." *Space and Culture* 13.3 (2010): 304–14. Print.

Lando, Fabio. "Fact and Fiction: Geography and Literature." *GeoJournal* 38.1 (1996): 3–18. Print.

Lee, Jack, dir. *Robbery under Arms*. 1957. DVD.

Leer, Martin. "At the Edge: Geography and the Imagination in the Work of David Malouf." *Australian Literary Studies* 12.1 (1985): 3–21. Print.

———. "Imagined Counterpart: Outlining a Conceptual Literary Geography of Australia." *Australian Literary Studies* 12.1 (1991): 1–13. Print.

Lefebvre, Henri. *The Production of Space* [1974]. Trans. Donald Nicholson-Smith. Oxford: Blackwell 1991. Print.

Lefebvre, Martin, ed. *Landscape and Film*. New York: Routledge, 2006. Print.

———. Introduction. M. Lefebvre, *Landscape and Film* xi–xxxi. Print.

———. "On Landscape in Narrative Cinema." *Canadian Journal of Film Studies* 20.1 (2011): 61–78. Print.

Lehmann, Courtney. "Strictly Shakespeare? Dead Letters, Ghostly Fathers, and the Cultural Pathology of Authorship in Baz Luhrmann's *William Shakespeare's Romeo + Juliet*." *Shakespeare Quarterly* 52.2 (2001): 189–221. Print.

Leitner, Gerhard. "The Aboriginal Contribution to Australia's Language Habitat." *The Habitat of Australia's Aboriginal Languages: Past, Present, and Future*. Ed. Gerhard Leitner and Ian G. Malcolm. Berlin: Mouton de Gruyter. 197–236. Print.

Leszczynski, Agnieszka. "On the Neo in Neogeography." *Annals of the Association of American Geographers* 104.1 (2014): 60–79. Print.

Levin, John. "Digital Humanities GIS Projects." *Anterotesis* 16 March 2011. Web. 11 June 2014. http://anterotesis.com/wordpress/2011/03/digital-humanities-gis-projects/.

Limbrick, Peter. "The Australian Western, or A Settler Colonial Cinema Par Excellence." *Cinema Journal* 46.4 (2007): 68–95. Print.

Lines, William J. *Taming the Great South Land*. Berkeley: U of California P, 1991.

Literary Atlas of Europe. Web. 12 June 2014. http://www.literaturatlas.eu.

Long, Christian. *The Imaginary Geography of Hollywood Cinema, 1960–2000*. Chicago: Intellect, forthcoming. Print.

Luhrmann, Baz, dir. *William Shakespeare's Romeo + Juliet*. 1996. DVD.

———, dir. *Australia*. 2008. DVD.

Lukinbeal, Christopher. "Cinematic Landscapes." *Journal of Cultural Geography* 23.1 (2005): 3–22. Print.

Lukinbeal, Christopher, and Stefan Zimmermann. "Film Geography: A New Subfield." *Erdkunde* 60.4 (2006): 315–26. Print.

Lydon, Jane. "A Strange Time Machine: *The Tracker, Black and White,* and *Rabbit-Proof Fence*." *Australian Historical Studies* 35 (2004): 137–48. Print.

Lynch, Tom. "Literature in the Arid Zone." *The Littoral Zone: Australian Contexts and Their Writers*. Ed. C. A. Cranston and Robert Zeller. Amsterdam: Rodopi, 2007. 71–92. Print.

MacEachren, Alan M. "Visualizing Uncertain Information." *Cartographic Perspectives* 13 (1992): 10–19. Print.

MacFarlane, Robert. *The Wild Places*. London: Granta and Penguin, 2007. Print.

MacLeod, Norm. *The Australian Kelpie Handbook*. 1st ed. Altona, Vic: N. MacLeod, 1978.

Maddox, Gary. "Iron Men." *Sydney Morning Herald*. Entertainment. 16 Jul. 2011. Web. 10 Oct. 2014. http://www.smh.com.au/entertainment/movies/iron-men-20110714-1 heio.html.

"Man Shot in Hand." *Barrier Daily Truth* 3 January 1953: 1. Print.

Map of Early Modern London, The. Ed. Janelle Jenstad. 27 Jul. 2012. Web. 9 Oct. 2014. http://mapoflondon.uvic.ca/map.htm.

Mapping the City in Film. Web. 1 June 2014. http://www.liv.ac.uk/architecture/research /cava/cityfilm/.

Mapping the Lakes: A Literary GIS. Web. 1 June 2014. http://www.lancaster.ac.uk/mapping thelakes/index.htm.

Mares, Detlev, and Wolfgang Moschek. "Place in Time: GIS and the Spatial Imagination in Teaching History." von Lünen and Travis, *History and GIS* 59–72. Print.

McAuley, Gay. *Space in Performance: Making Meaning in the Theatre*. Ann Arbor: U of Michigan P, 1999. Print.

———, ed. *Unstable Ground: Performance and the Politics of Place*. Brussels: Peter Lang, 2006. Print.

McCallum, John. "The 'Doll' and the Legend." *Australasian Drama Studies* 3.2 (1985): 33–44. Print.

McCallum, Robyn. "Cultural Solipsism, National Identities, and the Discourse of Multiculturalism in Australian Picture Books." *ARIEL* 28.1 (1997): 101–16. Print.

McGahan, Andrew. *Praise*. Sydney: Allen and Unwin, 1992. Print.

———. *The White Earth*. Brisbane: Playlab. 2009. Print.

McGahan, Andrew, and Shaun Charles. *"The White Earth"* (adapted for the stage by Andrew McGahan and Shaun Charles) *and "Bait"* (by Andrew McGahan). Brisbane: Playlab, 2009. Print.

McKean, Fiona. "Too Hot, Too Far, Too Much." MPhil diss. University of Queensland, 2015. Print.

McKee, Alan. "How to Tell the Difference between a Stereotype and a Positive Image: Putting *Priscilla, Queen of the Desert* into History." *Screening the Past* 9 (2000). Web. 15 Oct. 2014. http://tlweb.latrobe.edu.au/humanities/screeningthepast/firstrelease /fr0300/amfr09b.htm.

McKenzie, Catriona, dir. *Satellite Boy*. 2012. DVD.

McLean, Greg, dir. *Wolf Creek*. 2005. DVD.

———, dir. *Rogue*. 2007. DVD.

McMahon, Charles, dir. *For the Term of His Natural Life*. 1908. Short Film.

McMahon, Elizabeth. "Archipelagic Space and the Uncertain Future of National Literatures." *Journal of the Association for the Study of Australian Literature (JASAL)* 13.2

(2013). Web. 5 Nov. 2013. http://www.nla.gov.au/openpublish/index.php/jasal/article
/view/3154/3731.

———. "Encapsulated Space: The Paradise-Prison of Australia's Island Imaginary."
Southerly 65.1 (2005): 20–30. Print.

McRobert, John. "Discovery Flight." Hancock Prospecting. n.d. Web. 13 Apr. 2012. http://
www.hancockprospecting.com.au/files/discovery_flight.pdf.

Meinig, D. W. "Geography as an Art." *Transactions of the Institute of British Geographers* 8.3
(1983): 314–28. Print.

Méliès, Gaston, dir. *Captured by Aborigines.* 1913. Short Film.

Michaels, Eric. *Bad Aboriginal Art: Tradition, Media, and Technological Horizons.* Sydney:
Allen and Unwin, 1994. Print.

Michôd, David, dir. *The Rover.* 2014. DVD.

Milestone, Lewis, dir. *Kangaroo.* 1952. DVD.

Millar, Carly. "The Horror, the Horror: Tasmania's Cannibal History on the Silver Screen."
Metro 159 (2008): 17–21. Print.

Miller, George, dir. *Mad Max.* 1979. DVD.

———, dir. *Mad Max 2: The Road Warrior.* 1981. DVD.

———, dir. *Mad Max: Beyond Thunderdome.* 1985. DVD.

Miller, George T., dir. *The Man from Snowy River.* 1982. DVD.

Mills, Jane. "Mapping Australia: Cinematic Cartographies of (Dis)Location." *Senses of
Cinema* 55 (2010). Web. 20 Mar. 2013. http://sensesofcinema.com/2010/feature-articles
/mapping-australia-cinematic-cartographies-of-dislocation/.

Mitchell, Peta. *Cartographic Strategies of Postmodernity: The Figure of the Map in Contemporary Theory and Fiction.* Routledge Studies in Twentieth-Century Literature. New
York: Routledge, 2008. Print.

Mitchell, Peta, and Jane Stadler. "Imaginative Cinematic Geographies of Australia: The
Mapped View in Charles Chauvel's *Jedda* and Baz Luhrmann's *Australia.*" *Historical
Geography* 38 (2010): 26–51. Print.

———. "Redrawing the Map: An Interdisciplinary Geocritical Approach to Australian
Cultural Narratives." Tally, *Geocritical Explorations* 47–62. Print.

Mitchell, W. J. T. "Spatial Form in Literature: Toward a General Theory." *Critical Inquiry*
6.3 (1980): 539–67. Print.

Monmonier, Mark. *Rhumb Lines and Map Wars: A Social History of the Mercator Projection.* Chicago: U of Chicago P, 2004. Print.

———. "Cartography: The Multidisciplinary Pluralism of Cartographic Art, Geospatial
Technology, and Empirical Scholarship." *Progress in Human Geography* 31.3 (2007):
371–79. Print.

Mora, Philippe, dir. *Mad Dog Morgan.* 1976. DVD.

Moretti, Franco. *Atlas of the European Novel, 1800–1900.* London: Verso, 1998. Print.

Morris, Simon. "When Driven by Hunger." *Australian Geographic* 29 June 2009. Web.
15 November 2011. http://www.australiangeographic.com.au/journal/when-driven
-by-hunger.htm.

Mountford, Charles. *Ayers Rock: Its People, Their Beliefs, and Their Art.* Sydney: Angus and
Robertson, 1965. Print.

Mudrooroo [Colin Johnson]. *Long Live Sandawara.* Melbourne: Hyland House, 1987. Print.

Mulcahy, Russell. *Razorback*. 1984. DVD.

Mulvey-Roberts, Marie. *The Handbook of the Gothic*. 2nd ed. New York: New York UP, 2009. Print.

Murray, Robin, and Joseph Heumann. "Mining Westerns: Seeking Sustainable Development in *McCabe and Mrs. Miller*." *Journal of Ecocriticism* 2.2 (2010): 57–72. Print.

Noble, Allen G., and Ramesh Dhussa. "Image and Substance: A Review of Literary Geography." *Journal of Cultural Geography* 10.2 (1990): 49–65. Print.

Nowra, Louis. *Inside the Island*. Sydney: Currency, 1981. Print.

———. *The Precious Woman*. Sydney: Currency, 1981. Print.

Noyce, Phillip, dir. *Rabbit-Proof Fence*. 2002. DVD.

Ogilvy, George, dir. *The Shiralee*. 1987. DVD.

O'Carroll, John. "Upside-Down and Inside-Out: Notes on the Australian Cultural Unconscious." Barcan and Buchanan, *Imagining* 13–35. Print.

O'Neill, Errol. *The Mayne Inheritance*. Brisbane: Playlab, 2004.

"Open Season for 'Roos." *Barrier Miner* 29 January 1953: 11. Print.

O'Regan, Tom. *Australian National Cinema*. New York: Routledge, 1996. Print.

"*Outback* Theatrical Trailer." *Wake in Fright*. Dir. Ted Kotcheff, 1971. DVD Special Feature.

Palmer, Kingsley. "Petroglyphs and Associated Aboriginal Sites in the North West of Western Australia." *Archaeology and Physical Anthropology in Oceania* 10.2 (1975): 152–60. Print.

———. "Myth, Ritual, and Rock Art." *Archaeology and Physical Anthropology in Oceania* 12.1 (1977): 38–50. Print.

Palmer, Renee. "Director's Notes: *Wake in Fright* Program." Yabba Productions, Adelaide Fringe Festival. Holden St. Theatres, Adelaide: March 4–15, 2014. Print.

Parker, Merryl. "Bringing the Dingo Home: Discursive Representations of the Dingo by Aboriginal, Colonial, and Contemporary Australians." Diss. U of Tasmania, 2006. PDF.

Parsons, Tony. *The Kelpie: A Definitive Guide to the Australian Working Dog*. Ringwood, Vic.: Penguin, 2010.

Partridge, Eric. "Yabber." *Routledge Dictionary of Historical Slang*. London: Routledge, 2006. 5975. Print.

Paterson, A. B. "Banjo." "The Man from Snowy River." *Bulletin* 26 April 1890. Print.

Pavlich, Bob, adapt. *Wake in Fright*. 2012. Playscript. Print.

Pearce, Alexander. "Narrative of the Escape of Eight Convicts from Macquarie Harbour in Sep. 1822, and of their Murders and Cannibalism Committed During their Wanderings." Confession to Reverend Robert Knopwood, ca. 1824. Web. 20 Mar. 2014. http:// acms.sl.nsw.gov.au/item/itemDetailPaged.aspx?itemID=446620.

Peckham, Robert Shannan. "Landscape and Film." *A Companion to Cultural Geography*. Ed. James Duncan, Nuala Johnson, and Richard Schein. Malden, Mass.: Blackwell, 2004. 420–29. Print.

Perkins, Rachel, dir. *One Night the Moon*. 2001. DVD.

———, dir. *Bran Nue Dae*. 2009. DVD.

Pesman, Ros, David Walker, and Richard White, eds. *The Oxford Book of Australian Travel Writing*. Melbourne: Oxford UP, 1996. Print.

Phelps, William Lyon, ed. *Selections from the Poetry and Prose of Thomas Gray*. Boston: Ginn and Company, 1894. Print.

Piatti, Barbara, et al. "Mapping Literature: Towards a Geography of Fiction." *Cartography and Art.* Ed. William Cartwright, Georg Gartner, and Antje Lehn. Berlin: Springer, 2009. 177–92. Print.

Piatti, Barbara, and Lorenz Hurni. "Mapping the Ontologically Unreal—Counterfactual Spaces in Literature and Cartography." *Cartographic Journal* 46.4 (2009): 333–42. Print.

———. "Cartographies of Fictional Worlds." *Cartographic Journal* 48.4 (2011): 218–23. Print.

Pick, David, Bella Butler, and Kandy Dayaram. "Neo-liberalism, Risk, and Regional Development in Western Australia: The Case of the Pilbara." *International Journal of Sociology and Social Policy* 28.11/12 (2008): 516– 27. Print.

Pickles, John, ed. *Ground Truth: The Social Implications of Geographic Information Systems.* New York: Guilford, 1995. Print.

"Picture Studio Gossip." *Queanbeyan-Canberra Advocate* 9 Dec. 1926. Web. 27 July 2013. http://nla.gov.au/nla.news-article31691101.

"Pieman's River." *Launceston Examiner* 13 May, 1865: 4. Print.

Pilkington Garimara, Doris. *Follow the Rabbit-Proof Fence.* St. Lucia: U of Queensland P, 1996. Print.

Pocock, Douglas C. D. "Introduction: Imaginative Literature and the Geographer." *Humanistic Geography and Literature: Essays on the Experience of Place.* Ed. Douglas C. D. Pocock. London: Croom Helm, 1981. 9–19. Print.

———. "Geography and Literature." *Progress in Human Geography* 12.1 (1988): 87–102. Print.

Porteous, J. Douglas. "Literature and Humanist Geography." *Area* 17.2 (1985): 117–22. Print.

Price, Norman. *Urban Dingoes: A Performance Text.* Brisbane: Playlab. 2004. Print.

Price, Norman, and Lisa O'Neill. *Pineapple Queen.* Brisbane Powerhouse: La Boite Theatre. 29 Jul. 2009. Play.

Prieto, Eric. "Geocriticism, Geopoetics, Geophilosophy, and Beyond." Tally, *Geocritical Explorations* 13–27. Print.

———. *Literature, Geography, and the Postmodern Poetics of Place.* London: Palgrave Macmillan, 2013. Print.

Punter, David, and Glennis Byron, eds. *The Gothic.* Oxford: Blackwell, 2004. Print.

Queensland Gold and Minerals Limited Due Diligence Report. Brisbane: Environmental and Licensing Professionals, 2006. Print.

"Questions Answered." *Barrier Miner* 28 September 1937: 1. Print.

Rajewsky, Irina O. "Intermediality, Intertextuality, and Remediation: A Literary Perspective on Intermediality." *Intermediality: History and Theory of the Arts, Literature, and Technologies* 6 (2005): 43–64. Print.

Rankin, Scott [and the Namatjira Family]. *Namatjira.* Sydney: Curency, 2011. Print.

Read, Alan. *Theatre and Everyday Life: An Ethics of Performance.* London: Routledge, 1993. Print.

Redding, Oscar. *Convict 102.* Fitzroy, Vic.: A Poor Theatre Co. 2008. Play.

Redwood, Tom. "Warwick Thornton and Kath Shelper on Making *Samson and Delilah.*" *Metro* 160 (2009): 30–34. Print.

Reuschel, Anne-Kathrin. "Mapping Literature: Visualisation of Spatial Uncertainty in Fiction." *Cartographic Journal* 48.4 (2011): 293–308. Print.

Riggs, Damian. *Priscilla, (White) Queen of the Desert: Queer Rights/Race Privilege.* New York: Peter Lang, 2006. Print.

Roberts, Beth. *Manganinnie*. South Melbourne: Macmillan, 1979. Print.

Roberts, Les. "Cinematic Cartography: Projecting Place through Film." *Mapping Cultures: Place, Practice, Performance*. Basingstoke: Palgrave Macmillan, 2012. 68–84. Print.

Robertson, Pamela. "The Adventures of Priscilla in Oz." *Media International Australia* 78 (1995): 33–38. Print.

Robin, Libby. "Accounting for Deserts." Unpublished conference paper, Territorial Techniques Masterclass, U of Queensland, Brisbane, Qld. October 2003. Print.

———. *How a Continent Created a Nation*. Sydney: U of New South Wales P, 2007. Print.

Robson, Lloyd L. "The Historical Basis of *For the Term of His Natural Life*." *Australian Literary Studies* 1 (1963): 104–21. Print.

Roe, Michael. "Vandiemenism Debated: The Filming of *His Natural Life*, 1926/7." *Journal of Australian Studies* 24 (1989): 35–51. Print.

Roeg, Nicolas, dir. *Walkabout*. 1971. DVD.

Rolfe, Alfred, dir. *The Life of Rufus Dawes*. 1911. Short Film.

Rose, Deborah Bird. *Dingo Makes Us Human: Life and Land in an Australian Aboriginal Culture*. Cambridge: Cambridge UP, 2000. Print.

———. *Wild Dog Dreaming: Love and Extinction*. Charlottesville: U of Virginia P, 2011. Print.

Rose, Gillian. *Feminism and Geography: The Limits of Geographical Knowledge*. Cambridge: Polity, 1993. Print.

Rossetto, Tania. "Theorizing Maps with Literature." *Progress in Human Geography*. Online 19 Nov. 2013. Web. 18 July 2014. http://phg.sagepub.com/content/early/2013/11/19/0309132513510587 *Progress in Human Geography* 38.4 (2014): 513–30. Print.

Routt, Bill. "Bush Westerns? The Lost Genre." Public lecture, Australian Centre for the Moving Image, Melbourne. 3 February 2003. Web. 13 May 2014. http://www.routt.net/Bill/BushWesterns.htm.

Rowland, Michael James, dir. *Lucky Miles*. 2007. DVD.

———. *The Last Confession of Alexander Pearce*. 2008. DVD.

Ruoff, Jeffrey. "Introduction: The Filmic Fourth Dimension—Cinema as Audiovisual Vehicle." *Virtual Voyages: Cinema and Travel*. Ed. Jeffrey Rouff. Durham, N.C.: Duke UP, 2006. 1–24. Print.

Ryan, John. "An Interview with Kenneth Cook." *Westerly* 3 (1977): 75–83. Print.

Ryan, Mark David. "Writing Aussie Horror: An Interview with Shayne Armstrong and Shane Krause." *Metro* 159 (2008): 46–48. Print.

Ryan, Simon. "Inscribing the Emptiness: Cartography, Exploration, and the Construction of Australia." *De-Scribing Empire: Post-colonialism and Textuality*. Ed. Chris Tiffin and Alan Lawson. London: Routledge, 1994. 115–30. Print.

———. *The Cartographic Eye: How Explorers Saw Australia*. Cambridge: Cambridge UP, 1996. Print.

Said, Edward W. *Orientalism*. New York: Pantheon, 1978. Print.

Schepisi, Fred, dir. *The Chant of Jimmie Blacksmith*. 1978. DVD.

———. *Evil Angels*. 1988. DVD.

Schultz, Julianne. "Introduction: Beyond the Brisbane Line." *Griffith Review* Spring (2005): 7–10. Print.

Schuurman, Nadine, and Geraldine Pratt. "Care of the Subject: Feminism and Critiques of GIS." *Gender, Place, and Culture* 9.2 (2002): 291–99. Print.

Schwartz, Seymour I. "The Greatest Misnomer on Planet Earth." *Proceedings of the American Philosophical Society* 146.3 (2002): 264–81.

Scott, John, and Dean Biron. "*Wolf Creek*, Rurality and the Australian Gothic." *Continuum* 24. 2 (2010): 307–22. Print.

Scott, Kim. *True Country*. Fremantle: Fremantle Arts Centre P, 1993. Print.

Seddon, George. "The Persistence of Place—Western Australian Literature." *Westerly* 4 (1982): 62–72. Print.

Sen, Ivan, dir. *Toomelah*. 2011. DVD.

Sharp, Joanne P. "Towards a Critical Analysis of Fictive Geographies." *Area* 32.3 (2000): 327–34. Print.

Shields, Rob. *Places on the Margin: Alternative Geographies of Modernity*. London: Routledge, 1991. Print.

Shirley, Graham, and Brian Adams. *Australian Cinema: The First Eighty Years*. Sydney: Currency, 1983. Print.

Siemon, Rosamond. *The Mayne Inheritance*. St. Lucia: U of Queensland P, 2003. Print.

Simpson, Catherine. "Shifting from Landscape to Country in *Australia*, after Mabo." *Metro* 165 (2010): 88–93. Print.

Simpson, Catherine, Renata Murawska, and Anthony Lambert. *Diasporas of Australian Cinema*. Bristol: Intellect, 2009. Print.

Simpson, Jane. "Hypocoristics in Australian English." *Varieties of English: The Pacific and Australasia*. Ed. Kate Burridge, and Bernd Kortmann. Berlin: Mouton de Gruyter, 2008. 398–414. Print.

Skinner, Craig. "Ted Kotcheff Discusses *Wake in Fright*, Kangaroo Slaughter, and Existentialism." 2014. Web. http://www.filmdivider.com/237/ted-kotcheff-discusses-wake-in-fright-animal-welfare-and-existentialism/.

Smart, Ralph, dir. *Bitter Springs*, 1950. DVD.

Soja, Edward. *Postmodern Geographies: The Reassertion of Space in Critical Social Theory*. London: Verso, 1989. Print.

"Some Unrecorded Passages in the History of Van Diemen's Land (from a Very Old Stager)." *Courier* 6 Apr. 1854: 2. Print.

Sprod, Dan. *Alexander Pearce of Macquarie Harbour: Convict, Bushranger, Cannibal*. Hobart: Cat and Fiddle, 1977. Print.

Stadler, Jane. "Mapping the Cinematic Journey of Alexander Pearce, Cannibal Convict." *Screening the Past* 34 (2012). Web. 15 Apr. 2013. http://www.screeningthepast.com/2012/07/mapping-the-cinematic-journey-of-alexander-pearce-cannibal-convict/.

———. "Seeing with Green Eyes: Tasmanian Landscape Cinema and the Ecological Gaze." *Senses of Cinema* 65 (2012). Web. 15 Apr. 2013. http://sensesofcinema.com/2012/tasmania-and-the-cinema/seeing-with-green-eyes-tasmanian-landscape-cinema-and-the-ecological-gaze/.

Stadler, Jane, and Peta Mitchell. "Never-Never Land: Affective Landscapes, the Touristic Gaze, and Heterotopic Space in *Australia*." *Studies in Australasian Cinema* 4.2 (2010): 173–87. Print.

Steele, Kathleen. "Fear and Loathing in the Australian Bush: Gothic Landscapes in Bush Studies and Picnic at Hanging Rock." *Colloquy* 20 (2010): 33–56. Print.

Stenders, Kriv, dir. *Red Dog*. 2011. DVD.

Stevens, David, dir. *A Town like Alice*. 1981. DVD.

Stevens, David. *The Gothic Tradition*. 2nd ed. Cambridge: Cambridge UP, 2010. Print.

Stevens, John A. *Convict 1240*. San Francisco. 1885. Play.

Stewart, Keryn, and Helen Hopcroft. "A Band without Walls at the End of the World: The Green Mist, Next Stop Antarctica, and the Tasmanian Geographic Imaginary." *Transforming Cultures eJournal* 4.1 (2009): 138. Web. 2 Jan. 2012. http://epress.lib.uts.edu.au /ojs/index.php/TfC/article/view/1063.

Stewart, Rob, dir. *For the Term of His Natural Life*. 1983. TV.

Stratton, Jon. "Deconstructing the Territory." *Cultural Studies* 3.1 (1989): 38–57. Print.

Sui, Daniel Z. "GIS and Urban Studies: Positivism, Post-positivism, and Beyond." *Urban Geography* 15.3 (1994): 258–78. Print.

Tait, Charles, dir. *The Story of the Kelly Gang*. 1906. DVD.

Tally, Robert T., Jr. "Geocriticism and Classic American Literature." *English Department Faculty Publications, Texas State University* (2008). Web. 15 Apr. 2013. http://ecommons .txstate.edu/englfacp/14/.

———. *Melville, Mapping, and Globalization: Literary Cartography in the American Baroque Writer*. New York: Continuum, 2009. Print.

———, ed. *Geocritical Explorations: Space, Place, and Mapping in Literary and Cultural Studies*. New York: Palgrave Macmillan, 2011. Print.

———. *Spatiality*. Abingdon, Oxon.: Routledge, 2013. Print.

"Tasmania Invites You to Share Her Charms!" *Mercury*. 9 Sep. 1926. Web. 9 Aug. 2014. http://nla.gov.au/nla.news-article29458084.

Tasmania Legislative Council. *Boat Expeditions Round Tasmania, 1815–16 and 1824: Reports*. 1881. Web. 9 Sep. 2014. http://www.nla.gov.au/apps/doview/nla.aus-vn760576-p.pdf.

Taylor, D. R. Fraser, ed. *Cybercartography: Theory and Practice*. Amsterdam: Elsevier, 2006. Print.

Taylor, John, and Ben Scambary. *Indigenous People and the Pilbara Mining Boom*. Canberra: ANU E P, 2006. Web.

Thacker, Andrew. "The Idea of a Critical Literary Geography." *New Formations* 57 (2005): 56–73. Print.

Thielmann, Tristan. "Locative Media and Mediated Localities." *Aether: A Journal of Media Geography* 5 (2010): 1–17. Print.

Thomas, Allen James. "Camping Outback: Landscape, Masculinity, and Performances in *The Adventure of Priscilla, Queen of the Desert*." *Continuum: Journal of Media and Cultural Studies* 10.2 (1996): 97–110. Print.

Thomas, David, and Garry Gillard. "Threads of Resemblance in New Australian Gothic Cinema." *Metro* 136 (2003): 36–44. Print.

Thomson, Campbell. "Australia Is a Film about a Red Dog." *Overland Literary Journal* 208: 2012. Web. 17 Apr. 2013 https://overland.org.au/previous-issues/issue-208/poem -campbell-thomson/.

Thornton, Warwick, dir. *Samson and Delilah*. 2009. DVD.

Thrift, Nigel. "Literature, the Production of Culture and the Politics of Place." *Antipode*
15.1 (1983): 12–24. Print.

———. "Performance and Performativity: A Geography of Unknown Lands." *A Companion to Cultural Geography*. Ed. James S. Duncan, Nuala C. Johnson, and Richard H.
Schein. Malden: Blackwell, 2004. 121–36. Print.

Tilley, Christopher. *A Phenomenology of Landscape: Places, Paths, and Monuments*. Oxford: Berg, 1994. Print.

Tompkins, Joanne. *Unsettling Space: Contestations in Contemporary Australian Theatre*.
Basingstoke: Palgrave Macmillan, 2007. Print.

Tooley, Ronald Vere. *Maps and Map-Makers*. London: Batsford, 1952. Print.

Torres, Mitch, dir. *Jandamarra's War*. 2011. TV.

Trainor, James, dir. *Journey out of Darkness*. 1967. DVD.

Trau, Jörg, and Lorenz Hurni. "Possibilities of Incorporating and Visualizing Uncertainty
in Natural Hazard Prediction." *Proceedings of the 23rd International Cartographic Conference*. Moscow, 4–10 Aug, 2007. Moscow: ICC, 2007. 1–12. Print.

Travis, Charles. "Abstract Machine—Geographical Information Systems (GIS) for Literary and Cultural Studies: 'Mapping Kavanagh.'" *International Journal of Humanities and Arts Computing* 4.1–2 (2010): 17–37. Print.

———. "Transcending the Cube: Translating GIScience Time and Space Perspectives
in a Humanities GIS." *International Journal of Geographical Information Science* 28.5
(2014): 1149–64. Print.

Tuan, Yi-Fu. "Place: An Experiential Perspective." *Geographical Review* 65.2 (1975): 151–65.
Print.

———. *Place and Space: The Perspective of Experience*. Minneapolis: U of Minnesota P,
1977. Print.

Tulloch, John. *Legends of the Screen: The Narrative of Film in Australia, 1919–1929*. Sydney:
Currency, 1981. Print.

Tumarkin, Maria. "'Wishing You Weren't Here . . .': Thinking about Trauma, Place, and
the Port Arthur Massacre." *Journal of Australian Studies* 25.67 (2001): 196–205. Print.

Turcotte, Gerry. "Australian Gothic." *The Handbook to Gothic Literature*. Ed. Marie Mulvey-Roberts. Basingstoke: Macmillan, 1998. 10–19. Print.

Turner, Graeme. *National Fictions: Literature, Film, and the Construction of Australian
Narrative*. 2 ed. Sydney: Allen and Unwin, 1993 [1986]. Print.

"Unmitigated Boil of Horror, An." *Bulletin* 26 October 1963: 3. Print.

Urry, John. "The Place of Emotions within Place." *Emotional Geographies*. Ed. Joyce Davidson, Liz Bondi, and Mick Smith. Hampshire: Ashgate, 2005. 77–83. Print.

Valentine, Alana. *Head Full of Love*. South Brisbane: Queensland Theatre Company, 2012.
Print.

Venkatasawmy, Rama, Catherine Simpson, and Tanja Visosevic. "From Sand to Bitumen,
from Bushrangers to 'Bogans': Mapping the Australian Road Movie." *Journal of Australian Studies* 25.70 (2001): 73–84. Print.

Vinnicombe, Patricia. "Petroglyphs of the Dampier Archipelago: Background to Development and Descriptive Analysis." *Rock Art Research* 19.1 (2002): 3–27. Print.

Virili, F. L. (Enzo). "A Preliminary Report on the Aboriginal Sites and the Rock Art of the
Dampier Archipelago, W.A." Site Report for Dampier Salt, Ltd., 1974. Print.

Voigts-Virchow, Eckart. "*Metadaptation:* Adaptation and Intermediality—Cock and Bull." *Journal of Adaptation in Film and Performance* 2.2 (2009): 137–52. Print.

von Lünen, Alexander, and Charles Travis. *History and GIS: Epistemologies, Considerations, and Reflections.* Dordrecht: Springer, 2013. Print.

Walker, Thomas [Thomas Somers]. *For the Term of His Natural Life.* Royal Standard, Sydney: Alfred Dampier. 5 Jun. 1886. Play.

Watt, Harry, dir. *The Overlanders.* 1946. DVD.

———, dir. *Eureka Stockade.* 1949. DVD.

Weaver-Hightower, Rebecca. "Revisiting the Vanquished: Indigenous Perspectives on Colonial Encounters." *Journal for Early Modern Cultural Studies* 6.2 (2006): 84–102. Print.

Webby, Elizabeth. "Stage, Screen, and Other Versions of *His Natural Life,* 1886–1998." *Marcus Clarke: His Natural Life.* Ed. Lurline Stuart. St. Lucia: U of Queensland P, 2001. 591–605. Print.

Weddings, Parties, Anything, "A Tale They Won't Believe." *The Big Don't Argue,* Warner Elektra Atlantic, 1989. CD.

Weir, Peter, dir. *The Cars That Ate Paris.* 1974. DVD.

———, dir. *Gallipoli.* 1981. DVD.

Wenders, Wim, dir. *Until the End of the World.* 1991. DVD.

Westphal, Bertrand. Foreword. Tally, *Geocritical Explorations* ix–xviii. Print.

———. *Geocriticism: Real and Fictional Spaces.* Trans. Robert T. Tally, Jr. New York: Palgrave Macmillan, 2011. Print. Originally published as *La géocritique: Réel, fiction, espace.* Paris: Minuit, 2007.

Western Australia Dingo Association. "Dingo Dreamtime." Web. 17 Aug. 2013. http://www.wadingo.com/Dingoes_and_Aborigines.html.

White, Richard. *Inventing Australia: Images and Identity, 1688–1980.* Sydney: Allen and Unwin, 1981. Print.

Williams, Raymond. *The Country and the City.* London: Chatto and Windus, 1973. Print.

Williams, Stephan. *Alexander Pearce: A Brief Narrative of His Life Together with His Confessions of Cannibalism.* Woden, A.C.T.: Popinjay, 1986. Print.

Wincer, Simon, dir. *The Lighthorsemen.* 1987. DVD.

Winton, Tim. *Dirt Music.* Sydney: Picador/Pan Macmillan, 2001. Print.

Wittgenstein, Ludwig. *Philosophical Investigations.* Trans. G. E. M. Anscombe. Oxford: Oxford UP, 1978. Print.

Wright, Alexis. *Carpentaria.* Artarmon, N.S.W.: Giramondo, 2006. Print.

Wright, John K. "Geography in Literature." *Geographical Review* 14.4 (1924): 659–60. Print.

———. "*Terrae Incognitae:* The Place of the Imagination in Geography." *Annals of the Association of American Geographers* 37.1 (1947): 1–15. Print.

Wright, Robin. "Developing Our Own Space: Place and Identity in Recent Australian Cinema." *Working Papers in Australian Studies.* Ed. David Lowe. London: Sir Robert Menzies Centre for Australian Studies, Institute of Commonwealth Studies, University of London, 1993. Print.

Wright, Will. *Six Guns and Society: A Structural Study of the Western.* Berkeley: U of California P, 1975. Print.

Wulff, Toni. "Travel as Spectacle: The Illusion of Knowledge and Sight" *Issues in Travel Writing: Empire, Spectacle, and Displacement*. Ed. Kristi Siegel. New York: Peter Lang, 2002. 109–22. Print.

Yuhun, Pawinee, Andrew Taylor, and James Winter. "Alice According to You: A Snapshot from the 2011 Census." Darwin: Charles Darwin UP, 2012. PDF. http://www.cdu.edu .au/sites/default/files/the-northern-institute/Alice%2520according%2520to%2520you _FINAL.pdf.

Zampa, Luigi, dir. *Bello onesto emigrato Australia sposerebbe compaesana illibata [A Girl in Australia]*. 1971. DVD

Zimmermann, Stefan. "I Suppose It Has Come to This—How a Western Shaped Australia's Identity." *Crossing Frontiers: Intercultural Perspectives on the Western*. Ed. Thomas Klein, Ivo Ritzer, and Peter W. Schulze. Marburg: Schüren, 2012. 134–48. Print.

Zinnemann, Fred, dir. *The Sundowners*. 1960. DVD.

Zonn, Leo E. "Images of Place: A Geography of the Media." *Proceedings of the Royal Geographical Society of Australasia* 84 (1985): 34–45. Print.

Zonn, Leo E., and Stuart C. Aitken. "Of Pelicans and Men: Symbolic Landscapes, Gender, and Australia's *Storm Boy*." *Place, Power, Situation, and Spectacle: A Geography of Film*. Lanham, Md.: Rowman and Littlefield, 1994. 137–61. Print.

INDEX

Note: Page numbers in *italics* refer to illustrations.